Praise for *The Roads to Sata*

"Fluent in the language, well-informed and disabused, [Booth] is in the fine tradition of hard-to-please travelers like Norman Douglas, Evelyn Waugh, and V. S. Naipaul. A sharp eye and a good memory for detail . . . give an astonishing immediacy to his account."
—Frank Tuohy, *Times Literary Supplement*

"Alan Booth was not only the best travel writer on Japan, but one of the best travel writers in the English language."
—Ian Buruma, author of *The Wages of Guilt*

"[Booth] achieved an extraordinary understanding of life as it is lived by ordinary Japanese. . . . Frequently brilliant in his insights."
—F. G. Notehelfer, *The New York Times Book Review*

"One of the best foreign observers of Japan today . . . his book is unsurpassed."
—*Far Eastern Economic Review*

"To travel with Alan Booth is to travel in very civilized company indeed, but also close to the ground. He has a mind that illuminates and enlivens everything it encounters."
—Nigel Barley, author of *The Innocent Anthropologist*

"Booth's capacity for rueful, discerning observation will keep him in the front ranks of travel writers for years to come."
—*Kirkus*

ALSO BY ALAN BOOTH

Looking for the Lost:
Journeys Through a Vanishing Japan

THE ROADS TO SATA

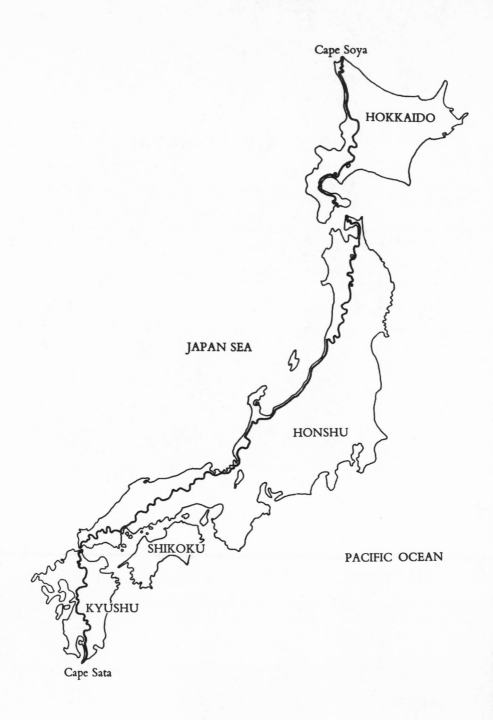

Cape Soya

HOKKAIDO

JAPAN SEA

HONSHU

SHIKOKU

PACIFIC OCEAN

KYUSHU

Cape Sata

THE ROADS TO SATA

A 2000-Mile Walk Through Japan

by Alan Booth

KODANSHA INTERNATIONAL
New York • Tokyo • London

I am lucky in having among my friends a discerning
publisher and a perspicacious editor. Though neither was
professionally involved with this book, they both read or
listened to all of it and were disturbingly frank in their
criticism and equally purposeful in their encouragement. So
my thanks to Ong Sok-Chzeng, for her incredulity and
laughter, and to Timothy Harris, who knows a cricket from
a grasshopper and was especially energetic in the removal of
an anapest.

Kodansha America, Inc.
575 Lexington Avenue, New York, New York 10022, U.S.A.

Kodansha International Ltd.
17-14 Otowa 1-chome, Bunkyo-ku, Tokyo 112, Japan

Published in 1997 by Kodansha America, Inc.
by arrangement with the Estate of Alan Booth.

First published in 1985 by John Weatherhill, Inc.

This is a Kodansha Globe book.

ISBN 1-56836-187-4
LC 97-71724

Manufactured in the United States of America on
acid-free paper

01 02 03 04   Q/FF   10 9 8 7 6 5 4 3 2

... the sundry contemplation of
my travels, which, by often rumination
wraps me in a most humorous sadness.

Jaques
in *As You Like It*

Contents

Author's Note

FEW PEOPLE (warns the publisher, grumbling) are likely to know where Sata is, so I had better locate it in this note. Sata is the name of the southernmost cape of the southernmost of the four main islands of Japan. I walked there from Soya, the northernmost cape of the northernmost island, and the roads between, and the things I saw and heard and did along them, are the subjects of this book.

Japan is a long country. If I had walked the same distance across the same latitudes in North America, the trek would have taken me from Ottawa to Mobile, Alabama; and if I had started in Europe, I would have marched from Belgrade through the Middle East to the Gulf of Aquaba. The distances I walked are given here in kilometers, not miles, because it is in kilometers that most Japanese think, and that I thought every morning, noon, and evening of my journey.

If I could, I would individually thank the men, women, and children who populate these pages, but I never knew the names of most of them, and I have thought it in their interests to alter those names I did know. Where names are used, they are used in the Japanese manner: family name first, given name last.

I have tried to avoid generalizations, particularly "the Japanese." "The Japanese" are 120,000,000 people, ranging in age from 0 to 119, in geographical location across 21 degrees of latitude and 23 of longitude, and in profession from emperor to urban guerrilla. This book is about my encounters with some twelve hundred businessmen, farmers, grandmothers, fishermen, housewives, shopkeepers, schoolchildren, soldiers, policemen, monks, priests, tourists, journalists, professors, laborers, maids, waiters, carpenters, teachers, innkeepers, potters, dancers, cyclists, students, truck drivers, Koreans, Americans, bar hostesses, professional wrestlers, government officials, hermits, drunks, and tramps.

THE ROADS TO SATA

❧ 1 ❧

Outposts

ONE OF THE NOODLE SHOPS at Cape Soya had a pair of loudspeakers perched high up above its door and out of these came, every five minutes, a song:

> *The ice floes melt, the spring wind blows,*
> *the sweet brier blooms, the sea gull cries,*
> *far out to sea the smoke of foreign ships*
> *delights the eye at Soya Cape.*
>
> *Snow storms abate, the chill is past,*
> *the shellfish stir along the shore,*
> *while men throw wide the doors of their hearts,*
> *and the sea roars on at Soya Cape.*

It was late in June so most of Japan was dripping and gray—the rainy season was at its height. But Hokkaido, the northernmost of Japan's four main islands, was cracking under a heat wave. The sea did not roar or even mutter; it was intense and blinding, like in advertisements for citrus fruit. Only with great reluctance did the people of Cape Soya venture out into the scorching sunshine. Most of them slouched in the shade of their doorways watching the trickle of honeymoon couples vainly trying with the aid of the coin telescopes to pierce the forty-three kilometers of heat-haze that separated their noodle shops from the Soviet Union. Four young motorcyclists in gleaming black leather sat sweating and drumming on a table outside one of the restaurants, picking flies off the rims of their cola bottles,

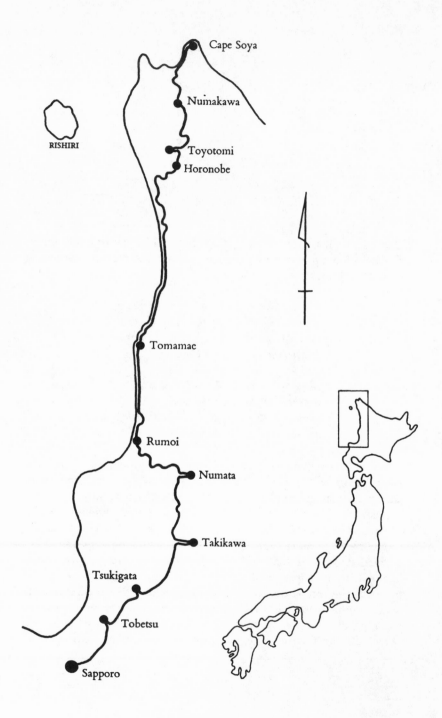

Cape Soya

Numakawa

Toyotomi

Horonobe

RISHIRI

Tomamae

Rumoi

Numata

Takikawa

Tsukigata

Tobetsu

Sapporo

listening to the taped voice shriek about shellfish, and gazing across at the four brand new Hondas they had parked within a yard of the end of Japan—latitude 45° 30′ N, the latitude of Milan, the Crimea, and Portland, Oregon—the furthest north you can get in Japanese eyes and still count yourself civilized.

When the sun set the flies retired to the hills, the taped voice snapped off in a burst of static, and the northern evening grew a fraction cooler. Through the open door of the *minshuku*—the lodging house—where I was staying, I could see the prawn boats on the flat pink sea, so far away and so still that they looked like matchwood.

"What time do you want to get up in the morning?" asked the owner of the minshuku. He was a tall man, brusque, unshaven, fiddling with his Dunhill lighter.

"I don't know. Seven, I suppose. I'd better get an early start."

"Are you catching a bus?"

"No, I'm going to walk."

"Are you walking far?"

"The length of Japan."

All night the wind blew into my room in the minshuku at Cape Soya and I couldn't sleep. The wind sang as it blew through the stovepipes till I thought there was a nest of birds singing: crafty birds, Japanese birds, transforming the pipes into their own loudspeaker. In the morning the owner of the minshuku gave me a small cotton handkerchief with a map of Hokkaido on it. It would come in handy if I took a wrong turn, he explained. Carefully, he unfolded the handkerchief and stamped the address and telephone number of his minshuku in the top right-hand corner.

"What's the date?" he called out to his wife in the kitchen.

"The twenty-eighth," she called back.

With great concentration he inked a second rubber stamp and neatly stamped "June 28" under his address, stepping back to admire the effect. But it still didn't satisfy him, so below the date he wrote in small red characters "7:00 start."

As though on cue the next-door speakers squealed into life and for the third or fourth time I retied my bootlaces.

"It's the twenty-ninth," I remembered.

"It's the twenty-ninth!" the minshuku owner howled, scratching through the last figure of the date with his ball pen and scrawling the new figure in on top of it so that the result was a barely legible mess.

"My wife is a donkey," he whispered.

⚮

One of the Japanese friends who celebrated my last night in Tokyo with me had been propped against the sakè shop wall by nine o'clock with bits of grilled liver stuck to his chin. But he contributed to the conversation. "Count the steps," he had advised. "Count all the steps from north to south and you'll know how many there are."

"What on earth would I want to know that for?"

"Then you could write a book about it. You can't write a book about a walk like that without knowing how many steps you've taken."

"But I'll have maps and a compass and the road signs should tell me . . ."

"Take my tip and count the steps. No one I've ever met in all my life could tell you how many steps there are from Cape Soya to Cape Sata. I bet no one's ever counted them before. I bet you'd be the absolute first."

He had gone to sleep after that with the liver still on his chin and two or three other friends had carried him out to a taxi, but the taxi driver had taken one look at him and sped off on a sudden urgent errand.

I never did count the number of steps, but I counted the kilometers as best I could, and on that first extraordinary morning, for fifteen kilometers, I walked beside the bright sea.

The walls and roofs of the sparse coastal villages were painted in what had once been primary colors, bleached to pale pinks and greens by the salt in the Siberian wind. The walls were made of plywood or cheap tin sheets printed to look like planks, and the roofs were patched with corrugated iron. Ahead of me to the southwest, beyond the invisible city of Wakkanai, loomed the awesome shape of Mount Rishiri, an island mountain far out to sea, its summit still covered with slivers of snow. The red doors of a fishermen's warehouse were open and on the floor sprawled a pile of large dead octopuses. I wished an old man in a kimono and a trilby hat good morning. "*Gokurosan*," he replied— "Thank you for taking the trouble."

Turning inland at midday, I stamped for another eighteen kilometers through fields of dazzling green. The blistering sun struck the bright blue silos and their Dutch barn roofs, the hayricks set out like the squares on a chessboard, the tractor constructing them, the white hood of the woman driving the tractor, the fork of the man's rake as he piled up the hay and waved to me, a cigarette stuck between his teeth.

By midafternoon my mouth felt like sandpaper and the empty beer cans by the side of the road were beginning to plague me like mirages. It was so hot and still that the stinking draft from the one truck that ground by was like a dip in the ocean. Hokkaido is the second largest of the Japanese islands, but it is by far the most thinly populated. A bare five percent of the population lives here—about one person to every four acres of land—and in the north of the island you can slog on for hours and meet only crows. Late in the afternoon a tractor stopped and, without a word, the young driver handed me a bottle of orange juice. I stood and gulped it in the middle of the road while the tractor purred and the driver grinned down at me.

"Where do you come from?"

"England."

"Ah, wonderful!"

"How far's Numakawa?"

"Just over the next rise."

And, satisfied that the last drop of orange juice was gone, he took back the bottle and purred off up the road, turning into a field where the evening wind had just begun to ripple the grass. Numakawa was over five rises and round eight bends, and in the entrance hall of the ryokan—the Japanese-style inn—I sat on the step and drank two bottles of beer before finding the energy to unlace my boots, while the owner's wife clapped her hands, wide-eyed with glee, and the maid stood choking on her giggles.

Communities in Japan have effective ways of warning you that you've slept too long. There are sirens that blast you out of your *futon*—your bedding—just as dawn has broken, foghorns in the coastal villages, and complete loudspeaker systems that broadcast favorite melodies like "Sakura, Sakura" and "Colonel Bogey." In Numakawa

7

there is a set of electric chimes that exactly duplicates the bongs of Big Ben and, if you sleep through the bongs, there is "Anchors Aweigh" for the children to troop into class to. The owner of the ryokan, Mr. Obata, was a teacher at the local primary school and had persuaded me to drop in on my way out of Numakawa the following morning to "show my face" to his pupils. By the time I reached the little single-story wooden school, the strains of "Anchors Aweigh" had long faded, for the school lay deep among the farms and the detour had taken me an hour out of my way. But the petrified squeaks and the breathless hush were definitely worth the extra boot rubber. The four children in Mr. Obata's class—three six-year-old boys and a seven-year-old girl—sat goggle-eyed on the edge of their benches while their teacher introduced them to the Thing from Outer Space.

"Now, children, here's an Englishman who comes from England. Do you know where England is, Kazuko-chan?"

"*Zutto muko* (far away)."

"And do you think you can find it on our map?"

A battered metal globe had been dragged out to the front of the class and the four children clustered round it, wriggling.

"No, Kazuko-chan, that's Saudi Arabia. This is England," said Mr. Obata, tapping Iceland. Mr. Obata rocked back on his heels as he addressed his four pupils, gesturing at them with large sweeps of his arms.

"Now, yesterday this foreigner walked thirty-three kilometers, all the way from Cape Soya. Where's Cape Soya, Kazuko-chan?"

"*Zutto muko* (far away)."

"Yes, and today this American is going to walk to Toyotomi. Where's that, Ryoichi-kun?"

"*Zutto muko.*"

"And after that he's going to walk all through Japan."

"Oooooooo!"

"How long do you think that'll take him?"

"A week."

"Two weeks."

"Six months."

"Five years."

And by this time my feet were beginning to tingle, so after the children had each tried to lift my rucksack (the little girl was the only one who succeeded), I drank a cup of thin green tea in the teachers' room, while the headmaster guffawed quietly at his desk, and then set off in earnest for Toyotomi.

The sun glared down on the unsurfaced road, on the white-cowled women constructing a drain, on the large brown snake that slithered miserably out of the way of a snorting tractor, and on me, my head wrapped in a sky-blue towel and my hands swollen to almost twice their normal size with sunburn, the skin slowly turning from scarlet to purple. I called at a farmhouse for a glass of water and received a tray of green tea and crackers and a recommendation that I see a doctor about my hands. In the wooded country above the fields flies clung to my face, and within seconds of taking off my boots and socks to bathe my feet in the exhilarating streams, my legs were mottled with spots of my blood the stream insects had sucked.

By the time—late in the afternoon—that I reached the hot spring resort of Toyotomi, with its one dusty street and its dozen old ryokans, I could hardly put one foot in front of the other. I had covered more than sixty kilometers in two days, through a heat wave everyone swore was unique and through country where often the only shade was in the clefts carved out of a quarry face. I managed to hobble from the ryokan to the public bathhouse—a feat in itself since the ryokan had provided me with a pair of the square wooden clogs called *geta,* which are not designed to soothe aching feet and which, anyway, were an inch and a half too short. But the sight amused the bathhouse attendants:

"Here, look at this foreigner hobbling along. I told you they can't walk in geta."

The bathhouse, mercifully, was almost deserted. Like a wall down the center of the huge tiled bathtub a cluster of gray volcanic rocks separated the men's portion from the women's, and out of these rocks trickled the natural hot spring water, a silky, morbid green. The bathhouse attendants had thoughtfully provided a net for skimming off the mosquitoes and flies that had died on the surface of the water, but I was too tired to bother and too badly blistered from the sun to do more than sit slumped on the tiled edge soaking my feet. I spent the best part of an hour in the bathhouse, limping back and forth between the bath and the cold-water tap where I emptied plastic bowl after plastic bowl of icy water over the burns on my face and neck.

The food in the ryokan was meager, the maid surly, the room undecorated, and the black-and-white television would only work if you kept stuffing hundred-yen coins into it. In the morning, as I left, forty or fifty pensioners on crutches were climbing painfully into two large buses, while a loudspeaker in the neighboring ryokan broadcast "Auld Lang Syne," and a small delivery truck roared past with "Happy's Coming" in bright yellow English across the back of it.

At ten to twelve the little restaurant opposite Horonobe station was empty. At twelve it was chock full. At one it was empty again. The third morning of my adventure had been a teeth-gritting twelve-kilometer limp along cinder paths, and I now sat in the restaurant drinking cold Sapporo beer and trying to reach a decision. My carefully plotted itinerary—plotted in Tokyo at a comfortable desk—and the neat little penciled numbers on my map all insisted I go on. My blisters, my sunburn, the joints of my toes, the arches of my feet, the balls of my feet, my ankles, my knees, my thighs, my gastrocnemii and the availability of Sapporo beer were eloquently persuading me to spend the rest of the day in Horonobe. I reached the decision at a quarter past three and passed the next two hours in Horonobe's tiny park, sprawled out under a neatly labeled tree, watching young children poke potato crisps through the bars of a cage at a newborn *bambi* (the post-Disney Japanese word for a fawn).

I had booked myself into a ryokan where the downstairs dining room was decorated with photographs of steam locomotives puffing through gorges and a large brownish reproduction of Millet's "Evening Knell." There were also some seashell pendants for sale inside each of which the teenage daughter had carefully glued a little cloth face, and there was a plastic mirror with "Tour Brings You Smile" printed across it in luminous letters. But, as I soon found out, the chief attraction of Horonobe (population 4,600) is its generous choice of bars (there are twenty-two). The third one I hobbled into that evening had a wonderful antique draft-beer cooling machine that the mama-san had to keep stoking with ice, a twenty-year-old Wurlitzer juke box, and a massive color television on which a red-bearded American wrestler was smashing a Japanese wrestler called Strong Kobayashi over the head with a ringside chair.

I ordered a draft beer but had barely sipped it when a voice at my elbow said "Hello, please, please, hello," and a bald, beaming gentleman was standing beside me, pouring me a glass of Very Rare Old Suntory.

"That's kind of you," I just had time to say, "but I don't drink whiskey. I prefer beer or sakè."

"Hello, please. You, hello."

Without any ceremony at all, the beaming man took a thousand-yen note from his wallet and dropped it on the counter, instructing the mama-san as he did so to fetch more beer and a saucer of peanuts. This sort of thing happens occasionally and there is little point protesting. I did not protest.

The beaming man produced his business card, explaining at the same time, since foreigners are not expected to be able to read Japanese business cards, that his name was Ogawa and that he was the town's Director of Public Works. He insisted that we drink together and steered me away from the counter to where his colleagues were seated at a corner table—four young men in white shirts and ties and one older man in Wellington boots and a boiler suit covered with smudges of mud who rose to hug me but fell across the table and upset two whiskeys and an ice bucket. He sat down again, missing the edge of his chair, and when he had scrambled out from under the table, was helped to his feet, dusted down, and conducted to the door, smiling and bowing and knocking over a dish of dried squid on the counter. At the door he turned to wave, dislodging the Playboy calendar, and was finally escorted, giggling, out into the night.

We raised our glasses in a toast. The red-bearded American wrestler was hauling Strong Kobayashi round the ring by his hair, Paul Anka was singing "Diana." Apart from that, a lull had settled over the bar. The man in the boiler suit was the Town Clerk.

"Thank you for coming to Horonobe. Thank you for going to see our bambi."

"It's a quiet town."

"It's a *peaceful* town," carefully amended Mr. Ogawa. "I go to Tokyo three times a year and I come back with my ears ringing. Horonobe is peaceful. It has twenty-two bars and a bambi, what's more, and the people of the world must try to be friends. If I may ask, where were you born?"

"In London."

"Ah, yes. What part of London?"

"Leytonstone."

"A splendid town! England and Japan have much in common. You have a queen and we have an emperor. We are islands. We have long histories. The Americans don't really understand us at all, but the people of the world should try to be friends. Do you think that Leytonstone might like to have Horonobe for a sister town? We have a bambi and so on."

"I could ask."

"It is essential, you see, that the people of the world be friends."

The red-bearded American had Strong Kobayashi entangled in the ropes and was bouncing the Japanese referee off a corner post. Mr. Ogawa slapped me gently on the back.

"It's not often we see a foreigner in Horonobe," he said. "It's a clean town, a peaceful town. We do our best. We give our residents the best we can. A bambi for the children . . ."

"And twenty-two bars."

"Let us drink"—Mr. Ogawa raised his glass—"to the friendship of all the people in the world."

We drank. Altogether about eight large mugs of beer and two full bottles of Suntory whiskey. And thus passed my fourth evening in Hokkaido. Truly, I thought, the people of the world are friends, for I was not permitted to pay for so much as the saucer of peanuts. It was still quite early when we left, but some of our party, Mr. Ogawa explained, had been out drinking till five or six that morning (the twenty-two bars of Horonobe are not subject to licensing laws) and it was felt that if the town hall's principal business of the next day—a baseball match against a team from Rishiri—was to be conducted with proper enthusiasm, the evening had better come to a fairly early end. We left arm-in-arm. The red-bearded American had long since been carried out of the cheering arena with blood all over his face.

The heat wave ended. The sky turned the color of bean curd and the rain came. Out on the lonely coast road where I stamped through the rain for the next six days, there was at least a sprinkling of bus shelters to rest in—shaky corrugated iron structures with nettles growing up out of the dirt floors and signs tacked to the rusty walls that said, in English and Japanese, "May Peace Prevail on Earth." Through holes in the corrugated iron I could watch the sea oozing gray and sullen up these far northern beaches, and in one of the lulls I took off my clothes and swam out till I could look back at the hulk of Mount Rishiri, its slivers of snow like cracks in a gutter.

The noodle shop I stopped in for lunch on the fifth day was run by one frail old lady who both cooked and served, and every time she came out to wait on a table she had to take off the clean slippers she wore in her kitchen and put on the grubby plastic sandals she used for walking on the concrete floor of her shop. She would set down her tray of bowls on the counter, lean back against the doorpost, and shuffle her feet in and out of the sandals without needing to use her hands. But this slowed her down, and at lunchtime in a crowded noodle shop slowing down is rarely tolerated.

"Oi! Where's my noodles?"

"What's up, then, grandma?"

"Why can't you get this table cleared?"

"Don't you give your customers glasses of water?"

"Does it take half an hour to open a beer?"

"You swam?" gasped the old woman incredulously when, on the stroke of one, the shop had emptied and she had flopped down to eat her own lunch of rice and pickles. The weather forecast had announced that morning that the sea off the southern tip of Kyushu, fourteen latitudes further south, was still too chilly to swim in.

"It wasn't any colder than an English sea," I explained.

"How courageous!" the old lady marveled.

I was finishing off my noodles when the Meiji Ice Cream man arrived to fill up the fridge. "All Englishmen," he told me, "*even fishmongers,* wear ties."

"Are you really from England?" the old lady sighed. "Is England further away than America? How long would it take to get there? How much would it cost?"

The ice-cream man had finished stocking the fridge and was lounging across the lollipops with a cosmopolitan air, shedding light on various foreign countries.

"What foreign countries are over there?" the old woman wondered, pointing out of the window at the sea.

"Russia," said the ice-cream man, "Korea, China . . . ," and then after a pause for thought, "Bulgaria."

Before I left he told me how the fishermen of Hokkaido exemplified the Japanese character. "Foreign fishermen," he explained, "will take

13

only the fish they know they can sell and throw the rest back. But Japanese fishermen will keep fishing till their boats are full, even though it means they'll have to sell their catch at half price. We Japanese are *waakaahorikku* (workaholics). We do everything with a vengeance." And the old woman and the ice-cream man both solemnly nodded.

Perhaps the vengeance of the Japanese fishermen is one reason why Hokkaido's famous herring shoals have almost totally disappeared and why the herring boats have had to turn in recent years to the much less romantic business of netting shrimps and crabs. No one writes ballads about shrimps and crabs, but the former glory of the herring fishers is the subject of Hokkaido's most popular folk song:

> *Ask the gull if the herring has come.*
> *The gull replies: I am a bird in flight—*
> *ask the waves.*

Through the curtain of the rain that still fell on the sixth day I began to make out a range of high mountains ahead of me, the summit of the highest still dismally capped with a gray-white blank of snow. My map, published seven years earlier, showed a road that skirted these mountains along the coast, though the key to the map, helpfully translated into English, warned that it was "difficult in traffic of motor car." This turned out to be a bit of an understatement for, as I was told, the road had yet to be constructed. I decided to give the mountains a wide berth, anyway, and turn inland when I reached the city of Rumoi, but Rumoi was still a good three days away and the rain showed no sign of letting up. I walked with the hood of my anorak zipped tight round my head, but the rain spattered into everything—boots, clothes, the cracks in the asphalt—dripping through the roofs of the bus shelters, imparting to the sea a texture like pocked lead.

Sometimes I would stop to rest at a small shop or to ask how many kilometers it was to the next village. And sometimes, especially when the shopkeeper was getting on in years, she would tell me she had no idea how many kilometers it was, but that it was perhaps a *ri* or a *ri* and a half. The *ri*, the old Japanese measure of distance, has disappeared entirely from road signs and maps, and within ten years it will have vanished from the language. One *ri*, say the conversion tables, equaled 3.927 kilometers, but that is nearly irrelevant. One *ri*—as I came to

14

know in practice—was the distance that a man with a burden would aim to cover in an hour on mountain roads. The kilometer was invented for the convenience of machinery. The *ri* was an entirely human measure, which is why it had no chance of surviving. We tell the time in digits and bleeps, and distance is not distance if you can't divide it by ten.

On the long empty road I would walk for hours and meet no one I could stop and talk to. Occasionally a car bounced past, ploughing up the loose pebbles and skidding round the ruts and pits. More occasionally I passed a gang of workmen high up on the protective netting of a cliff face who stared down at me and muttered to each other, too far away for me to hear what they were saying. On these first lonely days the little isolated shops were not only sources of information, but shelters, rest centers, snack bars, and, together with minshukus and ryokans, the only real indicators I had of how life is lived on the north Hokkaido coast. . . .

I unsling my pack and walk into a shop. The middle-aged woman who runs it is watching the midday quiz show on an eighteen-inch color television set. She can change the program by remote control, and in the lower right-hand corner of the screen there is a second screen, a tiny black-and-white one, so that she can monitor what is happening on other channels. Her wares consist of chewing gum, ice cream, soft drinks, cookies, and cellophane-wrapped bread rolls with bean jam in the middle.

"No beer?" I groan.

She does not sell beer but takes instant pity and raids her own massive three-door refrigerator.

"What a life!" she sighs. "It's ten past twelve and you're the only customer I've had all day. There's no point in having a shop here. All the fishermen and farmers have got cars so they drive into Wakkanai or Rumoi to do their shopping. It's a hard life for the poor like us." And she sighs again as the quiz show is interrupted by a commercial for digital watches.

In the back of one little shop I stopped in there was a woman with a smile so astonishingly lovely that it shot off her face like a beam of light. I glimpsed her while I was buying an apple. She was very tiny and had a grotesquely hunched back, and she sat in front of a huge electric knitting machine that someone had bought her as a present;

15

a brand-new electric computerized knitting machine—slip in a card and out comes a cushion cover. I don't think I have ever seen anyone look prouder than that little hunchbacked woman sitting there smiling at me, wanting me to notice her knitting machine.

There was a lull in the rain on the seventh day and I walked along the still empty coast road and saw an eagle ripping the guts out of a crow. On the main street of one village, an old woman in a dark kimono with a scarf round her head and no teeth in her mouth came up to me and, to my amazement, put her arms round my neck and, when I had bent down to her, put her cheek against my cheek and asked me where I lived.

"In Tokyo," I said, and she hugged me as tight as her shaky little body would let her.

"I have three grandsons in Tokyo," she said. "Three grandsons. Thank you. Take care. Good luck to you." And she patted me on the back, twice, smiling and then sighing, and the rain came down again and I walked on toward the snowy mountains.

It was dark by the time I reached the outskirts of the little town of Tomamae, and the rain was still pelting down, smacking the black gravel of the empty road and bouncing back in millions of crisp white explosions. I sloshed quickly past the rows of thin red-and-white striped poles that had been set up along the road for a festival, and under the strings of pink paper lanterns that bobbed and swung between them. The rain shook and spun the lanterns so that clouds of water cascaded off them. I passed a shrine where stalls had been erected and where one or two stallkeepers sat under their dripping canvas awnings, scowling at the shattered reflections of the lanterns in the puddles that swamped the gravel. I hurried on as fast as I could and met not a single reveler on the drenched streets.

In the ryokan three little children were screaming that they wanted to go out and buy candyfloss. We hung my dripping clothes over a stovepipe and I went down to the bathroom and wallowed for half an hour in water as hot as I could stand it. The hot smooth water nuzzled my thighs and shoulders and stomach, and first stung, then softened, the blisters on my heels and toes. I closed my eyes and the distant sound of a festival drum—a deep sodden thump of a sound practically drowned in the shush of the rain—came floating through the bathroom window. It went on for five minutes. Then it stopped,

16

and there was only the rain thudding on the glass and in the yard and on the tiles.

⚓

Occasionally the bus shelters I sat to rest in had posters on the corrugated iron walls. In one, a lively advertisement for gravestones was stuck up next to a recruitment poster for the "Self-Defense Forces" (the label coined in 1954 to get round the awkward problem of Japan's maintaining an army, navy, and air force while its postwar constitution specifically forbids them). The poster showed two men stripped to their vests arm-wrestling across a mess-hall table before an admiring audience of four uniformed women all of whom had gunmetal fillings in their teeth.

The mist lay so thick on the hills that it hid them, and the rain continued to flatten the sea. Fronds of dull green and orange seaweed were splattered, rotting on the stony beaches, and between the fronds of seaweed lay the usual beach ornaments: pink plastic detergent containers, a broken umbrella, white polythene bags, tires, beer cans, orange peel, and a rusty bicycle half buried at the line of the tide. I drank coffee at a drive-in that called itself a "pit-in," and the rain stopped, leaving the sea a silver calm.

The ryokan in which I spent my eighth night was an elaborate affair with an entrance like a Western-style hotel and a carpeted foyer stacked with pinball machines. The bath water had all the signs of coming from a natural hot spring—it was dull with thick black bits floating in it—and the guests ate their dinner in a small communal dining room, the first guests facing the color television set, the latecomers swiveling to watch it over their shoulders.

The program that evening was worth watching. An interviewer was talking to foreign students at a hostel in Tokyo. Most of the students had only just arrived and could speak little or no Japanese, so the interviewer was having a fine old time cracking jokes about their language and the color of their hair, and getting them to play Japanese children's games to the delight of the adult studio audience, who had not played such games since they were toddlers. But one young man from Greece spoke good Japanese and had obviously spent a lot of time studying the country and its culture. When the interviewer asked him

17

about his hobbies, he replied that his main hobby was learning to sing *enka*—popular Japanese ballads.

"*Enka! Enka!*" shouted the interviewer. The studio audience giggled in anticipation.

"And what singers of *enka* do you particularly like?"

"I quite like Mori Shinichi," said the young Greek.

"Mori Shinichi! Mori Shinichi!" The giggles turned to snorts and nudges.

"Sing us a Mori Shinichi song, then." And so the brave young Greek took the microphone and, in front of all the cameras, sang:

> *Is a flower not a woman,*
> *a man a butterfly . . .*

The rest of his song was lost in the howls of laughter from the studio audience and the noise made by the half a dozen diners in the ryokan who had put down their chopsticks and were chortling at the screen.

"Look at that! Ha ha ha! A foreigner trying to sing *enka!*"

After dinner, in the ryokan's little bar, while the juke box played "Unchain My Heart" and one of the diners crooned "Danny Boy," I had an interesting conversation with a myna bird who did a perfect imitation of a slightly hysterical Japanese woman laughing at a myna bird. To anything I said in a polite tone of voice, the bird would reply "*Ah, so desu ka?* (Oh, is that so?)" But if it thought I was being rude, it would screech, birdlike, and on one occasion drew a tasty spurt of blood from my finger.

"*Sayonara,*" it said politely as I went upstairs to get a bandaid.

The menu on the wall of the bar was headed "Fizz" and included one concoction called Blue Hawaii and another called Tennessee Waltz. There was a bust of Beethoven on the counter, with welts and cracks across its head that I suspect had been inflicted during the myna bird's rages.

"Why don't you teach Kyu-chan (the myna bird) English?" suggested the woman behind the bar. "He's as gentle as anything if he thinks you're sincere. And he's a very quick learner." The woman had stuffed two large dishes down the front of her dress for breasts and was dancing a rumba to amuse the three customers. I didn't want to guess which "Fizz" she was drinking, and anyway I was so dead tired—and the dishes seemed only to flatten her further—that I quickly decided to call it a night.

"That's all right," said the woman when I asked for the bill. "You can pay in the morning before you leave. That will be much more convenient, won't it?"

I supposed it would, and so it proved—convenient, at least, for the ryokan—since it enabled them to charge me for two bottles of beer I didn't remember drinking and a saucer of beans perhaps Beethoven had consumed.

"*Sayonara,*" said the myna bird, managing to sound wistful and not, I thought, too unlike Mori Shinichi:

> *When the flower falls the butterfly dies.*
> *Ah, how I should love to love so . . .*

The sea was ghostly in the mist, separated from the flat coast road by a wire fence that gave it the appearance of no man's land. High up on the cliff above the road a group of elderly workmen drilled the face with stuttering pneumatic drills. And a cannibal crow, its black eyes ecstatic, tore at the corpse of another crow that had been rammed flat to the road in the night. An old man on the island of Rebun once told me that the crows in Hokkaido attack human beings—but only schoolgirls, and only between four and five o'clock in the afternoon. It had something to do with their uniforms, he suspected.

By midafternoon I was sitting on a rocky beach staring down the coast at the first city I had seen for nine days—the city of Rumoi. I could see its chimneys, its cranes along the giant wharves, its antennas, its gas tanks, all shrouded in a mist that on the sea was pristine, but there, as it hovered round the factory stacks, was indistinguishable from the gray-white smoke belching out of them. I had spent nine days in the wilderness and was coming back to civilization.

"Ziss is a PEN! Ziss is a PEN!" screamed the children as I walked into the city. They giggled as they screamed that first sentence from their English textbooks, and if I answered them, they giggled louder. I came into Rumoi by what seemed to be the back way, trudging past

19

the Mobil Oil tanks, past the *Eastern Fuji* discharging its bilges, threading my way through a maze of narrow streets all of which seemed to
be under repair. Drills chewed up the tarmac, and women in white
scarves flagged down the cars.

"*Amerika? Amerika?*"

"England."

"Eh?"

"England."

"Wonderful! Wonderful! Thank you for taking the trouble."

The main shopping streets of Rumoi, as I discovered when I finally
found them, are like those of most other Japanese cities—a bewildering
exercise in juxtaposition. One shop sells electrical appliances: portable
radios with names like Mac, cassette decks and televisions all in one—
Zilbap, Cougar, Transam—so many knobs and digital counters they
look as if they require a pilot's license. Next door a shop sells lacquered
Buddhist altars, incense and candles to burn for the dead. Over the
road a pastry shop called Denmark and, next to that, a shop that sells
raw squid. A rack of bamboo *kendo* swords outside a toy store stocked
with baseball bats. The cinema posters display the same eclectic tastes:
Clint Eastwood squinting off one telegraph pole, two mottled dino-
saurs locked in combat on the next, and a half-naked Japanese Catholic
nun salivating as she fondles a black leather riding crop.

Rumoi seemed a lively enough city, I thought, though curiously
subdued in the early morning when I left it, striding off at the beginning of the tenth day of my journey past empty coal trucks and rows of
uniformed high school pupils, the girls babbling excitedly in their
neat full-skirted sailor suits, the boys in their shiny black blazers and
geta, dragging their satchels along the railings by the roadside and
waiting till I was well past before shouting out, "Hey, yooo!"

The morning brightened further from the city and the sun was soon
glinting on the inland rice fields, turning them into small square lakes
of green and silver. After more than a hundred kilometers I had left the
sea behind me and would not meet it again for a further three hundred,
when the sea would be the vast Pacific.

Outside a little railway station the stationmen were busy mowing
an already immaculate lawn, picking up the cut grass in their white-
gloved hands and placing it in a spotless red wheelbarrow. By the
time I turned off the main road into the mountains the blue sky was

20

cloudless and July was back. The road was a real dirt mountain road, twisting and turning, climbing and plunging, crossing and recrossing the single steep railway track that ran through the gorges from Rumoi to Numata.

"Do you want one of these? They're alive, you know," asked the man who owned the one village grocer's shop I stopped in, and he showed me a sea slug in a fat plastic tube. I opted instead for a packet of dried octopus and a bottle of chilled Sapporo beer: "Time honoured since 1876" said the label in English.

"You're my very first foreigner, you know," confessed a little girl on a tricycle, staring up at me with wide, serious eyes. She followed me on her tricycle out of the village until her attention was claimed by the Communist Party's loudspeaker van that was doing the rounds for the local elections, repeating the candidate's name over and over again in the ritual that serves, in Japan, for campaigning: "My name is Kodama Kenji. Vote for me. My name is Kodama Kenji. Vote for me. My name is Kodama Kenji. Vote for me. My name is Kodama Kenji. Vote for me...."

Four little boys on bicycles escorted me into the town of Numata at five o'clock in the afternoon and made me stop to look at their pictures of *suupaa-kaa* ("supercars").

"What *suupaa-kaa* do you have in England?"

I felt boastful: "Oh, you know ... Rolls Royces ... Jaguars ..."

"Is that all?"

"Well, er ... there's ... er ... Aston Martins ..."

"It's a shame he's not an Italian. *They've got Lamborghinis.*"

And with that accusation ringing in my ears, I was shown to a ryokan and promptly abandoned.

The island of Hokkaido is a comparatively recent addition to the Japanese homeland. Until the middle of the nineteenth century the only permanent Japanese settlements lay huddled in the extreme southwest of the island—at Matsumae, Esashi, and Hakodate—within a day's journey of mainland Honshu. A few loggers ventured further north, and a handful of merchants to trade with the Ainu, the aboriginal inhabitants of the Japanese islands who had been herded into Hokkaido by the close of the ninth century. But the loggers and the merchants returned south in the autumn, leaving the Ainu to brave the winter in their straw-walled huts and the Russians from Sakhalin to come trapping seals. It was not until 1869 that an official "Commissioner of Colonization" was appointed, and not until six years after that that a treaty with Russia established Japan's sovereignty over the island once and for all.

In the last three decades of the nineteenth century the settlement of Hokkaido became a major government policy. It was partly based on a desire to exploit Hokkaido's mineral and timber resources in the rush to develop Western industries, partly to ease pressure on an already-crowded mainland, and partly to establish a military presence that would serve to deter any Russian incursions. (Japan still bases approximately a third of its "Self-Defense Forces" in Hokkaido, including its one fully mechanized division.) The authorities engaged American cartographers to map the island, American agronomists to study how best the land could be used, American educators to found and lecture at schools and colleges. They imported steam trains from America and architecture from Russia, laid out new cities, set up new administrations, licensed Japan's first beer factory and a Trappist monastery.

But the island remained—and to some extent still is—an outpost, a frontier state. It is perceived even today as "un-Japanese"—in its climate, in the drift ice that grazes its coast, in the scarcity of cherry trees (a national symbol), in the absence of a clearly distinguishable rainy season, in the empty flat expanse of its plains, in its crops of potatoes, oats, and maize, in its lack of a local dialect (since settlers came from all parts of Japan, they tended to adopt the standard form of the language to facilitate communication), in the signs outside its dairy farms that boast of "Registered Holsteins," in the TV commercials for ski holidays that tout Hokkaido as "the Scotland of Japan." And even the folk songs of the Japanese settlers have an unmistakable echo of remoteness and suffering:

> *I wake to the sound of the sea gull's cry*
> *and see in my mind the mountains of Hokkaido.*
>
> *The plovers wail, shearing the moon,*
> *and the waves of the sea are choked with sobbing.*

22

Some of the villages and small towns I had passed through seemed outposts in a literal sense—the roads between them still uncompleted, cut off in winter by three yards of snow. The twenty-two bars of tiny Horonobe bore definite witness to its winter isolation (and twenty-two was not an especially large number, as I had learned to my satisfaction in other "frontier" towns). Conversation in these towns often plunged me out of my depth. I had spent seven years in Tokyo, an in-poster, displaying an in-poster's ignorance:

"In winter the snow is past the lintels."

"Oh, that must be pretty!"

But now I was emerging from the northernmost provinces into the valley of the Ishikari River—a valley that rapidly widened into a plain—and the sense of isolation, of moving from one frontier post to another, was increasingly swamped by the evidence of industrial development. The chimneys of the local power station are visible for twenty kilometers, car cemeteries flank the sprawling towns and the towns slide conspiratorially one into another, ponds and streams are in the throes of dredging, day and night there is a rumble of trucks on the highway, for the highway was now inescapable.

My eleventh day opened on a cloudy sky and four more little boys who pursued me on bicycles, screaming "*Gaijin! Gaijin!* (Foreigner! Foreigner!)" When they had overtaken me, they blocked my path with their bicycles and stood scowling up at me open-mouthed: "*Ufu! Mite! Eigo no hito da!* (Ugh! Look! It's an English-speaker!)" I suggested to them in Japanese that they might like to move their bicycles. They turned away, crestfallen: "*Ara! Eigo ja nakatta!* (Oh! It wasn't an English-speaker!)"

The wind made the pipes of my pack frame sing and muffled the noise the election vans made, though when the wind dropped you could hear them for miles over the flat plain: "My name is Kita Shuji. Vote for me. My name is Kita Shuji. Vote for me. . . ." I sat for ten minutes with a small white goat tethered to a railing by the side of the highway that munched grass from my hand, licked my knee, and bleated in despair when I left it.

The night brought a summer storm and in the morning a hard rain was still sweeping the streets outside my ryokan window. Less than five kilometers away the city of Takikawa offered shelter and a day of rest. I succumbed without much protest to the offer and fled across the girdered bridge, my anorak zipped up round my nose, the rain still drenching every square inch of me, so that when I swung my pack off in a coffee shop I practically swamped the floor. I sat for an hour drinking Kilimanjaro at a pound a cup, reading *Play Comic* ("No Cut!! No Black Out Porno!!") and listening to the Mozart flute quartets, which just about managed to compensate for the chill of my clothes and the smell of the overflowing drains.

At midday, with the rain still pelting down, I drifted into a cinema. It was three-quarters empty and I sat through a double bill, stiff, cold, but grateful for the dark and the rare bit of anonymity it lent me. The first film was about *yakuza*—Japanese gangsters—one of whom, to protest a gang decision, sliced off the tip of his little finger with a twelve-inch kitchen knife and slipped it to his boss in a cup of green tea. The result was mayhem. The second film, about a women's prison, climaxed in a scene where the prison superintendent chained one of the younger inmates to his bed and raped her while slashing her breasts with a broken bottle. When the lights went up I noticed that there were quite a lot of young children in the audience, some with their parents, so it was encouraging to remember that, according to the Japan National Tourist Organization, "Japanese cinema keeps in close touch with the people in its attempts to graphically express their hearts' desire."

The rain had stopped when I left the cinema but the streets still shone and the late afternoon light was a muffled gray. The ryokan I managed to find was of a type specially recommended for foreigners by the Japan Ryokan Association—a type I normally went out of my way to avoid. But I was afraid, being both wet and cold, that if I didn't get a bath and a dry kimono soon, my journey would be ending at Takikawa. They gave me a bed, a "Western-style" meal consisting of a cold chicken leg wrapped in aluminum foil on a pile of cold pink macaroni, and charged me twice what I was paying at minshukus. I bought a couple of cans of beer from a machine in the corridor outside my room (there being, in the "Western tradition," no service). They cost twice what I was paying at grocer's shops—about a pound a pint.

Broken bottles, comic books, and severed fingers that looked disturbingly edible danced about in my dreams all night. I found, when I woke, that my legs were not stiff, that my feet stopped killing me inside fifteen minutes, and that I could bow and smile politely while paying my bill. Clearly, I was becoming acclimatized.

Dark clouds still shrouded the mountains to the west, but the distant eastern mountains were bathed in a clear silver light. It was getting better. On the dead straight road, on my thirteenth day, I followed an open truck creeping along with a mechanical extension arm trimming the grass. On the back of the truck stood a mechanical policeman. He wore a real tie and a real helmet and was raising and lowering his flag in so lifelike a manner that, at first, I thought he was real as well. Further on, a large signboard on one side of the road showed an artist's conception of a holiday resort: a pristine blue lake, a pavilion with neat red-painted terraces, a children's playground, a tourist center, a complex of restaurants, pools, and shops. Through the trees behind the signboard I glimpsed a swamp in the first stages of being dredged— the choked remains of what must once have been a small lake, for little wooden steps led down to it and empty wooden benches over-looked it. I supposed that couples had come to sit on these benches on Sundays to gaze out over the lake towards the distant mountains. But they had done so for nothing, whereas lakes must pay their way.

A heavy lorry coming up from Sapporo swerved across to the wrong side of the road and growled to a halt in front of me. "My God," I thought, "what's coming?" The driver leaned out and gave me a pickled plum. Further up the road I passed a cattle truck parked outside a drive-in where the truck driver was eating his lunch of *nikomi* (gut stew), and in the truck the cows stood with shiny eyes, staring out at the stream of converted fish eaters, all speeding back in the wrong direction, towards Sapporo, away from the slaughterhouse.

It is not pleasant at the best of times to walk along a highway, but it can be educational. You notice, for example, the changing fashions in litter. I remember once, on a trip through Greece, being struck by the fact that the commonest kind of debris on the roads of Macedonia ap-peared to be squashed tortoises. On British roads I suppose it is squashed birds. On Highway 275 from Numata to Sapporo it is abandoned cassette tapes. They lie unraveled along the verges, sometimes for as much as half a kilometer, looking like lost bits of survey equipment. An educational experience, but a puzzling one.

I stopped at a grocer's shop for a beer and was invited into the back of the shop and given a wooden stool to sit on and a glass mug to drink from. The back of the shop doubled as a small savings club and an old man had come to deposit part of his pension. When he walked he bent almost double on his stick. When he listened he cupped his hand to his ear like a character in a cartoon strip. He wore baggy gray trousers and a spotless white shirt and he told me that he had been a sailor. Sixty years before, he told me, he had been to London, Glasgow, and Liverpool, and had visited the Vickers Company at Barrow-in-Furness. He pronounced this name with very great care, articulating every syllable so precisely that he made it sound like holy writ. The grocer was visibly awed, and when the old sailor said "Barrow-in-Furness" a second time the grocer's wife gave him a free packet of biscuits.

The evening was bright and good to walk in, but a daily average of thirty or so kilometers was starting to take its toll on my untrained body. I have always walked a lot, for pleasure and for exercise, but I had never before set out to cover 3,300 kilometers at a stretch, and the thought of the next four months, as much as anything else, was sending darts through my soles and calves.

The white-shirted manager of the Tsukigata Tourist Center, the only place with a vacancy for the night, tut-tutted and fussed as I staggered in: there were no slippers waiting at the automatic door so while I stumbled out of my boots some had to be fetched.

"So difficult to find trained staff," said the manager in the hearing of the elderly maid who had run to fetch the slippers. "You really must try to forgive us."

I asked the elderly maid if there was a washing machine that I could use. She smiled, bundled me up to my room, chatted to me while I changed into the *yukata*—the summer kimono—she had brought me, took my shirt, my jeans, my underpants, and stinking socks, washed them, rinsed them, dried them, ironed them, and had them in my room before breakfast next morning. So much for untrainables.

I wondered why Tsukigata, a nondescript little town by all appearances, should have such a thing as a tourist center. But as I lay soaking in the vast bath, looking out of the picture windows at the last light fading on the wooded valley, it seemed a pleasant enough place to be. And valleys must pay their way.

The younger maid who brought up my dinner kept holding her head in her knees and giggling. When it came to laying out the futon, she collapsed entirely, rolling about the tatami mats honking like a foghorn. She had clearly been at the sakè since lunchtime, and it was the older maid's turn, as she dragged the futon away from her, to tut-tut about the lack of staff training. But I didn't mind a bit. I liked them both—the old one's chatter, the younger one's bright red wobbling cheeks. And when the manager came sniffing along the corridor, picking tiny black midges off his crisp white shirt, I shut the door before he got to us.

I suppose there are still countries where children walk seven or eight kilometers to school. They must be very underdeveloped. In properly developed countries, the inhabitants regard walkers with grave suspicion and have taught their dogs to do the same. Shakespeare's Richard III complained that dogs barked at him as he halted by them and thought it had something to do with his hump. It made no difference whether I halted or not, the Japanese dogs that saw me flew into rabid frenzies. One dog owner guessed it was because my rucksack reminded them of a burglar's loot, although I preferred to think it stirred in them deep canine memories of the last Plantagenet. At any rate, I was thankful that dog owners in Japan keep their pets chained up on short leashes. It is a practice that has caused more than one foreign resident to vent his spleen in the English-language press. Let him try walking from Hokkaido to Kyushu.

The fourteenth day was brilliant hot—the sort of day when indolence was an even greater hazard than dogs. I turned off the road and tramped down a scorching path through fields to a small, sheltered hot spring where I lounged for an hour, trying to read the mineral analysis in the changing room, sipping what tasted like liquid sulfur from a dented metal cup on a chain.

I made an easy day of it, and after twenty-three slow, flat kilometers I strolled into the little town of Tobetsu. At the ryokan, there was a choice of slippers and the owner's wife greeted me with a kneeling bow and with a cup of green tea that I sipped as I perched on the upstairs window ledge, listening to the chirruping of the river. The owner's wife cut flowers in the garden and brought them up to me—two large white lilies and a blood-red camellia—arranged in such a casual way that no effort seemed involved at all. But I had watched her in the garden from my seat at the window, measuring the stalks, trimming them with her eye. There are ryokans and ryokans, but I found few like this one, where everything in sight had been chosen with care—from the handmade paper fan on my table to the scroll in the alcove with its two wild persimmons.

The owner had a soft round face and a quiet voice, and after dinner we sat in his living room together sipping beer that I knew his wife had gone out specially to buy. You could hear the river from the living room too, cooling the night with its plashing.

"My grandfather was a samurai in the province of Awa—nowadays the eastern part of the island of Shikoku. He kept a martial arts academy where he trained the sons of farmers. Awa was such rich country then. You could scatter seeds on the bare hills and watch them grow. Our family had lived there for centuries. . . ."

His wife brought us a dish of cherries.

"When the old feudal government fell and the restoration of the emperor took place—what year would that be . . . ? *Meiji gannen*— 1868 by Western reckoning—all the lords of Awa were dispossessed. One by one they lost their lands. My grandfather ended up a *ronin* . . ."

There was a flicker of embarrassment in the owner's smile.

"A *ronin*, you know—a samurai without a master. He was left with no lord, no responsibilities, no duties, no reason to stay in the place where he was born. So he packed his bags and came north to Hokkaido—two thousand kilometers, would it be? It must have been an extraordinary journey in those days. My grandfather was one of the pioneer settlers. He built a house here in Tobetsu. Married here, died here. . . ."

That night I lit a mosquito coil for the first time. Swarms of mosquitoes came up off the river and the old Japanese house with its gaps and cracks afforded no protection against them. It is often said that Japanese houses are built for summer, not for winter; and in this hard, far northern place, where the cool July drafts in the rooms seemed

28

evidence of that, I thought about the lives of the old pioneers and of the snow that covered their thin wooden lintels.

The smoke from the mosquito coil drifted through the little room, scenting the air with summer. Across the river, still faintly purling, children were letting off fireworks late into the night. But I was asleep five minutes after my head touched the pillow. I have only fond memories of Tobetsu and my dreams there were gentle ones.

⚡

There was a fierce wind on the bridge across the Ishikari River, and it took me nearly twenty minutes to battle it. Ahead of me, against the haze of the mountains, I began to make out the distant high-rises of the city of Sapporo, site of the 1972 Winter Olympics and the administrative capital of the island. The car cemeteries grew more and more frequent—acres of brightly colored metal, wheelless, impotent, still oddly condescending. It had taken me fifteen days to reach Sapporo— 370 kilometers from the start of my journey. It would have taken a motor car perhaps nine hours.

On the road into the city I was twice greeted in English. At a drive-in a young truck driver jumped out of his cab and said, "You foot, yes, and good for walk, but sun day—rain day, oh, Jesus Christ!"

Further on, a businessman stopped his car to offer me a lift and, clearly puzzled by my refusal, said, "Then what mode of transportation are you embarking?"

Japanese slipped out: "*Aruki desu.*"

"*Aruki?*"

"*Aruki.*"

A digestive pause.

"Do you mean to intend that you have pedestricized?"

I nodded. He drove away, shaking his head.

That evening, with my rucksack unpacked in a hotel room and twenty-four hours of lounging ahead of me, I strolled across the railway tracks to celebrate the completion of the first leg of my journey at the largest beer garden in Japan. The *Biiru-en,* or Beer Park, is actually the old disused Sapporo brewery, built in 1887, a dark, massive, red-brick complex like Victorian engine sheds sprouting ivy. The black brewery chimney bears the sign "Sapporo Beer," and the labels on the bottles

29

celebrate the holy trinity: "München–Sapporo–Milwaukee." Students and office workers crammed the trestle tables, slamming their tankards down on the wooden tops, shouting, singing, rolling from side to side, ordering beer (spelled "bier") by what looked like the gallon, and occasionally stumbling off in the direction indicated by two signs that said "Herren" and "Damen."

The tables out on the lawn were quieter than those inside, and I ambled towards them past a line of parked taxis where the taxi drivers slouched, chain-smoking, over their bonnets.

"Japan! Japan!" said one of the drivers, scowling and jabbing his finger at me.

"Pardon?"

"Japan! Japan! Japan! Japan!"

"*Amerika,*" giggled the office girls at whose table I sat, and as the waiter swabbed down the table in front of me, they gathered up their handbags, still giggling, and left.

I ordered the largest mug of draft beer on the menu and a dish of mutton-and-cabbage which the Japanese find so outlandish that they have dubbed it *jingisu kan* (Ghenghis Khan) after the grandfather of the greatest barbarian they ever jabbed at. The beer, as always, was about one-third froth, but a single portion of Ghenghis was so huge that it took an hour to eat—compensation for the loss of fluid ounces if not for the loss of office girls.

At eight the air took on a northern chill and the tables on the lawn began to empty. One by one the customers hailed taxis or threaded their way back into the jam-packed halls. I watched a young foreigner —I guessed an American—leading two Japanese girls toward the exit—one by the hand, gazing dreamily ahead of her, the other a yard behind, flirting with his back.

And all the people of the world are friends, I thought. Lovely sentiment, lovely girls. I watched them till they were out of sight, then I groaned and bent to my mutton.

✖ 2 ✖

The Savage Island

THE YOUNG WOMEN who operate the lifts at Sapporo Tower are well trained. As soon as the lifts are full they turn their backs on the passengers and politely address the instrument panels.

"Many thanks for your generosity in visiting us and a profound welcome to Sapporo Tower. We are now on our way to the observation platform. We are passing the offices on the second floor and the shops on the third floor. There is a souvenir stall on the observation platform and a tourist information bureau near the first-floor entrance. Please make free use of all our facilities." (An inclination of the head to the emergency call button.) "The television antenna that tops Sapporo Tower is 147.2 meters above the ground. The observation platform is 90.8 meters above the ground. The digital clock on the outside of the tower is 69.98 meters above the ground."

The lift floats to a halt, the doors swish open, the instrument panel is thanked for its patronage, and the passengers drift across to the plate-glass windows and grin down at the city spread below them.

Sapporo was laid out in 1869 and has a street plan like New York's. Its straight roads cross at right angles, its blocks are numbered according to the cardinal points of the compass. The result is a checkerboard that was considered at the time of the city's founding to be "modern" and "Western." Ironically, the Japanese city that Sapporo most resembles in this respect is Kyoto, laid out on an exactly similar pattern in the year 794 in imitation of China's three-thousand-year-old capital of Ch'ang-an. "Modernity" is an oddly blinkered concept. The little stream that flows through Sapporo has been made to flow in a dead

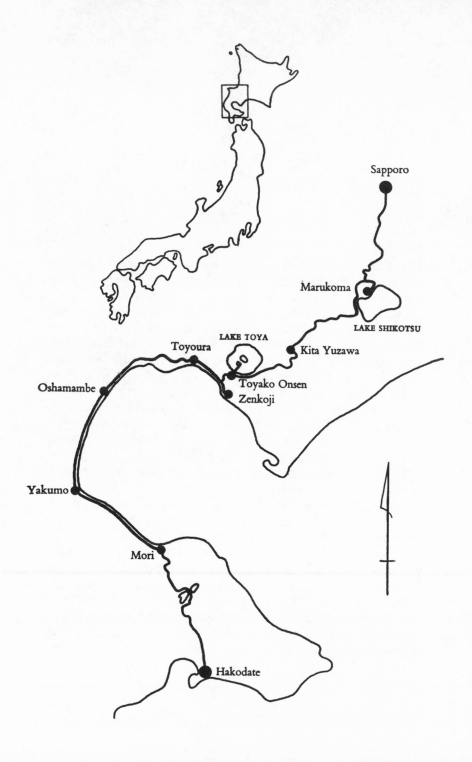

Sapporo

Marukoma

LAKE SHIKOTSU

LAKE TOYA

Toyoura

Kita Yuzawa

Oshamambe

Toyako Onsen

Zenkoji

Yakumo

Mori

Hakodate

straight line. The broader avenues are lined with trees, and the trees have been planted exact distances apart. The city viewed from Sapporo Tower is a clear contradiction of the distaste for symmetry that Japanese aesthetics are held to embody. It is a model of cleanliness and order and, as such, seems only to underscore the "foreignness" of Hokkaido.

One point of interest not visible from the tower is a narrow avenue of shops that stretches across eight of the city's central blocks. The high-rise buildings have hidden it from sight and, in any case, it has been roofed over and converted into an *aakeedo*—an arcade. It is called *Tanuki Koji*—Badger Alley—and I spent an hour strolling up and down it.

The badger is a magical animal in Japan, able to take on human form. So is the fox, but the fox is malevolent whereas the badger is simply mischievous. He is best known for his phenomenal sakè consumption, for the equally phenomenal size of his scrotum, for the nighttime drumming he performs on his belly, and for his skill in tricking innocents out of their cash. In the early 1870s a parcel of land was sold to a man called Matsumoto Daikichi who built a theater on it. Japanese theaters have been notorious since the seventeenth century as magnets for seekers of illicit pleasure. That is one reason why, in 1629, the government banned public performances by women, and why male actors still traditionally perform the female roles in Kabuki (thus encouraging a still more illicit pleasure). But government edicts did not prevent the theaters from continuing to attract fans of "the floating world," and the area round Mr. Matsumoto's theater was soon dotted with tea shops, bars, and places that specialized in less public entertainments. Sapporo was a boom town then, and many of its residents were frontiersmen who had come to Hokkaido in search of their fortunes. These hard-working, hard-drinking trappers and miners found themselves irresistibly drawn to the new pleasure quarter. There, beguiling creatures of the night, their powdered necks magical in the glow of the lanterns, proved able to spirit away their cash quite as competently as any badger. They first called the area *Shirokubi Koji*—White-Neck Alley—in honor of its principal attractions. But perhaps at the instigation of the city fathers the name was changed to *Tanuki Koji,* and it was known after that, as the badger is, for its nocturnal liveliness, its enchantment, and its trickery.

Today, nothing much is left to indicate *Tanuki Koji*'s virile past. It has become an avenue of fashionable clothing shops and early-closing pizza restaurants.

It was well after midday on the fifteenth of July—the seventeenth day of my journey—when I walked out of Sapporo. In the broad park avenue that stretches from the tower—with its gum machines and its ashtrays that say "Smokin' Clean" on them—workmen were putting up pink paper lanterns for the summer Festival of the Dead. It was a bright hot afternoon. The mountains stood clear and violet on the horizon. Beyond them lay the southern lakes. I walked quickly past the sprawling pink concrete housing estates with their thousands and thousands of tiny apartments that the Japanese, straight-faced, call "mansions," past the vast Ground Self-Defense Force barracks with its rows of tanks that Japanese politicians, straight-faced, call "Special Protected Vehicles," past the salarymen practicing their golf swings with invisible clubs at the pedestrian crossings, past a girl wearing a jacket that said on the back of it "Let's Summer and Punk," past the intriguingly named Bar Madonna, by which time I was out of the suburbs, it was five o'clock in the evening, and the road stretched bare ahead of me with neither ryokan nor minshuku in sight.

I tried a motel. The owner explained that, since he was a member of the Japan Motel Owners' Association, I had no need to worry—his rates were all fixed and aboveboard. Between eleven o'clock at night and ten o'clock the next morning I could stay there for 4,800 yen (about fourteen pounds). For each hour before eleven o'clock I must pay another 500 yen. It now being five o'clock, I would be most welcome to stay at a total cost of 7,500 yen (about twenty-two pounds). This, of course, did not include meals. In fact he did not serve meals. But I could easily drive the five or six kilometers to a restaurant he would be glad to recommend. It was at this point, I think, that he realized—from my boots and rucksack and general demeanor, and from the fact that I was standing and not sitting behind a steering wheel—that I didn't have a car. He looked up and down the drive for a moment, cocked his head thoughtfully to one side, and suggested that I go and amuse myself for six hours and come back shortly before midnight.

"Thank you," I said. "Do you get many customers?"

"Oh, lots," he assured me.

The restaurant that I finally found was closed, but the tail end of the day's business was dragging on at the grocer's shop next door.

"I wonder if you can tell me where the nearest ryokan is?" I said, smiling encouragingly over the rim of my beer glass. I knew perfectly well where the nearest ryokan was. It was thirty kilometers away on the shore of Lake Shikotsu.

So I ended up helping with the evening deliveries, lugging beer crates two at a time up the fire escape to a tiny bar that smelled as though the lavatory had been clogged for a fortnight. My muscles groaned and all I wanted to do was sleep, but I was enticed back to the same bar after dinner, where the grocer, nudging me under the counter, announced that I was his long-lost son and that he'd fathered me at a grocers' conference in Edinburgh.

"Is he really your son?" whispered the awe-struck mama-san.

"What do you think? He speaks Japanese, doesn't he?"

"Oh, yes—he's obviously not a foreigner."

"Well, then . . ."

"Well, then, he must be."

I had the living-room floor to myself. In the morning when I went out to look at the garden pond, the kind grocer turned the waterfall on specially for me. Wildlife abounded. A huge Saint Bernard in the next-door yard couldn't make up its mind whether to mother me or kill me, and in the kitchen the grocer's wife was replacing long fly-papers that were black two layers deep with flies.

The eighteenth was a bright day and the road ran high through wooded country. Often I stopped to bathe my feet and drink the water of the mountain streams. The water was colder than any I had ever drunk, and I could not keep my feet in it for more than a minute or two without them turning numb. Clouds rolled over to rake Mount Eniwa, and a young cyclist stopped to take our photos with an automatic camera.

"How many kilometers do you walk a day?"

"About thirty as a rule."

"You should walk at least forty."

"But I'm not in a race."

"At least forty, I should say, with legs as long as yours."

I buried my face in the Izari River and lay for a while on its gravel bank looking up at the gray clouds scudding.

At three I glimpsed Lake Shikotsu for the first time far below me, absolutely flat, the color of breeze-blocks. As I clumped down to it along the winding asphalt the clouds parted to let through white slanting rays of sunlight that mottled its surface. By the time I reached the picnic spot on the shore of the lake and was kicking my way through the beer cans and lunch boxes, the sun had reappeared entirely and the lake had brightened to a glittering blue.

It was a Saturday. The lodge at Marukoma Hot Spring was crowded with two large groups of young women holding class reunions and with a much less appealing group of some fifty businessmen who already, at four in the afternoon, were merrily drunk and clapping their hands to the one Hokkaido folk song everyone knows:

Yaren soran soran soran soran soran hai hai!

The staff of the lodge were rushed off their feet, and so as not to inconvenience them I agreed to have dinner at whatever time they chose to serve it. They chose to serve it immediately—at a quarter past four—with the result that I left about half of it on the tray. But it wasn't wasted. It was finished off in front of me by twenty-six nonchalant flies.

After dinner I took a towel and explored the long corridors of the lodge till I emerged on a rock platform at the edge of the lake. There, to one side of the natural ledge, in a cove sheltered by the overhanging cliffs, thermal water came bubbling out from under the rocks at a temperature delightful to lie wallowing and singing in. I used it like a sauna, sitting for five minutes on a submerged rock in the hot slimy pool, then wading out and sitting for five minutes in the lake.

"Are *you* going to do that?" scoffed a nude businessman to his companion.

"What do you think I am . . . ," his nude companion grumbled, "a foreigner?"

They grumbled together, though not for very long. The pool was too hot and too slimy and too dirty and too small and too crowded for them (I was the only other bather there), so I soon had it to myself again.

The sun set behind me and a soft gray light settled over the hills on the distant shore. Along the wharf outside the lodge the guests who had spent the afternoon scouring for prawns were packing up their nets and strolling back to the baths inside. I sat for a long time in the hot spring, watching the light fade till I could no longer see the smoke drifting out of the crater of Mount Tarumae and, then, till Mount Tarumae itself was hidden in the dusk.

There were no rooms vacant at the lodge so I made do with a bunk bed in a small wooden outhouse. The bed was hard and there was no service of any kind—no shower, no television, no maid, no futon—but it was quiet and I had my own sleeping bag to crawl into. I was a little surprised in the morning when the matronly old lady who ran the place presented me with a bill for full board and lodging that amounted to more than twenty pounds, and even she must have experienced a twinge of guilt about it for, as I stamped grumpily out of the door, she gave me—quite free—a packet of picture postcards.

The path I had planned to follow along the lakeshore turned out to be a fiction of the mapmakers; at least, two of the three people I asked about it swore there had never been any such thing, and the third—the matron of Marukoma—remembered it vaguely from her childhood, but told me it had been impassable for the last thirty years. Since most of the lake is bounded by cliffs, and the chances of scrambling along them looked very remote, the only alternative seemed to be to skirt Mount Eniwa to the north, and so I set out, grudgingly, back along the same road I had tramped down the day before.

It was a brilliant Sunday morning and the shimmering surface of the lake was dotted with boats. As I rose above it, the sound of young men's voices came floating up to me—"*Sutaato! Sutaato! Sutaato!* (Start! Start! Start!)"—all hugely amplified through bullhorns and clearly, unconcernedly, audible for miles. "Left! Left! Left! *Sutoreeto!* (Straight!) *Sutoreeto! Sutoreeto!*" I was glad when I rounded the hulk of Mount Eniwa and the voices no longer reached me.

But relief was short-lived. The sky clouded over with malicious speed, and by the time I had reached the highest point of the road and the car park with its little observation platform, the sun had entirely vanished and the air had acquired an electricity that was tangible. For a while the storm merely threatened, though the one or two motorists who passed me seemed to sense it at their backs, for they steered their cars like mad things between the potholes, spewing up the stones and gravel of the worst road I had so far walked along.

The first thunderclap broke with no warning at all. It bounced off the bald face of the mountain, off the flat sounding board of the lake four hundred yards below, and rolled for what seemed an incredible time through the hills and trees as though seeking an escape route. It brought with it a sudden rising of mist. The lake, when I glimpsed it, was indistinguishable from the sickly sky, and the borders of the visible world shrank until I could see little but the potholes in front of me. I hurried on as the first rain spat, counting the snakes squashed flat to the gravel. The raindrops were huge and smacked like hail, but there were few, and the real onslaught was concentrated in the thunder.

My tally had reached six snakes, four of them babies, when quite without warning the mist rose and the storm was gone as suddenly as it had come. The lake was tranquil again through the pines. The evening had begun to gather.

I tramped on past the debris that accrues to tourist sites—rubbish tips in the clefts of the hills, abandoned cars, their windows demolished, bonnets up, wheels gone. By the time I reached level ground again it was clear that there were no more hot springs, no outhouses, no ryokans, no grocers in search of long-lost sons. Through a stretch of the trees I glimpsed the lakeshore, flat between a break in the cliffs, and so I left the road and walked half a kilometer over soft fallen pine needles and emerged into a sandy clearing that turned out to be a campsite. Two fishermen sat smoking on the nearby beach, and an old caretaker had come out of his wooden hut and stood staring at me as I trudged towards him. I nodded.

"Do you mind if I sleep down there on the beach?"

"You can if you want."

"I haven't got a tent."

He was lighting a cigarette. "Haven't got a tent?"

"Will I have to pay?"

The old caretaker squinted at the pack on my back.

"I've got a sleeping bag."

He shrugged, said nothing, and went back into his hut.

I chose a spot away from the fishermen and laid out my groundsheet on the damp sand of the beach, weighing it down with my boots and with stones. I unfolded my waterproof sleeping-bag cover and pulled it carefully on over the thin quilted bag. Then I crawled into it and lay for a while as the last light faded and the insects began to come in off the lake. The sound of the lake water was peaceful and the lights of the little fishing boats out on the surface of the lake seemed as distant as stars. There were no stars in the sky. I zipped the bag tight round my head and tried to go to sleep.

The rain began at midnight. It was light at first and felt like a breeze, but it was rain. I heard it on the waterproof cover of the sleeping bag and swore at it (that, incidentally, being the first English word I had uttered in nineteen days—Japanese is a very adequate language for complimenting the autumn moon and things like that, but it is sadly deficient in words for expressing a less harmonious relationship with nature). I uttered more English about thirty minutes later when I discovered that my waterproof sleeping-bag cover was definitely not waterproof.

Still the rain was light and I decided to try and stick it out, which was a stupid decision. By two o'clock I was thoroughly soaked and the drizzle had turned into a downpour. I got up, spewing out English like lava, and began gathering together my saturated belongings. It took me three journeys to drag everything over to the dry concrete step under the eaves of the caretaker's hut. I had a small electric torch, but still managed to lose my way on the second journey and spent ten minutes fighting a forest of wet thornbushes. I ended up leaving my groundsheet on the beach, throwing down my sleeping bag on the narrow sheltered concrete, crawling oozily into it, and trying once again to go to sleep. I found it impossible to keep my eyes closed. The rain thump-thumped on the iron roof, and under the damp sleeping bag the concrete was a torment.

A light went on in the hut. Through the condensation on the window I could see the wood stove the old man had burning. I saw his shadow move across the dry wall and watched him peer out through the lighted window and stare at me lying on his step. Then I heard him move to the door. The door opened a little and, by turning an inch, I could see his face silhouetted in the doorway. He stood there for what seemed a very long time and I tried to think of something to say, but in the end, I was spared the necessity of saying anything. Quietly but firmly he closed the door of his hut and turned the key in the lock.

It was light by five and the rain had stopped. I got up, shivering, retrieved my groundsheet from the beach, beat the sand off it with a sodden branch, and began to pack my rucksack. The caretaker sat staring at me through the window of his lodge. He looked as though

39

he had been sitting there all night. His old face was tired but his eyes were remarkably sharp. I knew he was staring at me as I rolled up my sleeping bag and strapped it to the pack and as I folded the groundsheet and laced my boots.

"*Sayonara,*" I said as I got up to leave.

I expect he was still staring when I reached the trees.

The man who told me about bears had lived on the shore of the lake for thirty years. He had been a prisoner of the Russians on Sakhalin, and the Russians had told him that he would never go home again. In the end they had released him after two years, and he had gone back to Sapporo where he had found no one he knew, he said, and no way of making a living. So he had settled here on the shore of Lake Shikotsu, a wiry brown-faced hermit, and an amiable one.

Like most Hokkaido people, he knew the value of hot water. He had an oil stove going now, in mid-July, and he poured the water that he had pumped up out of the ground very carefully into his small metal teapot and set it on the stove to boil.

Bears, he said, are the most predictable of animals—far more predictable than human beings, whom he confessed he had not much interest in and whom he thought overrated as a species.

"There are dozens of bears in the hills around the lake. They come down almost daily to the road over there."

He pointed at the road I had just walked along, and I said "Oh really?" with a great deal of nonchalance.

"You want to whistle or sing when you walk," he said, "or have a bell and ring it from time to time, or bang a stick. They won't come near you unless they're really hungry, and then it's only your food they'll want."

I nodded pleasantly, having no food.

"If you turn a corner and you see a bear and it's thirty meters away from you, you've no need to worry. The bear will run away. It'll be far more frightened than you are."

"Well, well!" I said, and sipped my tea.

"If you turn a corner and you see a bear, say, twenty meters away, there's still a good chance it won't bother you. It'll roar a bit just to let you know it's there, but if you stand quite still it'll probably get bored and go back into the forest."

"Mm," I said, giving the forest a very uncursory glance.

"And then, of course, if you turn a corner and you see a bear and it's five or ten meters away from you . . ."

"Then, presumably, I should start to worry," I said, chuckling my most British chuckle.

"Not really," he said. "You've no need to worry. Bears are the most predictable of animals. If it's five meters away it'll certainly kill you. There's no point in worrying at all."

From a distance Mount Shiraoidake must have looked like a Sung Dynasty painting. It looked a bit less like one at close range. Two motorcyclists came down the dirt road, their headlamps full on in the noon mist. One fell on the turn and hadn't the strength to lift his machine. When I passed him he was in tears. The road over the mountain was wild and high, crags and outcrops of sharp black rock, a sheer drop on one side, a sheer cliff on the other. Incredibly, a bus came bouncing down, hooting every four or five seconds, lurching on the turn, forcing me flat against the wet rock. Visibility was less than fifty yards and a drizzle had been falling since midmorning. I met a middle-aged Japanese couple in full Alpine gear—knickerbockers, knobbly canes, and Tyrolean hats with feathers in them. They were quivering under a single bright yellow poncho—the bus had missed them by fractions of an inch.

At three in the afternoon I emerged into green open country and the first cultivated fields I had seen since before Sapporo.

"Look at it! Look at it!" gasped the three little boys who had followed me to the door of a noodle shop and now had their noses pressed flat against the window. "What's it eating? What's it speaking?"

"Go away," said a woman, "and don't be rude to customers."

"It's all right," belched a fat man, "they're only kids."

The evening breeze bore a whiff of sulfur that spiked the blander smell of the apple orchards. At the hot spring resort of Kita Yuzawa clouds of white steam came hissing off the river. The drizzle had stopped and one or two people in ryokan yukatas were dipping small

41

string baskets of eggs into the scalding pools in the riverbed. I asked for a room at the *kokuminshukusha*—the government lodging house—but it was booked solid by an old age pensioners' glee club. The clerk phoned a ryokan.

"Hello, ah, I'm sorry to trouble you only, the fact is, well, uh, could you . . . I mean to say . . . it would be very good for international relations . . ."

There was a small refrigerator in the ryokan room containing bottles of Coca-Cola and beer. This is an increasingly common provision. The guest helps himself to whatever he needs, and in the morning the maid counts the empty bottles. It is an efficient arrangement that saves time and energy and reduces the pleasure of human contact to an absolute minimum.

The bath was fine. The men's and women's sections were separated this time by a jungle of plastic flowers and leaves so realistic I had to float up and touch them before I was sure they weren't real. From the bathroom I could see the steam rising off the river for more than a kilometer. There were benches on the opposite bank, and wooden bridges, and colored fairy lights in the trees. One guest succeeded in washing the whole of his body, face, and hair without taking the cigarette out of his mouth. I very nearly applauded.

"Why do all foreigners have such beautiful faces?" asked the middle-aged maid as she laid out the futon. I couldn't think of a suitable reply. "Men, women—they all look the same—such beautiful faces."

In the morning she counted the bottles twice and opened the refrigerator door to make certain.

The weather had improved. The gray clouds were sponged white, and Mount Shiraoidake stood the picture of innocence behind me. In midafternoon I caught a glimpse of Lake Toya, sparkling and clear, and the deep green knobs of the islands in its center. I trudged down past a row of souvenir shops selling carved wooden bears with salmon in their mouths.

The Ainu used to revere bears as gods. They would capture a young cub and keep it for years in a wooden cage in their village, treating it with great kindness, letting their children pet it, till it was tame as a puppy. Then they would dress up a stake with evergreen leaves, noose the bear, and lead it out into the village compound where they would let it skip about on a long leash. Some of the men, dressed in their finest robes, would shoot harmless decorated sticks at it in imitation of a hunt. They would then tie the bear to the green stake, kill it with arrows, ceremonially strangle its corpse, decapitate it, skin it, scrape out its innards, drink its blood for the mystical strength in it, and display the head of their god on its mangled hide.

Until 1879 this northernmost island was not called Hokkaido, but Ezo. The word *Ezo* is written with two Chinese characters. The first means "prawn," the second means "alien" or "savage."

For twelve hundred years of their history the Japanese left Ezo alone. It was too frigid, too wild, too much trouble to civilize, fit only for habitation by barbarians. The title Shogun, an abbreviation of *Seiitai-shogun*—literally, "Great Barbarian-Subduing General"—was earned in the genocidal campaigns that were waged against the Ainu in the eighth and ninth centuries, and which succeeded in pushing them out of their homelands in Honshu into these northernmost wilds. The Ainu were altogether a different race from the Japanese. They spoke a different language, practiced a different faith. Ainu men—reputedly the hairiest in the world—grew thick beards that covered their chests. Ainu women tattooed their faces. To the Japanese who glimpsed them, spearing their fishes, murdering their gods, they must have seemed utterly alien.

Added to their savagery was the savagery of the Ezo volcanoes, a savagery that still threatens. In 1910 Mount Usu erupted with such violence that a new mountain was formed in the convulsions. In 1944 it erupted again and a second new mountain grew up beside the first. To the Japanese people who have finally settled here, the island must resemble a half-wild animal. They have tried to tame it, and now they love it. But they can never be sure that it will not turn against them.

Lake Toya lies at the foot of Mount Usu and on the shore of the lake stands the hot spring resort of Toyako—a mess of ten-story Western-style hotels, Western-style coffee shops, and Western-style bars. The hotels have names like Villa and Palace, the bars have names like Julie. There is an amusement park called *Samaa Rando* (Summer Land), a club called *Kurabu Nuudo* (Club Nude), and a "Ladies' Corner" called Don Quixote.

I took a sightseeing cruise in the early morning of my twenty-second day, when the mist had not yet cleared from the water. The hotels were quickly lost to sight and we chugged through a world in which nothing was visible but the lake, the sky, and the gray humps of the islands.

"Good morning, everybody," said the guide through her microphone. There were three of us on the boat—two old ladies and myself. "If you will kindly turn and look to your left, you will see Mount Yotei."

We turned to our left. The mist was so thick that we couldn't even see the shore.

"What a beautiful mountain—the Mount Fuji of Ezo! And to the right you can see Mount Usu and the new mountains called Meiji Shinzan and Showa Shinzan."

We turned to the right and stared at a gray wall. No mountains, no buildings, no land of any kind.

I recall the blue waters of Izu and Miura
at the distant hot spring town of Toya.

The mist had begun to clear by the time we reached the little island called *Kannon-jima*—the Island of the Goddess of Mercy. We moored next to the six swan-shaped tunnel-of-love paddle boats, and I left my rucksack on the jetty while I strolled up to look at the Goddess of Mercy's shrine. It was a single small building of unpainted timber standing on the top of a pleasantly wooded hill. In the trees that ringed it hung two loudspeakers out of which came a stream of advertisements for the hotels and bars in Toyako, followed by "Black is black I want my baby back," followed by more advertisements, followed by "Oh mammy oh mammy mammy blue oh mammy blue." It was, in short, a typical sanctuary, so I refrained from pummeling the two old ladies who had followed me up the slope, and we returned intact to the jetty.

On our way back the mist had cleared enough for the new mountains behind the resort to be visible: Showa Shinzan, its cone belching smoke, Meiji Shinzan like a burial mound.

The sound of trapped fire—
the breath of the mountain
ascends toward Heaven . . .

44

The Goddess of Mercy has a lot of problems to contend with, not the least of them having to do with gender. *Kannon* is actually one of the male attendants of Amida Buddha, but he is generally depicted with so tender an expression on his face that, in the Japanese imagination, he has undergone a sex change. The bewildering variety of his own incarnations must be another source of consternation. There is, for example, a Horse-Headed Kannon, ringed with fire, who defies evil spirits. There is an Eleven-Faced Kannon who, for some reason, always has twelve faces, and a Thousand-Handed Kannon who only ever has forty hands (the argument being that each hand has the power to save twenty-five souls). Kannon's most familiar form is that of a tranquil, feminine spirit seated benignly on a lotus leaf, crowned with the crown of everlasting compassion, and glowing with the eternal tolerance of Buddha.

But in this savage island the Goddess of Mercy can be equally savage.

Eighteen days after I left Lake Toya, Mount Usu erupted for the third time this century. The eruption hurled ash and stones nearly three hundred kilometers to the south and east. Lava ran down the slopes to the shoreline. Smoke rose nine kilometers into the sky. A thick gray layer of what appeared to be moondust settled over the fields, and the vegetable, wheat, and rice crops were ruined. The five thousand inhabitants of Toyako Hot Spring were evacuated from their homes in army lorries and had to camp out in schools and temples till the eruption had ceased. Fish died in the lake, young trees died in the forests. Roads and railways were impassable. Fourteen cities and towns sustained damage. The hotels, coffee shops, and bars were closed and the boats no longer went out to the islands.

The loudspeakers in the Goddess of Mercy's shrine had been savagely, mercifully, silenced.

In the compound of Zenkoji—the oldest Buddhist temple in Hokkaido —a light breeze rustled the red paper lanterns advertising Asahi Beer. The temple is the only dwelling on the island without *amado*—wooden shutters. There is nothing between its corridors and the northern winter but paper screens.

"It was a storm, a storm at night, and there was no one in the temple

45

but me when he came. He was about your age. The rain was pouring down and he stood in the entrance hall and rapped on the door with his knuckles."

I watched, startled, while the tiny old lady with a face like a crab apple hauled herself up to her feet and stood tiptoe on the green felt carpet. The light coming in from the shaded temple garden turned her eyes bright emerald under the lids. She stood straight as a cane.

" 'I'll stay,' he said. 'You're welcome,' I said. The rain poured off his face. He didn't even wipe it. He was carrying nothing. He wore straw sandals. He had spent five years walking all over the island. He didn't even carry a satchel. He slept out there in the corridor and wouldn't accept a pillow."

She lowered herself down onto the cushion again. We sipped our tea.

"They were splendid then, before the war, the Rinzai priests. We are Jodo Shinshu, but he was Rinzai. They had such extraordinary faces. He told me he walked twenty *ri* a day."

Nearly eighty kilometers.

"He went up the mountain behind the temple and meditated for a week without eating or drinking. I don't know anything about India, but in Japan three days was considered the limit. He sat there for a week. We thought he would die."

Her eyes flickered out over the garden, over the red lanterns bobbing in the afternoon wind.

"He slept in the open for five years."

Her clock ticked.

"Summer and winter."

The old lady said nothing after that and I watched her tug herself back from a long way off to the July day and the room of the temple we were sitting in.

She gave me three tangerines and I left Zenkoji, found the Pacific, and walked along the coast road that smelled of strawberries. There were at least a dozen strawberry vendors by the side of the road and two of them gave me samples. The evening sun sparkled on the sweep of Uchiura Bay, a minor dent in the Japanese coastline, about the size of the duchy of Luxembourg.

The old woman who ran the grocer's shop in Toyoura got her grandson to take me to a ryokan where they were very pleasant, except that I couldn't understand a word the husband said. Over dinner his wife sat helping me drink my sakè and telling me her troubles, which grew more horrendous the more sakè she drank.

"My husband's Korean."

"Ah, that explains it."

"Couldn't you understand him?"

"Not very well."

"Neither can I most of the time."

I poured her another cup.

"I've got Korean nationality, you know," she said.

"Do you speak Korean?"

"Not a word."

"Have you been to Korea?"

"No."

She twisted round on the cushion and looked out of the window. You could just see the Pacific over the iron roofs.

"I'm a foreigner, too," she said.

"Well," I said, "it could be worse."

She was still looking out of the window at the sea. I refilled her sakè cup.

"This is very nice fish," I said. "What's it called?"

"A gaijin," she said, staring out of the window.

I went out for a walk. On the beach, in the last light, a young woman with no front teeth nursing a baby strolled up and asked me if I spoke Japanese. When she found that I did she took me back to the coffee shop she ran with her husband, and they gave me Coca-Cola and three cups of Kilimanjaro. The shop was called Hot and was decked out in Scandinavian wood and posters of the Bay City Rollers. We closed it at nine and took a few bottles of beer back to the young couple's flat. On our way out of the door we bumped into a man in a white shirt unzipping his flies.

"I wonder if you'd like to go somewhere else," the husband suggested.

The man in the white shirt said "Warrgggah!" to the husband, "Gaijin!" to me, and stumbled off round the corner. The wife swabbed the step.

They were a nice couple. They wished they had run into me before I booked the ryokan, they said. I could have stayed with them. They promised to drive down the coast the next evening and meet me at Oshamambe, where the young man's mother lived. I got back to the ryokan at midnight to find that the woman had left a pile of comic books by my pillow—*Comics for Men* and *Comics for Ecstasy*. In *Comics for Ecstasy* naked women were having their breasts sliced off with garden shears, being torn apart by bulls, and rammed with red hot irons. In *Comics for Men* they were only being bound and raped. I lay awake for a long time, not really ecstatic, looking at the moonlight on the corrugated roofs.

The smell of strawberries was even headier in the morning, and the Pacific sparkled as it lapped up the white beach. I longed to swim but the road ran several hundred feet above sea level and there seemed no way down. I came out of a tunnel a mile long that I got through with the aid of a pocket torch, climbed over the dented white guard-rail, and sprawled out on the baking hot grass of the cliff top. I fished for my sunglasses to ward off the glare and spoke briefly in English when I discovered I had sat on them. In the end I found a way down to the beach and swam for an hour in the crashing surf.

There were no other customers in the little restaurant at Oshamambe when I reached it, long after dusk, so I had a quiet, confessional chat with the plump old lady who was grilling me a mackerel. She told me about her visions.

"Coming back from Muroran in the car before evening I saw the mountains like a naked woman with long thick hair and enormous round breasts."

She mimed them.

"She was lying on her back staring up at the sky, and the clouds were a young man waiting to pounce. What d'you reckon?"

My mouth was full of mackerel.

"I saw it again coming up from Hakodate. Breasts like watermelons."

I began looking round for the comic books. She was leaning over the counter in front of me in her apron and I was going to say something clever, but then I looked down at the counter and her knuckles were bone white.

"I've not told anyone ever before," she said. "I think it's *akuma*."

Akuma is the devil.

"You have special eyes," I said. "That's all. It's a gift."

"The best thing," she said, "was the watermelons."

By the time the young couple from Toyoura arrived we had moved on from visions of breasts to folk songs. They could hear us quite plainly in the street, they said, which is generally the case when I am singing "*Soran Bushi.*"

Whatever their stature, men are men—
it makes no difference if they're four foot ten . . .

They had with them the husband's sixteen-year-old sister, smoking like a chimney, sipping whiskeys-and-water, and a spotty girl I remembered from the coffee shop who, the wife intimated with nods and winks, was not in the habit of coming out on evening drives and had put on a new dress and a great deal of makeup, so there must be a "very special reason."

It had taken me a long day to reach Oshamambe—thirty-seven kilometers from where the young couple lived. It had taken them in their car less than thirty-five minutes. That fact was enough to start me yawning, and I was inelegantly draped over the restaurant counter when my friends decided I should go to bed. We said goodbye at the ryokan door and in less than ten minutes I was sound asleep. It wasn't until I was nibbling my seaweed at breakfast that her very special reason occurred to me.

The traffic was heavy on the morning of my twenty-fourth day, and a fat little boy with a huge pair of spectacles looked in constant danger of being smashed flat by the trucks. For one thing, he was riding his bicycle with no hands on the wrong side of the road. (Cyclists in Japan seem not to be subject to any form of highway code. They can ride on either side of the road, on pavements, through traffic lights, and across pedestrian crossings as the mood takes them. Bicycles are the second largest cause of injuries in Japan. The first is falling down flights of steps.) For another thing, his spectacles were riveted on me, and we were deep in yelled conversation. I shouted to him to keep his eyes on the road, but no mere road was going to distract him. He was studying.

"How do you say 'My book is a boy's is my brother' in Japanese?"
"I don't know."
"Eh?"
"It doesn't make sense."

"We learned it at school."

"It's not English."

"Our teacher wrote it on the board."

"He must have had an off day."

"All right then, how do you say *jitensha?*"

"Bicycle."

"*Yama?*"

"Mountain."

"*Kintama?*"

"Balls!" ("Testicles" would have been better pronunciation practice, but I had my own mood to think about.)

The fat boy swirled his bicycle round in a U-turn, eliciting a wail of desperation from a fish lorry, and pedaled furiously away shouting "Balls!" at the top of his voice.

Orange blood leaked out of the fish lorry and spattered onto the hot road. The tires of a military convoy spread it thinly into the tar. I walked on to a village where a little faded vermilion bridge spanned the sea between an outcrop of gray rocks and the beach, and on the rocks stood a tiny battered orange-roofed shed that was a shrine. Shrines like this are a common sight on the tops of small hills and on rocks by the sea. The gods they house are placated with rice balls and tins of Coca-Cola that the rain turns brown.

"How do you write your name?" asked two gaping schoolboys.

I took out my alien registration certificate and showed them my name.

"What's that?"

"A fingerprint."

"Whose?"

"Mine."

"Why do they need your fingerprint?"

"It's the law."

"They've never taken *our* fingerprints."

"It's a privilege reserved for foreign residents."

A grocer in the same village gave me some sweet corn and told me about the winter.

"In Asahikawa it freezes so bad that the Coca-Cola bottles explode when you move them. Here it's not as cold as that, though we've more snow than further up the coast. We light our oil stoves around the twentieth of August, which is why Hokkaido people catch colds when they go to Tokyo. Here, the least sign of a chill brings the stoves out. There, the fools shiver till November."

On the steaming rocks at the edge of the beach an old woman in a dark blue headscarf and sea boots was laying out strips of mud-colored seaweed to dry in the mid-July sun. I walked on and swam near the next little village and lay on the hot beach and forgot the winter.

"Are you going to walk all the way to America?"

"Not all the way. I'll have to swim part of it."

"What will you do when you're tired of swimming?"

"Flap my wings and fly."

At Yakumo, in the restaurant where I had my evening meal, the Yakumo Farmers' baseball team was celebrating the afternoon's loss. It was a hearty celebration, partly because the team, in their emerald-green and orange tracksuits, were all naturally hearty, backslapping people, and partly because the night was hot and the restaurant served draft beer in large frosted mugs.

"Haven't sin you for ages!" roared the coach as he pummeled my shoulder blades and splashed beer over my Swiss Army knife. "Com'n have a little drrrrink!"

I went and had a little drink.

"What you doin'n Yakumo?"

"Having a little drink."

"Well, have annnnother!"

Later on we went to what the first baseman described as "a *genuinely real* Japanese bar." It was called the Music-In. The mama-san wore a low-cut satin ballgown and the centerpiece was a grand piano. In the absence of a pianist, I spent ten minutes fiddling about on the keys and was rewarded with an earsplitting ovation, a lot more beer, and two very bruised shoulder blades.

The pinch hitter who had stood beaming over me as I sat at the keyboard began to stroke my knee under the table.

"What year were you born?"

"Forty-six."

"*Showa* forty-six?"

"*Showa* twenty-one."

"The same as me! He's the same as me! What month? What month?"

51

"December."

"Aha!!"

My left thigh received a sharp pinch hit.

"*I* was born in *June*, so *I'm* the *sempai!* Hear that, everybody? *I'm* the *sempai!*"

And being my "senior" caused him such delight that I had to move round the table a couple of feet to ensure that my left leg would be usable in the morning. He made up for it in the street outside.

"When are you leaving Yakumo?"

"Tomorrow morning."

"Early?"

"Eightish."

He threw his arms round my neck.

"Why don't you pop in and see me in the morning? I'm a car salesman up at the Nissan showroom."

"That's nice," I said. "I'll certainly do that. I could buy a Nissan while I'm there."

"I've a very good line in Cherries," he said, and he patted my cheek and kissed me goodnight.

The morning was cool and overcast. I left before the showrooms opened.

I don't know what it was that upset me that morning. A note in my diary says that I was sick of being stared at; but I had been in Japan for seven years and was thirty, which meant that I had been stared at daily for nearly a quarter of my life; so there must have been more to it than that.

"We don't see many foreigners here," explained one old lady on a bicycle, "and a lot of the children have never seen any."

As I walked on through the villages I began to take more notice of the posters in shop windows. In the camera shops Yul Brynner was advertising Fuji Film and Candice Bergen was cocking a Minolta. In the grocers' shops Kirk Douglas, Paul Newman, Pat Boone, and Telly Savalas were sniffing different brands of instant coffee. In the clothing shops Alain Delon, Peter Falk, James Coburn, and Giulliano Gemma were all sporting Japanese three-piece suits, and in the chemist's Charles

Bronson was splashing himself with a Japanese after-shave called Man-dom. Sophia Loren was straddling a Honda, Olivia Hussey was pursing Kanebo lips, and Jimmy Connors had just won a tournament without needing to remove his Seiko watch. In the sakè shops a varied crew that included Orson Welles, Sammy Davis, Jr., Herman Kahn, Paul Anka, and Alexis Weissenberg all vied in their praise of Suntory or Nikka with phrases like "Quel bon whisky."

"We don't see many foreigners here," explained the old lady as she pedaled off. "That's why the people stare at you. That's why the children shout."

I stopped at a drive-in for some noodles and beer. The two waitresses giggled and disappeared into the kitchen. I waited five minutes, and when they still didn't reappear I stormed up to the serving hatch and bawled the order at a horrified cook.

Two minutes later a chastened waitress brought me a strawberry milkshake and two pairs of chopsticks.

"I ordered beer," I snapped.

The waitress bit her lip.

"And why have you brought me two pairs of chopsticks?"

"One set's for your friend," the waitress whispered.

"I haven't got any friends," I snarled. "I'm a gaijin."

Whatever impression I had made on the waitresses was certainly buttressed by the time I left. If I had been them, I would have cowered in the kitchen too. I stamped off down the coast road in as foul a mood as an overcast day, two silly women, and seven years of being a side-show can provoke. It was in this mood that I met Sammy.

He was called Sammy, he told me, because he looked like Sammy Davis, Jr., in the Suntory whiskey commercials. He was very dark-skinned for a Japanese, had a small bristly beard, and at some point in his youth he had badly broken his nose, which had bent it like a parrot's beak and given his voice a high-pitched nasal whine. This, together with the natural lisp he had, made his speech a little hard to under-stand, but, like everything else about him, it distinguished him and seemed only to add to his charm. Sammy was one of the pleasantest people I met on my journey—and the only other long-distance walker. He was hiking back from the university in Sapporo, where he was a third-year student of agriculture, to his home in Ibaraki—a distance of about a thousand kilometers that he reckoned would take him a month. He wanted, he said, to write a book about his walk in which he would list the numbers of all the cars that had stopped to offer him lifts. I felt thoroughly ashamed, and the sun came out.

We walked along together singing "Let It Be," and every so often Sammy would stop and set up his tripod by the side of the road, screw his camera onto the tripod, and take a picture of us sitting, sweating, on our packs, or standing, grinning, with our arms round each other. Whenever we passed a railway station, Sammy would slip into it and buy two platform tickets as souvenirs—one for him and one for me.

Near the end of the day we sat on a grass bank and looked out over the silver Pacific towards Muroran and at the peaks of Mount Komagatake to the southeast, rearing up in front of us like devils' teeth. Sammy pried pebbles out of the ground and told me that his one real dream was to live in a house with a chimney.

"What are you going to do when you leave university?"

"I don't know," he said. "Work in the open."

He was quiet after that, and when he spoke, his funny voice had a note in it that I was hearing for the first time. He tossed the pebbles down at the sea.

"I don't want to be a salaryman," he said.

I parted from Sammy at the town of Mori and looked for a place to stay. The first three ryokans told me they were full, and I was in such a good mood that I half believed them. The fourth had a room. I spent five minutes grinning and squabbling with the wife about who was going to wash my underpants and socks until, in the end, she grabbed them and ran into the kitchen and I laughed and went back to lie in my room and watch the sun set over the pylons.

There had been many such days during the past seven years: days I began in the foulest of moods and ended laughing, or days when I woke up feeling perfectly at ease and went to bed wanting nothing more frantically than to leave Japan on the first plane out. It was not a special day, but it is one that sticks in my memory. Sammy will not be a salaryman.

I remember the apprentice barber
of Hakodate—
how good it felt when he shaved my ears.

54

That is a poem by the *tanka* poet Ishikawa Takuboku. It is not, perhaps, one of his best poems, though in the circumstances—a barber's chair in Hakodate—it was one that flitted conveniently into my head. Takuboku was born in the north of Honshu and all of his best poems have something of the warm-cold spirit of the north in them.

> *Dune flowers on a northern beach*
> *reeking of the sea—*
> *I wonder, will they bloom again this year . . . ?*

He lived in the city of Hakodate for about four months during 1907. In a life of almost unrelieved misery, these were months of comparative contentment. He had a job at a local primary school, had begun to edit a small magazine, and could afford for the first time to rent a house large enough for his family to move into. He even had a lightning love affair with a teacher on the staff of the primary school who later married a dairy farmer. But in August a fire destroyed both the school and the office of Takuboku's magazine, and he left the city to go further north in search of work. Looking back on it, he was compelled to view his time in Hakodate through the filter of sorrow that attended him everywhere.

> *Ah, Aoyagi in Hakodate!*
> *How sad it was!*
> *My friend's love song. . . .*
> *The wild cornflowers. . . .*

His baby son died in October 1910; his mother, who had spat blood for seven weeks, died in the spring of 1912; and his young wife, who had been ill for months with pleurisy, was not expected to survive the winter. Takuboku knew with absolute certainty that he, too, had little time to live. He had been in hospital for a month the previous year and had been diagnosed as suffering from incurable tuberculosis. In his last poems, the loneliness of this certainty attains an extraordinary peak of eloquence.

> *When I breathe in*
> *there is a sound in my body*
> *sadder than the winter wind.*

55

Takuboku died in April 1912 at the age of twenty-six. His last literary act was to arrange the sale of his most recent collection of poems for twenty yen, in order to buy medicine.

By the sea wall at Omori, just east of Mount Hakodate on what was once a sand beach, there is a monument to Takuboku. He sits on a stone with his shoulders hunched and his chin in his hand, staring down the coast at the distant mountains, his back towards the burnt-out city. On a tablet is inscribed his poem about the dune flowers. Such monuments to dead writers are not uncommon, and there are picture postcards for sale too.

I took a cable car up Mount Hakodate. It was a hot day and I had a clear view of the city stretching back towards the mountains I had walked across, pale green beyond the mass of squat red and blue roofs and tramlines sandwiched between two curving mirrors of sea.

Unlike Sapporo, which was a city from the moment the ground was broken, Hakodate is simply a coastal village that has grown to fill out its natural boundaries—to the west the Bay of Hakodate, to the east the northern reaches of the Straits of Tsugaru, and to the south its own mountain, bulking up above the thin neck of its peninsula like an island or, more to the point, like a fortress. The superb protection the mountain affords the harbor must have been one of the chief reasons why, in 1859, among the first proclamations that marked the end of feudal isolation was one that opened Hakodate to commerce with foreigners. From the terminus of the cable car I could look down at the massive slate-gray roof of the Buddhist temple Higashi Honganji and see it flanked on one side by a Catholic church and on the other by the white walls and pale green knobs of a Russian Orthodox cathedral.

In the city museum stood case after case of decorated Ainu tunics, their arms stretched out on frames like crucifixes. It was pleasanter to stroll down by the wharves, past the women with their melons and fish spread out on straw mats across the pavement, content in the breathing space of the northern summer and not appearing to care much whether they sold the stuff or not. In the fish market a circle of men and women were practicing for the coming Dance of the Dead, and the smell of glue and the sweet smell of vegetables rotting in plastic bags drifted through all the narrow streets west of the station.

I left Hakodate on the twenty-seventh of July and took the ferry to Oma. In four weeks I had walked the length of Hokkaido, a distance of about 660 kilometers. During the first week my feet had ached like murder and I had had to lance blisters every night. In the second week my left shin had swollen and turned yellow, but the swelling had gone down after four or five days, and canaries, I remembered, are that color all the time. I still occasionally suffered from shooting pains in the toes of my right foot that kept me awake at night. And for the rest of the journey I would find it difficult to walk for the first ten minutes of each morning and have to hobble up and down the corridors of minshukus until my feet could flex again and I could bear to lace my boots.

But I had also notched my belt two notches tighter, my sunburn had turned into a healthy-looking tan, and I was feeling fitter and stronger than I had felt for years.

The ferry edged away from the quay with its speakers blaring "Auld Lang Syne" and I sat in the stern drinking cool beer and rubbing oil into the leather of my boots. Across the shrinking city, beyond Mount Hakodate, I imagined Takuboku sitting hunched on his sea wall watching the ferry grow smaller and smaller till it was lost against the thin blue shimmer of Honshu.

> The white-capped waves roll in and roar
> on the beach of Omori in Hakodate. . . .
> Remembering. . . .

I strolled toward the prow of the ferry and watched the blue shimmer grow green.

3

Death in the North

THE NORTHERNMOST PENINSULA of Honshu is shaped like an axe and in the middle of the axe blade stands a mountain called Osorezan. Osorezan means Terrible Mountain. I had climbed Osorezan twice before and I knew why it had that name.

The road up from the coast was a dirt track that wound through steep wooded hills till it leveled out on a plateau where the grass was thick and white with dust. Red-and-black snakes came out onto the dirt road to die there. One, a baby, hissed as I passed and refused to budge till the tires of a delivery truck flattened it. The truck churned on up the road leaving a dense white cloud like a fog behind it. My hair and shirt were white with the dust, and the water of the mountain streams was too bitter to wash the dry taste off my tongue. Higher, the dead stumps left by the loggers were bone white, and the smell of the old volcano, like a moldy larder, had forced its way into every copse. No forest is ever wholly silent. There is always the sound of the wind in the trees, the sound of the branches as they move, the minute sounds of the scavenging lizards, the sounds the birds make when they stop singing. But on the road to Osorezan these sounds had all died. There was not the slightest hint of a breeze nor of any form of animate life, and the twigs and branches were stiff as stone. I was alone on the road to Osorezan, but I felt a greater loneliness than comes from merely being alone.

Try to imagine the landscape of the earth on the third morning of creation, before any green shoots have appeared above ground—an earth still shuddering from the shocks of form and light. That is the landscape of Osorezan. The ground is the same dead white as the dust, stained yellow in patches from sulfur springs that bubble up through rifts and cracks in the lava. A stream crawls through banks of lime-green clay that seem both putrid and unripe. You approach the temple Osorezan Bodaiji across a small vermilion drumbridge—the same bridge that the newly dead must cross, and it is said that a man who has lived an evil life will not be able to cross the bridge, for he will not perceive it as a bridge at all, but as the merest thread of mist.

Strewn across the waste of earth are hundreds of mounds of small round pebbles, built up carefully a pebble at a time, each tiny pebble a prayer. This is the land of Sai no Kawara, the dismal limbo of the Buddhist underworld. The mounds are built by the souls of children who have died before they can repay their parents for giving them life, and so must make up for it in death by eternally piling pebble upon pebble, the only service they are capable of performing. Here and there among the mounds stand figures carved out of the soft volcanic rock who stare at the visitors, and at the still lake in which fish do not live, and at the stained wooden buildings of Osorezan Bodaiji. They wear red aprons that have faded to a yellowish pink and caps that give them the appearance of costers. The wind and rain have blown so long against their faces that, though they stare, they stare without eyes. It is said that blind witches live on the mountain and that these witches can speak with the spirits of the dead.

There were few visitors to the temple that day. The festival of Osorezan had ended five days before, and the ground was still littered with the tiny one-yen coins that worshipers had strewn about. Three or four elderly women picked their way among the mounds of pebbles and lit candles in front of a small charnel house that contained the teeth of countless dead; and a middle-aged man in a business suit strode confidently up and down taking pictures of the eyeless figures and announcing to everyone within earshot, "Ah yes, I see. Ah yes, I see."

Near the temple lies a pool of crimson water called Chi no Ike—the Pond of Blood. It is guarded by a group of small stone figures whose aprons are a bright unfaded scarlet and who protect the spirits of women that have died in childbirth. Around the figures dead flowers lay scattered, and among the flowers a few dried biscuits. Hot yellow steam hissed up through the crust of the earth as though the earth itself were straining to split before it, too, died with a living thing inside it.

"Ah yes, I see. Ah yes, I see."

Osorezan
Tanabu
Mutsu Yokohama
Noheji
Shichinohe
Towadakomachi
LAKE TOWADA
Yasumiya
Oyu Onsen
Hanawa
Tamagawa
Matsuba
LAKE TAZAWA
Kakunodate
Omagari
Hiraka
Yuzawa
Yokobori
Mamurogawa

The businessman snapped a picture of the Pond of Blood, and I turned back through the gates of the temple, along the avenue of yellow stone lanterns, and went out across the drumbridge and up the road that leads into the hills where the trees looked green.

Osorezan is the most disquieting place I have ever visited. Of course the temple and the lanterns and the eyeless figures were shaped and placed here for a human purpose. We know their dates and the names of the priests who built them, and we know the uses to which they are put. Still, this easy knowledge is belied by their power to intimidate and to awe. Like the yellow stream and the Pond of Blood and the silent trees on the road over the mountain, they are awesome because there is an old god in them—a dusty, crouching, terrible god who does not often reveal himself in the world.

The road to Tanabu was alive with breezes and the ground was dark and soft with loam.

"Ah yes, I see. Ah yes, I see."

What did he see, I wondered.

An old man walked up to me on the road to Tanabu with his hand stretched out for me to shake.

"Look at my teeth," he said, and he showed me his fillings, wobbling the loose ones backward and forward with his finger and laughing at me as I stood there gawping into his mouth.

"Have you ever eaten adders?"

"Er . . . no . . . I haven't."

"I have. Been up to the woods and caught 'em live. Skinned 'em and ate 'em while they're wriggling about. Don't taste up to much but they're good for your constitution."

He reached up, giggling, and peeled a bit of burnt skin from my nose.

I asked about ryokans at a grocer's shop in Tanabu, and another old man who was drinking white liquor there offered to draw me a map. He asked for a ball pen and a sheet of notepaper and sketched an elaborate network of roads on it with an arrow pointing to where we were and a square to represent the ryokan. Then he began to write the two characters for "ryokan," got halfway through the first and stopped suddenly, squinting at it with his head to one side.

"Ummm . . ."

"It's all right. I'm sure I'll be able to find it."

He scratched out the half-finished character and started to write another.

"Araa . . . schhhh . . ."

He scratched through the second character with a violence that ripped a hole in the paper and tried a third.

"*Nanda ga okasii naa* (that's odd) . . ."

He screwed the sheet of paper up into a ball, explained that it wasn't big enough to draw a proper map on, and fled from the shop before anyone could stop him. Five minutes later he was back with a large square of cardboard on which an anonymous calligrapher had drawn, in neat blue pencil, the same set of roads, the same arrow, the same square, and the two characters for "ryokan."

"Right," he said. "That'll get you there."

The ryokan turned out to be three minutes' walk away at the end of a single, dead straight road, and I was greeted there by a woman crawling about on all fours. She told me her legs had been playing her up something wicked, so I offered her the tube of ointment I carried for muscular aches and pains. The ointment was called Rub, which is how Japanese people pronounce the English word "love"—a coincidence that startled the crawling woman, caused her young niece to bounce up and down shrieking with laughter, and eventually so endeared me to them that they washed three pairs of my socks.

The slim neck of the Shimokita peninsula—the shaft of the axe—is a bridge of rich, well-nourished farmland. Cows graze between the long paddies, and the haze of the low hills in the center softens the brilliant green swathes of unripe rice. The sea on the morning of my thirty-second day was an eye-murdering blue. The white specks of the fishing boats out in the straits were like blisters popped up in the scorch of the sun. I tramped down the flat coast road and sat for a while at a small wayside shrine, peering through the wooden lattice of the shed at the dark, musty, holy inside.

It was good to be in Aomori again. Aomori was one of the first prefectures I ever came to in Japan and it has a special place in my affection. I love the powerful shamisen music of Tsugaru, the acres of apple orchards around Hirosaki where each apple is sealed in its own little bag against the birds and early frosts and the winds that blow in autumn. I love the late-blossoming cherries of the north, and the Nebuta lanterns on summer nights, and I love the dialect of Aomori and occasionally try to speak it, though never with much success and always with trepidation. It's a bit like a Japanese walking into a Yorkshire pub and saying, "Eee, by gum." But no one minds, and on this sparkling day I exulted in the sights and sounds of Aomori and celebrated my body with kilometers and beer.

"I'd live nowhere else," said a village grocer. "Not if you paid me. I've tried it and I don't like it. I've lived in Kyushu and I've lived in Tokyo and you can keep 'em. All that heat and noise. We've no rainy season here, or, at any rate, not much more than a week. The typhoons rarely get this far and the wind's too strong for the snow to lie deep."

He gave me two salami sausages and I walked on, waving to an old ice-cream vendor who stood up quickly and bowed four times, till I came to the town of Mutsu Yokohama and found a sensible ryokan where they made no fuss about my being a foreigner and lent me a yukata and a pair of geta to go out for an evening stroll in.

By a rare chance, my stroll took me into a bar—a tiny bar about five yards by three in which the elderly mama-san mothered me and two friendly customers insisted that I dance.

"Go on and dance with her."

"But I'm wearing geta."

"You're a real Japanese!" they cried in admiration.

Unable to dance, I was urged to cuddle the mama-san, but I felt compelled instead to sing a Japanese folk song:

> Mount Bandai of Aizu is a mountain of treasures. . . .
> Its bamboo grass is laden with gold. . . .

The bar was hardly larger than a cupboard, but no sooner had I begun to sing than I found a microphone thrust practically up my nose and the orchestral accompaniment for a quite different song coming out of the *karaoke*. The *karaoke*—literally, "empty orchestra"—has become standard equipment in Japanese bars. It consists of a cassette recorder, an amplifier, a microphone, and a set of tapes that contain the accompaniments for a selection of popular songs. It makes no difference that the bar is cupboard-sized. One would no more think of singing there without a microphone than one would think of standing up to drink if there were no vacant stools, though I have seen one customer in a bar where the microphone was broken pick up his chopsticks and croon into them instead.

I laid the microphone down on the counter. It was snatched up and held two inches from my face. I took it and placed it in the ashtray. The battle won, we eventually rejoiced. In fact, we rejoiced rather more than was good for us since, despite the fact that the next day was Sunday, one of the customers had to drive a truck to Akita, the other had to cement the rims of a dozen manholes, and I had thirty kilometers to walk if I was to reach the town of Noheji by evening. Alas . . .

> *Ohara Shosuke-san . . .*
> *how has he squandered his fortune away?*
> *By getting up late, by drinking early,*
> *and by taking baths first thing in the morning.*
> *That's how he's squandered his fortune away.*
> *Ah, mottomo da! Ah, mottomo da!*

There are few worse enemies to a hangover than a scorching hot day and a Japanese breakfast. The breakfast in Mutsu Yokohama consisted of a bowl of bean-curd soup, a dried plum, a small dish of pickled cabbage, a salty piece of hard-boiled fish, a large bowl of sticky white rice, and a raw egg that one is supposed to crack and stir into the rice to make a thick yellow goo. Seven years in Japan had still not reconciled my stomach to this lot ten minutes after waking up, so I nibbled a bit of fish, sipped the soup, hid the raw egg, and took an aspirin.

It was the hottest day since Cape Soya. The air trembled like tight-ropes over the road, and by half closing my eyes and shading them with both hands, I could just make out the shivering peak of Mount Hak-koda to the southwest, a bump of pale mauve jutting up into the burning blue sky, and the sky was a steam iron threatening to flatten it.

I looked for a place to swim, but the beach at Mutsu Yokohama was a mess of plastic bags and cans, and it was not till midday, a dozen kilometers down the road, that I found a path across the railway track down onto clean white sand. You could have roasted coffee beans on that sand. I spent an hour floating on my back in the tepid sea, gazing down the coast towards Mount Hakkoda and thinking about a bacon sandwich.

"Some of these fishermen just don't wanna know. We try and be friendly and all, and some are O.K., but I guess speaking the lingo'd make a helluva difference. D'you speak it?"

"Yes," I admitted, half apologetically.

The middle-aged officer and his wife had come up from the American air base at Misawa to comb the beach for glass fishing floats.

"I'm just crazy about this blue-and-white china," said his wife. She unwrapped a small round dish and held it out to show me. You could have bought it at any pot shop for a couple of hundred yen. "We've tried to make friends with a farmer's wife back down the highway. Last week we brought her some American cookies. I wanted to ask her if she has any of this blue-and-white china, but she just doesn't understand. Today I brought this dish to show her, and I held it up like this and kept pointing at her kitchen, you know. But she still didn't seem to get the message. I guess if I knew the word for 'dish.' What's the word for 'dish'?"

"*Sara.*"

"*Saru?*"

"*Sara. Saru* is a monkey."

"Oh, gee. I guess we'd better not."

"We pick these floats up on the beach," said the officer, "ship 'em back to the States, make a helluva profit. There's a real demand for this kinda stuff."

"Doesn't it cost a lot to ship them back?"

"Not a cent." The officer winked. "Some of these fishermen, when you try to buy 'em, they ask, like, three thousand yen. That's *twelve dollars!* Out here on the beach it's a rare Sunday we don't find two or three. Over the four years we've been here I guess we've shipped back maybe a hundred."

"What do they sell for?"

"Thirty, forty dollars."

We went for a swim.

"What brings you up here?"

I told them.

"Oh, gee!"

We popped a bottle of fifty-cent Korean pink champagne. My hangover disappeared in a panic.

They stood on the beach waving to me like windmills, as I climbed back over the railway track onto the road. It was slick and empty in the midafternoon heat. An adder had been squashed flat to the middle of it and an eagle was trying to rip it free, but it was stuck down hard and slowly frying.

I asked for a beer in a little sakè shop. An old woman hauled herself to her feet and fetched me a bottle from the refrigerator. I asked for a glass. She fetched me a glass. Then she fell down on her knees on the concrete floor of the shop with the beer bottle in one hand and the glass in the other. I helped her to her feet and took the bottle. She dropped the glass and the glass broke into slivers on the concrete. I put the bottle of beer down on the counter and began to pick up the slivers of broken glass. The old woman fell down on her knees in the middle of them.

"I'm sorry," she said.

An old man came out of the back room holding a dustpan and brush.

"Excuse me," he said.

He gave me another glass and began to sweep up the broken slivers. He never once touched the old woman, nor spoke to her.

"I'm very sorry," the old man said to me.

The old woman stood up and limped away into the back room with blood coming out of her hands.

※

It took a long noisy morning to get off Highway 4, and when I finally managed to, at the dusty little town of Shichinohe, no one seemed able to tell me which road I should take. I wanted to get to the town of Towadakomachi without having to go through Towada City.

"You can't," said a petrol pump attendant, flatly.

But after a half-hour conference with four of the staff at a second petrol station, each of whom drew plans on scraps of paper and none of whose plans resembled any of the others', I finally found the road I was looking for and set off through flat wet rice fields that the over-cast sky had turned a deep bottle green. Mount Hakkoda brushed the clouds to the west, and the hills that surrounded it were layered in tones of gray like cardboard cutouts.

"To Kyushu?" spat a workman in an orange helmet. "I wish I was going to Kyushu. There's thousands of Turkish baths in Kyushu. The cheapest Turkish baths in Japan."

He spat and grinned and squinted sideways at me.

"I don't need to tell *you* what goes on in Turkish baths."

"Well . . ."

"Nothing like that round here," he mourned. "I'd invite you out to one if there was. Don't miss the ones in Kyushu, though. I bet you'll end up staying a fortnight."

A grandmother in *mompe*—traditional loose-fitting "mountain trousers"—was out on the country road playing baseball with some young children. She was showing them her catcher's crouch.

"Where are you going?"

"Lake Towada."

"Look after yourself. Take care of yourself."

My judo friends tell me that, once upon a time, it was the dream of every schoolboy in Japan to be a judo champion. This remained their dream until the 1964 Tokyo Olympics—the first Olympics to include judo—when a foreigner, the Dutchman Geesink, beat the all-Japan champion and took the gold medal. Since then, they tell me, all the schoolboys have wanted to be baseball players.

In the dusk a man stood bare-chested on a bridge that crossed a stream, staring down into the water as though he had drowned his child in it.

"Excuse me, could you tell me . . ."

He didn't move a muscle.

I tramped on and found a sweet shop. The woman in the shop phoned a ryokan for me, and the man at the ryokan offered to come and fetch me in his car. It was seven o'clock and dark. I had covered twenty-eight kilometers that day and the ryokan was still an hour away.

"I'll walk," I said.

The man in the car came anyway.

"No, I'll walk," I insisted.

When I got to the ryokan they were waiting outside in the street for me.

"That was splendid," the man said, seriously.

"What?"

"After I'd come out to fetch you, and all. Have you walked very far?"

"Just from Noheji."

"Splendid," the man said. "Let me take your pack."

He carried the pack up the narrow stairs for me.

"What's it weigh?"

"About fourteen kilograms, I think."

"And you've walked from Noheji. Splendid! Splendid!"

In an upstairs room four workmen were grilling liver. They saw me on my way to the bath. Three plates of liver and five cups of sakè later I made it down to the bathroom.

"What do you think of Aomori?" asked one of the men. He was a young man with short cropped hair and a deep, livid scar that ran down his right cheek.

"I like Aomori very much."

"What about the stars?"

"Stars?"

"You can only see them in the north. You can only see stars like this north of Fukushima. What about the people?"

"I like them too."

"Aomori people are the best. People in Akita and Iwate are all right. South of that they're a lot of bastards." He rubbed his scar and nodded at me. "Fukushima people are bastards, but it's not their fault. They can't see the stars."

I ate dinner downstairs with the family. The youngest son kept running in and out announcing that there was an *obake* in the house. An *obake* is a ghoul, a monster, a freak. This went on for about five minutes and I glared at him every time I caught his eye.

"A *real obake!*"

His parents ignored him.

"A horrible, fearful, *real obake!*"

Slamming down my chopsticks and swinging round on my cushion to berate the little horror, I came face to face with a second son, about eight years old, whose head and neck were entirely sheathed in a large green rubber Frankenstein mask.

"Wwwaaa!" he said. The youngest son whooped. The parents slapped their thighs. I nibbled a pickled radish.

It rained all night and it was still raining when I set off the next morning for Lake Towada. My shirt was drenched in half an hour, and I caught myself sneezing. "Watch Out for Kids" said a road sign in English outside one village. I knew what that meant.

The sky cleared towards midmorning, and I sat on the bank of the Oirase River, my shirt drying over a gate, and listened to the low trickle of the water through a concrete dam. Above the dam the river widened quickly to a still deep green, and there were trout pools and ice-cream stands and expensive-looking drive-ins. But once past the crossroads it narrowed again into the steady rapids that gurgle steeply out of the three-pronged lake. This is a stretch of the Oirase River made famous by tourist posters and by dabblers in the traditional forms of Japanese poetry. In autumn the road will be jammed with cars, bumper to bumper, and fathers will wish they had stayed at home, and children will wail for Coca-Cola, and mothers will lean out of car windows to snap the red and gold trees with Instamatic cameras. Nothing will daunt the poets, though, and they will see and hear only what thousands of others have wanted to see and hear before them:

> Shrill in its rapids, sobbing in its deeps,
> the Oirase water sings.
> Stand for a moment in the shade of a tree
> and listen, traveler.

But autumn was months away, and except for the coach parks with their crowds of snapping people and their mounds of empty cardboard lunchboxes, the little footpath that follows the river was quiet and the sounds of the waterfalls and the river bubbling over moss-covered rocks held their own against the motor horns.

At the lake an irate bus driver was persuaded to phone a minshuku for me, while the waitress I had first asked hopped from one foot to the other as though in urgent need of a lavatory.

"Look here," barked the bus driver, "there's a gaijin here . . ."

The minshuku sent their apologies for being full.

Lake Towada lay gray and still in the evening, swallowing the last halfhearted shafts of sunlight. I marched round its southern bank, recalling the words of another poem I had seen printed on a picture postcard:

69

For life, the Land of the Rising Sun.
For disporting oneself, Towada Lake.
It is a three-and-a-half-ri walk along
the Oirase River.

Some poems, I supposed, were written on commission.

Eventually I found a minshuku and spent the night there, trying to ignore the unearthly noise made by two frantic mongrels in heat. A mongrel accompanied me on my trudge next morning—the thirty-sixth morning of my journey—trotting on ahead of me for a while, then sitting and waiting at a bend in the steep road till I caught him up. When I caught him up, he would eye me indulgently and trot on ahead again, looking round at me often, but never once letting me touch him. In this way we reached the lakeside resort of Yasumiya together. He took one look at it and bolted into the trees. I, less free, trudged down to explore it.

Lake Towada is a caldera lake, formed two million years ago in the collapsing cone of an extinct volcano. It is surrounded by steep wooded hills and divided like a webbed foot along its southern shore by two promontories, one thin and flat, the other steep and mountainous. Famous for its crystal blue water, for its maple leaves in October, and for its proximity to the hot springs of Kuroishi, Hakkoda, and Hachimantai, the lake is the most popular tourist attraction in the north of Honshu, and since 1936 it has been the center of a national park. Yasumiya (literally, "Rest Shop") stands at the base of the thin southwestern promontory. It is not picturesque, nor does it command a good view of the lake, most of which the promontory blocks from sight. But it offers everything that a Japanese holidaymaker could wish for: souvenir shops, sightseeing cruises, high-speed motorboats, restaurants that charge five hundred yen for a medium-sized bottle of beer, tiers of wooden benches on which groups of people can have their photographs taken against a background of other groups of people, a shrine, a crowded beach, and the comforting sense that you must have come to the right place because this is where everybody else is.

On a large square plinth near the end of the beach stands a bronze monument erected in 1953 called *The Maidens of the Lakeside*. It depicts a pair of young women with prohibition hair and breasts like

70

ovens, standing stark naked playing pat-a-cake. This is one of the lake's most popular attractions. All the souvenir stalls stock plastic replicas of it and people stand in line to have their photos snapped in front of it. It has been celebrated, too, in a postcard poem:

> Have they dropped from Heaven?
> Are they clustered foam?
> These maidens on this sad, strange shore—
> face to face, of what do they speak?

And there the poet's imagination fails him.

A breeze began to blow in across the lake and turned slowly into a wind. I strolled down the beach past two black families sitting huddled round a monster radio tuned to the American Forces' transmitter at Misawa, nibbling *kiritampo* (baked mashed rice) and looking thoroughly miserable. The wind carried their music out over the beach and you could hear it as far back as *The Maidens of the Lakeside*.

"Soul," said a maiden, "I wanna go home."

"Oi, you you you!" barked a Japanese man in an Aloha shirt. "You you you, oi, camping, camping!"

I hitched up my pack and trudged out of Yasumiya, and at three-thirty I crossed the prefectural boundary from Aomori into Akita.

The lakes and ponds of ancient Japan were known to be the haunts of dragons, and the moods and changing colors of the lakes were attributed to the dragons' rages and calms. A sightseeing boat ploughed out of Yasumiya, with its amplified commentary audible for miles describing the lake in our own century's terms:

"... forty-four kilometers in circumference, 334 meters deep at its center ..."

For the first time since I found my packet of picture postcards, I felt moved to admire one of the contributing poets:

> The sky too is deep,
> the water immeasurably deep.
> Of heaven and earth we know nothing.

The northern third of the island of Honshu is called *Tohoku*—"east-north." It used to be known as *Michinoku*—literally, "the end of the road." From the point of view of the court in Kyoto, or even of the Shogun's government in Edo (Tokyo), the name was both a literal description and a dismissal. The roads north were narrow, wild, and unpoliced, the inhabitants of the north little better than beggars. You might come to Michinoku out of despair or out of curiosity or to hide from hostile eyes, but not unless you were stark mad would you forsake the delights of the civilized south and bring your family to scratch a living here.

The six prefectures that make up Tohoku are today among the least developed in Japan. (In terms of per-capita income, Aomori is the second poorest of all the forty-seven prefectures, Yamagata is the ninth, Akita the sixteenth.) This is partly due to the long, harsh winters, the heavy snows of the Japan Sea coast, and the fogs that roll in from the north Pacific to blight the towns and sour the farmers. Most Japanese, for all their complaints about population density, have grown so used to big city comforts that they no more want to live in Tohoku than they want to live in Hokkaido. The climate is too bitter, the living too hard. And so in recent years as the old cottage industries of rice-straw weaving and charcoal burning have declined to the level of picturesque jokes, and as television has broadcast throughout the country its slick versions of the urban gospel, the population of Tohoku, despite the region's size and the richness of much of its soil, has dwindled to a bare eight percent of the nation's total.

Yet go into any bar that has a *karaoke* and you will hear customers who have never been further north than Tokyo singing soulfully about "A Northern Inn" or "The Straits of Tsugaru in Winter." The north exerts a profound attraction on the armchair imaginations of many Japanese people, because it epitomizes what they call *furusato*— "the old home country" and its influence on their lives. The Tohoku of their imagination is a perfect *furusato*—a place that is content to be old-fashioned, that doesn't alter with each new twist of "progress," where nature, though harsh, is also generous, and where time is measured by the changes in the seasons:

> *A white birch, a blue sky, a wind blows from the south,*
> *and in the deep north blooms the magnolia—*
> *ah, the deep north spring!*
> *In cities the seasons pass unnoticed*

72

save for a package from my mother;
ah, shall I go back to that old home country?
Shall I, shall I go back?

Offer the singer a one-way ticket to Akita in January and you'll soon have an answer.

The road down from the Hakka Pass was practically a wilderness. The migration of farmhands south to the cities had left fields lying fallow even now in early August. Next to a swathe of sturdy green rice would lie a square of dead brown stalks cropped off at the mud level in the previous autumn and not ploughed since. The buildings were few and miles between, but they presented the same stark contrasts. Most were the cheap aluminum-paneled shacks that I had seen along the coasts of Hokkaido. The outhouses were corrugated iron, the roofs were insane blue plastic. At intervals I would come across a wooden farmhouse falling apart at the eaves, and I would stop for a minute to admire the pale green moss that grew on the thatch, and the wide dark pillars and half-timbered walls that reminded me of my own *furusato*. The orange-and-yellow pyramid-shaped cabins of the Towada Car Lodge gave warning that civilization was again at hand, and at about four-thirty in the afternoon I walked into the little hot spring village of Oyu, passing under a white banner stretched across the road that advertised the triple delights of "Apples, Skiing and a Stone Circle."

My experience of Japanese youth hostels is not wide. One reason is that the people I meet in youth hostels have mostly come from Tokyo, so the amount I can learn from them about anything is minimal. Another reason is that, despite the legend, the cost of staying in a youth hostel, if you eat two meals and are loaned a sheet, is only marginally less than that of staying in an ordinary country minshuku. A third and a fourth reason are that, in the few Japanese youth hostels I have stayed at, the food has been uniformly dreadful and alcoholic beverages have not been allowed on the premises. Fifth, sixth, seventh, and eighth reasons were made plain to me during the course of the night I spent at the youth hostel in Oyu.

I did not risk eating there, but wandered up and down the one village road till I found a little *akachochin* (drinking shop with a red lantern outside) where I was able to persuade the mama-san to pop

73

out to the fishmonger's for a couple of trout. I agreed to look after any customers that came in while she was away and she went off happily, leaving me to mind the business. An old man who wandered in for some sakè seemed not in the least surprised to have me serve it to him, and even asked me if I knew where he could get hold of a decent eel-trap. The trout were good, and so was the old man, and it was with great reluctance that I left the shop to attend the hostel's evening meeting, but the warden had already chided me for not telephoning to reserve a bunk, and I thought that, if I missed the meeting, I might blacken the gaijin image for years to come.

We sat round the walls of the meeting room on metal chairs, and the warden told us where we should go in the morning, what time we should leave, what buses we should catch, what we should do when we got there, and what souvenirs we should bring back with us. He then divided us into three teams and we stood up, sat down, clapped our hands, and hopped in circles whenever the name of our team was called. After this, the forty or so university students who were staying at the hostel, and who ranged in age from nineteen to twenty-four, began with noisy enthusiasm to play a game of musical chairs. I excused myself on the grounds of suddenly intolerable thirst and fled back to the *akachochin* where I drank three beers in quick succession and bought the old man another jug of sakè.

That night we slept twelve to a room. The sheet I had rented was absurdly small and there was no toilet paper in the lavatory—only a sign forbidding me to throw cans or bottles down the pan. At 6:30, piped birdsong that sounded like factory whistles wafted into our rooms, to be replaced at 6:35 by the Beach Boys and at 6:40 by the warden who came bursting in to scold us for not being up. In the meeting room at 6:55 the television was on full blast, two students were listening to transistor radios tuned to competing stations, the rain which had begun to fall in the night was thunderous outside the plate-glass windows, and to spice the cacophony the members of a cycling club had discovered a set of wooden skittles and were bowling them down with a determination approaching cruelty to inanimate objects. Each member of the club wore a T-shirt with the words "TIT CYCLIST" printed across the front of it. I took the most studious-looking member aside and quietly explained the implications. "No, no," he insisted, "it means Tokyo Institute of Technology." With that, I drank a cup of black coffee beside a vending machine called "Nuts is Best," and despite the rain's still falling in torrents, I left the hostel at Oyu and ate a breakfast of tangerines in the doorway of a chemist's shop.

The rain was falling even harder by the time I reached the Oyu Stone Circle, or rather the two stone circles, one on either side of the narrow prefectural road. I found the custodian in his tiny museum, borrowed his umbrella, and wandered about in the rain for half an hour, peering through the wire-mesh fences at the spoked-wheel and sundial patterns of the stones, and splashing through the ditches of a recent excavation.

The stones—the tallest are no more than three feet high and most are laid, or have fallen, flat—were discovered in 1932, but a proper investigation had to wait until six years after the end of the war. It revealed two rough circles—one 44 yards in diameter, the other 50—formed of boulders taken from a dry riverbed and mostly shaped into crude oblongs. The circles are thought to be late Neolithic (about four thousand years old) and the usual theories have been advanced to account for them—that they are part of a burial complex, that they are part of a place of worship, that they have some vague astronomical significance. It never seems to occur to people that primitive man might have made things like this to amuse himself, as we amuse ourselves with musical chairs and statues of nude women on plinths by lakes. The signboard on the wire fence apologizes for the mystery: "Not even the professors," it moans, "are certain. . . ."

"Of heaven and earth we know nothing," I chuckled, splashing off through the rain towards Hanawa, down a road that was straight as a ley.

The road began to curve, though the land was flat and the mountains of Hachimantai reared up like a stage set. In the brief intervals between the torrents of rain, the layers of cloud that hovered round the mountains would rise and fall as though on pulleys. First the clouds would hide the peaks so that the mountains looked flat-topped like tables, then they would sink to hide the slopes and the peaks would jut up above the clouds like a landscape in a charcoal painting. When the rain ceased, the light had the chilling quality of old silver, but when the rain came on again it smothered everything—the peaks, the clouds, the distant farms. I sheltered for an hour in someone's back shed and scooted on again to find a grocer's shop where I sat, sodden, eating apples while the thunder drove the grocer's children frantic.

In a lull I reached the town of Hanawa. It was a little after midday. I ate lunch in a restaurant where the walls were covered with posters announcing a festival, and the restaurant owner stamped about, cursing the rain and worrying that the festival would be canceled.

"You mean it's today?"

"Today and tomorrow."

"Here?"

"Over towards the station." The owner squinted at me from behind the counter. "You mean to say that's not what you've come for?"

"I'd no idea."

The owner scoffed. "There's no other damn reason to come here. You might at least stay for that."

I needed no persuading. The weather was foul to walk in and the prospect of a festival—however threatened—was the perfect excuse for a dry afternoon. I took a room in a ryokan near the station, hung my dripping clothes over an oil stove, and spent a couple of hours sprawled on tatami mats, sipping green tea and listening to the thunder ripple across the valley.

By early evening the rain had stopped and I strolled out of the ryokan to find the road in front of the station transformed into an open-air bazaar. It was lined with dozens of pink-draped stalls, all hung with red-and-white paper lanterns, selling fireworks, goldfish, stag beetles, terrapins, candyfloss, robot masks, octopus, and ginger. There were rifle ranges and hoopla stands, and in a shelter between the pumps of a petrol station sat six or seven policemen with megaphones, sipping tea and trying not to look enthused. Beyond the stalls, on the main street of the town, was a collection of large wooden platforms on wheels, and on each of the platforms stood a huge *taiko* drum. Hordes of young children in bright summer yukatas were clambering over the platforms and beating the drums with curved wooden sticks. Out of the shops and houses flocked the fathers—firemen, bank clerks, postmen, farmers—dressed either in yukatas or in white shorts and the belted blue tunics called *happi*. There was mayhem as the fathers tried to wrest the drumsticks from their wriggling sons, and the noise of the drums and the screams and the laughter had reached a climax when the downpour began again.

It fell without thunder but it fell as solidly as it had fallen for most of the day, and the cries of the children when their mothers scuttled forward to drag them off the streets mingled with the curses of their fathers as they swarmed onto the platforms and struggled to haul tarpaulins over the drums. The tarpaulins were sodden and heavy with a day's rain and the drums were twice the height of a man.

I fled into the first dry space I could see—a canvas tent that turned out to be the festival organizers' headquarters. The organizers sat behind a row of trestle tables, scowling at the rain, complaining to their wives, and drinking large quantities of beer. We gaped at each other for a few seconds, till I was invited to sit down at one of the tables and submit to beer and questions.

"What do you think of festivals?"

"I like them when it doesn't rain."

For a long moment my presence was ignored.

"That is to say, I like them anyway. Especially festivals in small towns."

An organizer topped up my glass.

"I like festivals where tourists are not important, festivals where they'd just as soon tourists didn't come. The festivals I've seen in large cities like Kyoto and Kanazawa seemed mainly for the benefit of the tourist trade, whereas a festival in a small town like this one is an event for working people and their families. That," I continued, growing radical, "is what a festival ought to be, not an annual bonus for some travel agent."

This heady speech earned me a plate of salami and a bottle of beer I was allowed to pour myself.

"And what do you think of Akita *bijin?*"

Akita is famous for its beautiful women (*bijin*), a fact that I had noted long ago and tended to dismiss as a partisan myth until, wandering about the streets of Hanawa in the rain, I found that my mouth kept dropping open and that I was devoting about a quarter of one eye to the taiko drums.

"My daughter is a *bijin*," an elderly festival organizer chuckled. "She's twenty-four."

"How very nice . . ."

"It's a pity she's married. You could have married her."

His wife, I supposed, was the woman choking in the corner. His daughter stayed wisely out of sight. And before I could ask about nieces

77

and distant cousins, the rain stopped as suddenly as it had started, and the organizers packed me off to the station square where "the real festival," they said, was about to commence.

In the station square stood eighteen of the wooden platforms in a semicircle facing the gathering crowd. Nine of the platforms supported taiko drums, and on the other nine stood rectangular paper lanterns, all taller by half than the massive taiko, and lit from inside by candles so that the red-and-gold hand-painted pictures on them glowed and flickered with life. Some were of heroes from the Kabuki theater with masses of black hair, white-and-blue faces, and bright scarlet eyes. Others were of feudal warriors, grimacing under fierce horned helmets. On some, the warriors were locked in combat, a tangle of long white-bladed swords and black, glinting halberds. On others, a single warrior rode in arrogant splendor, his horse's jaws a mass of foam, his armor bristling with arrows.

The nine drums thundered in unison, pounded by the fathers now, not the sons. Each drum required two men to beat it, and they hammered out a single rhythm that had already reached a powerful crescendo and was still mounting as the noise and excitement of the crowd mounted with it. Sweat poured off the faces of the drummers and the trails of it glistened in the light of the candles. So violently did they hurl themselves at the drums, and so powerfully did each stroke take its toll on the whole body, that a man could not play for more than three or four minutes before stumbling away, as another took his place, and collapsing on a bench to tip cold sakè down his throat and bury his face in a towel.

The taiko is an instrument that demands more than technique. It is an obstinate instrument. It will resist and resist the drift of the music until the sheer energy of the man who plays it at last excites the god in the drum, and the rhythms then flow naturally from him till his arms grow weak with exhaustion. The wise player circumvents the drum's resistance by taking so much sakè into his body that the god in the drum has no alternative but to assume command at the outset.

I have to suppose that the god in the drum can also read minds, for as I moved in and out of the crowd, past the lanterns and the benches and the crates of bottles, a young man wearing a white plastic raincoat came up and thrust a paper cup of sakè into my hand and asked me if I would like to play. I said that I would, but that I would require more sakè. More sakè came. The crowd around us began to bubble. Three drummers offered me the use of their sticks, and after I had drained a third paper cup I took my place by the side of a drum and waited for the right-hand drummer to tire. Then, when my turn came, I stepped up to the drum, saluted it with the sticks, and whacked it.

The crowd went silly. "Look at this! Look at this! A gaijin! A gaijin playing the taiko!" Flash guns went off, crates were upended, parents pushed their children forward and craned their necks and stamped and clapped, and I felt the sakè curl in my stomach and grinned at the drummer on the left of the drum, a middle-aged man who said "Yah!" and grinned back, and the god in the drum was kind to us both.

I have no idea how long I played. Twice the left-hand drummer changed and twice the drumsticks slipped out of my hands. When I came away I was drenched in sweat, and I sat on a bench with a towel round my head, guzzling sakè and laughing like an idiot.

They had seen me from the ryokan windows, and when I got back, they danced about the entrance hall while I beat the floor with a pair of slippers. Then they ushered me into the front parlor where a college professor in a suit and spectacles presented me with his namecard and commenced to give us all a lecture.

"You see, the festival is a Tanabata festival and so it has its origins in eighth-century China where it commemorated the annual union of the two stars Altair and Vega. Up to the nineteenth century . . ."

Someone had poured me a cup of sakè.

"Up to the nineteenth century the festival was celebrated on the seventh night of the seventh month, but when Japan adopted the Gregorian calendar Tanabata was incorporated into the general celebrations of August. The Nebuta lanterns of Aomori . . ."

"Excuse me, professor . . . ," I said, grinning inanely while the parlor audience held its breath, ". . . but have you ever played the sakè after three cups of drum?"

The professor expressed his puzzlement.

"I mean to say," I said, attempting a northern dialect to hisses of delight, "have you ever played the taiko after drinking three cups of sakè?"

The professor admitted that he never had.

"The professor knows an awful lot about festivals," said the mistress of the ryokan, beside herself with joy.

In the streets the fathers were lighting fireworks for their sons. I felt happy for the firework sellers, who were the only stallkeepers that had not been doing a brisk trade. In the bath, when I let my ears sink under the water, the water throbbed to the rhythm of the drums, and when I got out of the bath and stood drying on the mat, my hands were still tapping out the rhythm on the windowsill. It was a long time before I could get to sleep, but I didn't mind. That night I knew an awful lot about festivals.

The most significant summer festival in Japan is the Festival of the Dead, which is called O-Bon. To many people O-Bon is the most important time of the year, for at O-Bon they leave the cities where they work and go back for a few days to the towns and villages where they were born. There they meet their families again and visit the graves of dead family members. They place parcels of food and drink on the graves and invite the spirits of the dead to come back to their houses. In the villages and towns they dance to amuse the dead, and to amuse themselves. And so O-Bon is a happy time.

> *O-Bon is coming*
> *and then we shall go.*
> *If Bon comes soon*
> *we shall soon go home.*

But O-Bon is a strangely sad time too, for thoughts of death are everywhere—even in the lullabies sung to children . . .

> *And if I die*
> *who will cry for me?*
> *The cicadas will cry*
> *in the mountain pines.*
>
> *No, not the cicadas;*
> *my sister will cry.*
> *Ah, sister, don't cry,*
> *for it grieves me so.*

"We were going to have a Bon dance this evening," said the waiter in the dining room at Tamagawa Hot Spring, where I spent my thirty-ninth night. "We'd already strung out the lanterns and there's a space down by the stream just right for a dance. All the guests were looking forward to it, and now they've gone and canceled it."

Tamagawa is described in the official guidebook as a "primitive" resort, where most of the guests lodge in cheap wooden dormitories. The majority of guests are elderly or ill, and many come for weeks at a time, for the strong acid sulfur and radium springs are said to cure various forms of neuralgia, gastroenteritis, and diseases of the stomach. Those who stay in the wooden dormitories cook their own food, wash their own clothes, and emerge from their rooms four or five times a day to lie for an hour at a stretch in the steamy wooden bathhouse. Through the windows of the dining room, I watched a group of women gathering in sheets and airing straw pallets. The diners were dressed in yukatas and geta and the waiters wore black dinner jackets and bow ties.

So I asked the waiter why they had canceled the dance. He struck me as genuinely simple-minded. I had been chatting to him about my journey, and he had written down everything I had said to him on small scraps of paper which he pulled out of his pockets and spread on the table. "How many kilometers from here to there?" "What will be the date when you get to Kanazawa?" The dining-room manager seemed not to mind that he was sitting with me instead of waiting on tables and, in fact, came up and joked about how well Shigeru could speak English. Shigeru smiled and pocketed his scraps of paper.

"Or can it be Japanese you're speaking? I expect it is, isn't it, Shigeru? I can see this guest speaks Japanese. I can see it from the way he uses his chopsticks."

"Why did they cancel the Bon dance?"

Shigeru looked round to make sure the manager was out of earshot.

"One of the guests died in his room this morning. He'd been here about three days with his wife and she found him lying dead on his mattress. It's a good thing he didn't die in the bath. They were an old couple. It happens sometimes."

Shigeru went off to eat his dinner and I sat picking at a dish of raw tuna. Outside, in the hissing bed of the stream, metal pipes and a wooden trough stained bright yellow by the sulfur carried the hot spring water to the baths. The water is a bare two degrees below boiling when it comes out of the earth, and so the stream is practically invisible, shrouded day and night in billows of white vapor. The smell of the springs is overpowering, and in the huge wooden bathhouse where you grope your way to the pool of your choice through a permanent curtain of cloying steam, the stench is so heavy it chokes your throat till, after a while, you learn to breathe very gently and regularly as in a sauna.

But perhaps the most remarkable thing about Tamagawa is the fact that men and women bathe together. This was often so before "Westernization," and its survival here must be one of the reasons why the Japan Travel Bureau is so sniffy about "primitiveness." I found nothing primitive about it. I thought it a joy to lie and watch old women with breasts hanging down to their bellies giggling like schoolgirls while they scrubbed their husbands' backs and eyed the one or two muscled young men who skipped self-consciously from pool to pool dangling hand towels in front of their crotches. The beauty of the Akita *bijin* does not appear to suffer much with age; the grandmothers' faces were often as radiant as sixteen-year-olds'. The younger *bijin* stayed irritatingly out of sight—though, on reflection, that was probably just as well, since it enabled my enthusiasm for the primitive to continue at a cerebral level.

I sat in the hottest of the bathtubs chatting to a young man from Niigata who was anxious to explain to me the effect of pH on boiling points, but I told him that we didn't have that sort of thing in Britain and so was able to change the subject.

"Did you hear about the old man who died this morning? Apparently it happens from time to time. They were going to have a Bon dance, and now they've had to cancel it."

"Why?" asked the young man from Niigata, surprised.

"Because of the old man dying."

"And what do they suppose Bon dances are for? The whole point of O-Bon is to please the dead. They should have gone ahead and held the dance. It is no easy thing to die in a strange place. I would have danced. We should all have danced. The old man would have wanted it cheerful."

But the hot spring seemed especially silent that night. No one stayed up to pass the time. One by one, the elderly left the baths and went back to their lodgings, gathering up their pallets and locking the doors quietly behind them. By nine I was quite alone in the bathhouse, and from the windows I could hear no voices at all—only the cicadas in the mountain pines.

I locked the door of my own room before sleeping. It was a quiet death and no one danced.

I don't know what magic properties the Tamagawa water possessed, but the next day—the fortieth—I walked faster and further than on any day since the start of my journey. I had begun to think of my legs as having gears, and I would pore over my maps each morning and calculate the gears I needed to use during the day. The road from the Hachimantai plateau to Lake Tazawa was almost all downhill, so I was in top gear within twenty minutes of leaving Tamagawa. I followed a stream down through thick woods, wiping away my sweat on a towel that reeked of sulfur, as it would for weeks to come. The water that trickled out of the rocks was cold enough to make my head ache if I drank it, and when the land leveled out and the stream widened into a still pool of brilliant turquoise, I stopped to rest on the road above a dam and sat looking out over the pale green rice towards the dark hills that surround Mount Taihei. In all my journey I found little to compare with the hills and valleys of Akita, and for all the heartaches of the northern winter I envied the people who looked out on them each day.

Occasionally a car would stop to offer me a lift and I would have to put up a lengthy defense for not accepting. The couple who stopped for me just after the dam were particularly insistent.

"Get in!"

"No, as a matter of fact I've walked all the way from . . ."

"We saw you at Osorezan."

"Yes . . ."

"You accepted a lift at Osorezan."

"I didn't."

"You did. We gave you a lift then. Why won't you accept one now?"

"I haven't been inside a car for six weeks."

"You've forgotten. Get in!"

"You must be mistaken . . ."

83

"Ooo . . . he's a liar!"

The woman wound up the window and the man at the wheel accelerated away, leaving two pebbly ruts in the loose-surfaced road and the familiar dense white fog of dust.

Down in the valley the houses of the first village I came to had professional wrestling posters tacked to their plywood walls: Mil Mascaras in black-and-silver tights would destroy Giant Baba in the *Samaa Akushon Shiiriizu* (Summer Action Series). There were posters, too, for a Lake Tazawa festival that said, in English, "Let's Do Your Trip," and on the veranda of the little grocer's shop an elderly woman made me a tiny pot of green tea, pouring the water from a red thermos flask that had "Lequel voulez-vous du café ou du thé" printed on it in fancy white letters.

When, at dusk, I tramped down a narrow farm path and settled myself into the minshuku at the end of it, I realized with a shock that I had walked thirty-nine kilometers in top gear that day and hardly noticed it. I logged the fact with a complacent flourish in my diary, drank one too many jugs of postprandial sakè, and went to bed tingling like an athlete. The next morning I woke up with stomach cramps and diarrhea.

It was ten o'clock before I dared leave the haven of the minshuku, and by then my torments had been crowned with rain. Spots of it fell on the short road down to the lake and pocked the gray beach where small groups of holidaymakers sat squinting at the sky from under faded orange parasols. The lake itself was the color of a battleship. Four couples rowed aimlessly about on its surface, this way and that, determined to enjoy themselves. A speedboat howled past, cutting as close to the rowers as it possibly could and sweeping off in a tight, bumpy circle as its wake just failed to capsize them. I sat down in a small wooden pavilion, next to a trashcan full of dead fireworks, and thought seriously about stretching out and going to sleep. A squall of rain came in across the lake, carried by a wind that turned a sharp 180 degrees, uprooting a parasol and tugging it out into the water. Two holidaymakers retrieved it with a lot of flapping, and the rest snatched up their belongings and began to move quickly up the slope towards the car park. The squall had spun the trashcan over, and the charred fireworks lay scattered across the pavilion floor. I stood up gingerly so as not to jolt my bowels, held my breath while I hoisted my rucksack, and began a sullen trudge round the lake's northern shore.

Lake Tazawa, an almost perfect circle with a circumference of twenty kilometers, is the deepest lake in Japan—425 meters at its center. You do not begin to suspect its depth until you leave the beach and walk round towards the Gozanoishi Shrine, where the sand gives way to a sheer wall of boulders that descends almost vertically into the water. Apart from its depth, the circular lake—on this unseasonal August day—had nothing special to recommend it. The hills that surround it are less spectacular than those at Lake Towada and the souvenirs at the shabby restaurants were well below standard for a prefecture boastful of its handicrafts: the commonest items were plastic pinball games and replicas of yet another mystical lakeside maiden—clothed this time, but in a clinging garment that left nothing to the imagination. In the shrine a set of tinny loudspeakers endlessly broadcast a tape loop of *"Etenraku"*—the only piece of shrine music most Japanese can recognize—and a gaggle of sightseers rinsed their hands in ritual water before lining up for a commemorative photograph.

A dirt track led me away from Lake Tazawa, up into a short, high stretch of woodland, then down into a thin valley full of precast concrete blocks. The rain came on again, bringing out the snakes for an afternoon shower. One—a yard long—I almost trod on. It curled out of my way in two elegant sweeps of its mud-colored body and then stopped just short of the long grass and turned to stare at me, totally unafraid. A cemetery of rusted car chassis marked the approach to a village and the railway track that runs south to Omagari. By the time I came out onto a surfaced road, the rain had gathered such spiteful force that, having eased my other complaints in the lavatory of a restaurant, I found the prospect of going out into it again too depressing to face. I flopped down at one of the restaurant tables and sat scowling out at the grizzling sky and slowly sipping my way through a chilly beer that I would gladly have swapped for a mouthful of beef stew.

"Where are you going, then?"

"South."

"Where to?"

"Saimyoji, I think. Is there a minshuku there?"

"No."

"A ryokan?"

"No."

"Shit."

"Pardon?"

"Sorry, I was thinking in English. Are you sure there's nowhere to stay in Saimyoji?"

"Quite sure. I'm the village policeman."

I looked up. He was a stocky man in his late thirties, wearing a pair of sodden faded trousers, Wellington boots, and a brown fisherman's anorak. He nodded.

"Of course, I'm not in uniform. I only wear uniform for special occasions. But it's true all right. Have another beer."

He ordered another bottle of beer and left the oil stove he had been hovering over to come and sit at the table.

"Why do you want to go to Saimyoji?"

"To get out of the rain," I said.

"You're out of the rain here."

"I mean for the night."

It was still only a little after two in the afternoon, but he must have caught a note in my voice that conveyed a certain weariness with cross-examination.

"Of course," he said, after a thoughtful silence, "there's a ryokan here in Matsuba."

"I saw nothing on the road except this restaurant," I frowned.

"No," he agreed solemnly, "you wouldn't have. This is the new road, sort of a bypass. The old road runs to the east, through the village."

There was no other road—not even a track—on the map.

"It's not on the map," he agreed, equally solemnly, "but it's there all right. Want to give it a try?"

I said I did. In less than a minute he had phoned the ryokan, booked me a room, ordered two more beers, and gone out on a call leaving three full bottles and a large plate of beans.

"That's the policeman," gasped an old man who had been listening intently from a seat in the corner. "He's got a patrol car in his garage. He's got a fourth dan in judo, a second dan in kendo, a first dan in karate, and a first dan in sumo wrestling. He drinks whiskey—sometimes a bottle a day, sometimes half a bottle—and he hunts bears with a rifle on Sundays and holidays. His wife's pregnant. Do you mind if I ask you a question?"

The old man shuffled over, sat down wheezing, leaned across the table, and said, "Do you believe in Nessie?"

A recent Japanese news bulletin had announced the capture of the Loch Ness monster by a Japanese fishing boat just off New Zealand. Since then, questions about the monster (in Japanese, *Neshii*) had acquired a tone of anxious concern. I said I wasn't sure but was prepared to be convinced. The old man shut one eye in a curious squint and said in a whisper, "I believe in the *Tsuchi-no-ko Hebi* (literally, 'Child-of-the-Earth Snake')."

"The what?"

"The *Tsuchi-no-ko Hebi*." He opened his squinting eye and examined my face to see if I was smirking. I definitely wasn't doing that.

"I've seen it," he said, nodding and glancing over his shoulder. "I've seen it on Mount Taihei. That's where it lives. I saw it when I was up there for mushrooms. It's shaped a bit like a *kokeshi*, except you can't tell where the head ends and where the body starts." (A *kokeshi* is a wooden folk doll usually made from two pieces of wood, one a cylinder for the body, the other a globe for the head.) "It doesn't move fast, but I still couldn't catch it. I wish I had. There's a 400,000-yen reward for it. It's about the size of a beer bottle," he ended ruminatively.

I poured him a beer.

"Sounds like you missed a good opportunity."

"Ah," he said, "it bit an old woman from Yatsu. Her hand went green."

Later on, at the ryokan, the policeman confirmed the 400,000-yen reward, though he doubted the old man had actually seen the creature. Only two women, he said, had reported seeing it, and they had both come shrieking away in fright.

Outside the window, in the still falling rain, an old woman in a conical straw hat and straw cape was carefully weeding her vegetable patch. In the ryokan room, the policeman sat with me, drinking beer, till dusk came down. The rain was still pounding as I lolled in the bathtub, letting the hot water knead my stomach and feeling the aimless depression of the morning seeping out of me and drifting off with the steam. There are few complaints, whether of body or soul, that a Japanese bath will not help ease. It is simply a question of separating the functional from the hedonistic. You do not take a Japanese bath in order to wash. You wash before you get into the bath, thus freeing yourself from the obligation of doing anything in the tub itself but wallowing, reviving, gossiping with your neighbors, drowsing, humming, listening to the evening rain.

Thus it was that, stomach cramps gone, diarrhea a fading nightmare, I emerged from the bathroom fully prepared for the evening revels of the Matsuba Phoenix Baseball Team who had just won the village tournament and had taken over the upstairs floor of the ryokan for what already sounded like Akita's answer to Balshazzar's Feast. Top of the bill on the circus program, I sang for them, played the taiko for them, attempted to explain the rules of cricket to them (an explanation doomed from the start by their unshakable conviction that cricket, croquet, and polo were the same game), drank a lot of their sakè and most of their draft beer, and ended up being put to bed by two ryokan maids who told me that I had a good voice but rather loud, and that I should try to avoid the downstairs guests in the morning. It wasn't so much that they had complained; more that they had been "a bit surprised."

In the night I made the beginner's lavatory mistake. Whatever the style of Japanese lavatory—whether Western or the traditional hole in the floor—you never go into it wearing the same pair of slippers that you wear along the corridors. Another pair of slippers—often helpfully marked "lavatory"—is laid out for you there, and you change into them as you enter. The beginner's lavatory mistake is this: stumbling half-pissed into a hole-in-the-floor-type lavatory at night, he kicks one of the lavatory slippers down the hole. This, I suppose, happens fairly regularly, but for a veteran of seven years to commit this blunder was an immediately sobering embarrassment. In fact, it was so embarrassing to be left hopping about in a single lavatory slipper that I kicked that down the hole to follow the first. My plan was to disclaim all knowledge of the slippers so that the maid would be accused of having forgotton to lay them out. This, I congratulated myself, was a cast-iron defense, but in the searing light of morning it struck me that I might well be resorting unawares to an instantly recognizable "beginner's lavatory feeble ploy," so I avoided not only the downstairs guests but the entire domestic staff as well.

In the late afternoon of my forty-second day I went to see the old samurai houses in the town of Kakunodate. They line the sides of one long, unspoiled street between the station and the river. Standing back in the shade of their own gardens, some are still lived in, some deserted and empty, their gnarled raindoors stashed away, the odd leaf blown through open screens onto the faded tatami. The rooms are bare, devoid of furniture. The rough, worn wood of the beams and posts is dark and grained, and the creamy white plaster of the walls is cracked and, in several places, has crumbled away to reveal the daub-and-lath construction still very common in Japanese houses. The paper screens are yellow with charcoal smoke, the ends of the rooftiles black and hollow. The whole is silent, and the sound of a sparrow is enough to startle you as you stand there moping.

The classical Japanese house attains its somber beauty by decaying in stages until it offers both the congenial textures of age and the sense of natural order that attends the first hint of ruin. Tatami are the color of green tea when new. Only gradually do they acquire the mellow gold-straw color that warms and softens rooms such as these. In time, the gold fades to the color of old hay, and the rich, smooth patina of wear grows lusterless. The glow dims out of the brown-and-white spaces, and the rooms die as these have.

In the silent gardens of the old houses in Kakunodate the tops of the stone lanterns are lumpy and green, the stone wells drip with dark water drops that congeal in the summer heat. The moss is black-green and thick as a poultice. Not a single flower blooms, though the cherry trees are in full leaf, and beyond the mounds of twig and rock stands a small, empty veranda from which to view their blossoms. All of the colors are the colors of decay—decay, not the full-blown colors of maturity. Their tranquility stems from the brush of death on them.

Across the road, in an open workshop, two young craftsmen sat hammering cherry bark, one making *suzuribako*—flat square boxes for writing instruments—and the other decorating geta. Behind them in a small dripping lumberyard a pile of logs lay under jets of water dousing them to separate the ripe bark from the wood, and as the young craftsmen worked they sang "Blowin' in the Wind."

On the road the next morning I passed a Buddhist nun in a filthy white robe striding towards Kakunodate station carrying a round, flat, fan-shaped object called an *uchiwa-daiko*—a stained, single-skinned drum. She was beating it for alms as she strode along, and no one was paying her the least attention. To the southwest the white, snow-riddled peak of Mount Chokai teased its way up through a fine mountain mist. Chokai is known as Dewa Fuji—Dewa being the old name for Akita and Yamagata—just as Yotei is known as Ezo Fuji, Bandai is known as Aizu Fuji, Iwaki is known as Tsugaru Fuji, and so on through at least a dozen "Fujis" that in some way, if only in the imagination, call to mind the famous prototype. Each of these lesser, provincial mountains is beautiful because it imitates Fuji. That, it has been decided, is the epitome of natural splendor, so that is what the rest shall aspire to. I sat and drank a bottle of beer in a drive-in and watched the largest, most beautiful moth I had ever seen—deep purple and orange, and huge as a bat—curl up and die on the windowsill.

At the Omagari Batting Center a machine lobbed pitches to a solitary batter who whammed them into a frayed green net, and in the avenue to the south of the station a few soiled Tanabata lanterns bobbed on strings, and grit blew into the doorways of the Sony shops and the shops selling cherry-wood boxes.

Early on the forty-fourth morning I seized the first opportunity to get off the dusty highway onto a flat country road that rambled through farms and slate-tiled villages, and on which, from midmorning till late afternoon, I saw not a single motor vehicle. Houses older than those in Kakunodate stood, lived-in and contained behind high tile-topped walls. Dark iron fire towers teetered over the village streets, and beyond the villages lay the fifty-kilometer sea of rippling green rice that filled the wide Yokote valley.

On the outskirts of the villages stood little shops selling giant radishes and plastic spaceships. I learned to tell from a considerable distance which shops stocked beer. Those that did not had large red Coca-Cola signs or blue Fanta Grape signs tacked to their walls. Those that did displayed advertisements for the local brands of sakè in bold black calligraphy: Full Bloom, High Spring Water, Heavenly Longevity, Akita's Glory. There is an ancient dispute among the men of Tohoku as to which of the six prefectures produces the best sakè. The keenest rivalry is between Akita in the west and its larger Pacific-coast neighbor, Iwate. The men of Iwate state flatly that their sakè is better because their rice is better. The men of Akita counter that their sakè is better because their water is better. I have studiously avoided taking sides in this dispute because I have found that, by maintaining a noncommittal silence, I have cup after cup of free sakè urged upon me in an effort to elicit the judgment I shall never give. Solomon in all his glory lacked this simple wisdom, or perhaps wasn't thirsty.

At a fork in the road at Kakumagawa I asked two old grandmothers sitting under a tree which road would take me to Hiraka. The one I asked first turned to her companion and giggled into her scarf. Her companion smiled toothlessly and jerked her thumb with no apparent conviction towards the road on the left.

"Are you sure?" I asked.

The first giggled, the second nodded. I set off down the road to the left. Thirty minutes later I was back at the tree. The grandmothers had disappeared.

"Hiraka?" said a young man tying six boxes of apples over the rear mudguard of his bicycle. "No problem at all. Road on the right."

Obtaining directions is an artful business and I had blundered. I had named a town twelve kilometers away whereas, had I asked the grandmothers the way to the next village, I might have saved myself half an hour of boot rubber. The trouble was that, much of the time, I couldn't read the characters for the smaller villages, and when I showed my map to grocers and truck drivers and restaurant owners, it turned out that they couldn't read them either.

Along the road, small wayside shrines held empty twisted candlesticks. Wax had guttered down them and they looked as though they had been basted with pus. At Nozaki—a village so completely hidden among trees that it appeared to have been walled to withstand a siege—a woman told me that in winter the snow is as high as the second-story windows and the villagers tunnel from house to house and from shop to shop like moles. At the next village a pretty girl in Levi shorts skipped up to me, panting, and asked me to write my name in her notepad. She was, I suppose, eighteen. Her notepad had teddy bears printed at the bottom of each page and I signed it with her luminous orange pen.

"I . . . I saw you from my window," she gasped, hopping from one foot to the other, ". . . and I . . . couldn't let a chance . . . like this . . . go by." I handed back her pen with a smile whose charm would have melted a two-story snowdrift. She fled.

From far away across the late afternoon fields came the sound of shotguns, double-echoing through the valley. Three lank black crows hung high in the wind, flapping from a clothesline. And then I saw a man of straw. He was standing in one corner of a ripening field beside a small farm crossroads. He wore a long straw cape and a tattered conical hat, and the stick in his belt proclaimed him a warrior. His belt was made of twisted rope like the rope that decorates the gateways of shrines. A thicker rope was nailed to the tree above his head and from it hung the white twists of paper that, in Shinto, are the universal charm against evil. He had a face of stuffed white cloth. His features were carefully outlined in black ink, and he stared, not at the crows in the field, but at the deserted crossroads. I started with surprise when I saw him, and I shivered when I turned away and his eyes were on my back.

Outside Hiraka a little girl, perhaps ten years old, had just pulled her knickers down and was getting ready to piss in her front garden. Her two schoolfriends were ecstatic.

"Oooo! Are you going to? Are you really going to?"

I passed the front garden. The little girl saw me, hoisted her knickers, and with a wail of despair vanished into the woodshed.

The great trunk road to Fukushima shudders with the constant pounding of container trucks, and the dust they raise clogs the air in the narrowing valley and swirls in the bottlenecks of the gray Omono River. A day of it coating the roof of my mouth made me long for the cool of the uplands and hills or the sea that was still a week away. But Michinoku plays hide-and-seek among the trucks and clogging dust. The old sakè warehouses of Yuzawa have the elaborate frontage of ancient ryokans. The windows are slatted with smooth, grained wood, and the roof tiles are stamped with the crest of the Satake clan, the former daimyo of the valley. In the jammed main street of the old commercial city, narrower than some of the country lanes I had tramped down, the beer shops sell bean curd and the hardware shops sell eel baskets. Through the dust and petroleum haze of the street, the foothills and slopes to the east of Mount Chokai looked as distant as they had from Kakunodate, though I knew they were less than a day away and that by tomorrow night they would lie behind me.

In the early hours of the forty-sixth morning rain began to fall. I hung about after breakfast in the ryokan at Yokobori, drinking cups of green tea and watching the sky. But when I finally set out it was through a slicing rainstorm that hammered the highway and gave the trucks swishing through it the appearance of snowploughs. The rain would ease, then hammer, then ease. In the lulls I could see the splashes of white and gray mist that clung to the slopes of the nearer hills. The further hills were lost to sight, and before the mist could part to reveal them, the rainstorm descended like a net and it was more than I could do to look up from the streaming road.

As the road climbed more and more steeply into the hills, the storm drains beside it swirled faster and faster till the water was churning too fast to be contained and spilled out of them over boots and gutter. There was some shelter under the snowshields that protected the hairpin bends in the highway as it crawled blindly up the flooded mountain. At midday I entered an unlit tunnel and stamped through the chill of it to emerge in front of a battered white signboard that told me I had just crossed the prefectural boundary from Akita into Yamagata.

The rain still eased, then slashed down, then eased. I stopped at a restaurant for lunch, but there was no food. I stopped at a village to buy some food, but all the shops were closed. The road twisted sharply down through the hills until it reached the northern edge of the flat plain of Shinjo, where a narrower road forked off to follow the railway in a sweep to Mamurogawa. August thirteenth—the first day of O-Bon—and on the Shinjo Plain the narrow road was quiet, the railway line curved away gray and gleaming, and the paddies shone like polished slate. If the dead are abroad, I thought, it's because they've been flooded out of their graves.

But the rain had not kept the living at home, and as the afternoon wore on, more and more families came out of their houses and marched to the graveyards. I passed children skipping along in cotton yukatas, fathers carrying babies on their backs, mothers loaded down with kettles and flowers, and grandmothers splashing through the puddles in rainboots, chatting to each other under paper umbrellas. Everyone I saw wore bright summer clothes, the children giggled excitedly, all of the women chuckled and joked, and when I passed them they nodded sagely to each other and said, "Look, he must have been up in the mountains. Look, he's just come down from the mountains."

In the first graveyard a mother and her daughter had set up a small bamboo table in front of a grave. On the table they had placed handfuls of cooked rice wrapped in lotus leaves, slices of watermelon, a tomato, some beans, crackers still in their cellophane wrappings, and a little cup of the cold green tea they were sitting drinking. The rain ran down their umbrellas and pattered onto the plastic sheets they sat on, but they laughed as they talked and drank their tea.

In the next graveyard the same makeshift tables had been set up for half a dozen graves, and although they were a good way back from the road, I could hear the noisy chatter of the families, spreading their mats, unwrapping their riceballs, trying to light sticks of incense in the rain, trying to keep their candles dry for evening. Children played hide-and-seek among the trees, the girls in pink, the boys in blue. By the time I reached the third graveyard the rain had given way to a fine damp mist and dusk had started to gather.

One by one the candles on the graves flickered and settled into a glow. In the distance the tiny pricks of light pinpointed another graveyard and, beyond that, another, stretching back towards the dark shape of the mountains. The rusty cola tins in the wayside shrines had been replaced with bright red new ones, candles scorched the cobwebs inside the shrines, and the old guttered wax melted slowly into life. From the nearest graves the dry sweet smell of incense leavened the odd stench of burning I had smelled all day. Across the darkening fields came the sound of a shotgun, like a ripple back and forth down the valley, and as I walked into the little town of Mamurogawa I could hear the low steady note of a temple bell.

"Look at the sky," a barber told me, standing rooted in the road outside his shop. I turned and looked. In the space of perhaps five minutes the entire western sky had turned a brilliant flaming orange, the color of tangerine peel, the color of bonfires.

"I've seen that once before in my life," said the barber, hardly moving his lips. "Only once. This is the second time."

At a ryokan I slid open the door and called out in a loud voice from the entrance hall. There was no reply. I called out again; there was no reply. I waited a minute and called out again; there was no reply. I heaved off my pack and stamped about in the damp entrance hall, making as many loud noises as I could. A voice asked me to wait. I waited three minutes and called out again. There was no reply. I called out again. Finally, the screen inched slowly open and an old man in blue-and-white striped pajamas peered round the doorpost.

"Are there any rooms free?"

"Rooms?" the old man wheezed.

"Rooms, yes."

"But today is O-Bon."

"You mean you're closed?"

"Of course we're closed."

The old man shook his head and started to chuckle. He was still chuckling as I trudged off towards the station.

At the second ryokan I got exactly the same response, but this time I was dealing with a motherly woman and with motherly women I am on firmer ground.

"What terrible weather! What an exhausting day! Would you believe I've walked all the way from . . . "

In two minutes I had a room, a dry kimono, and was slipping into a warm bath, my mind adrift among hillocks of hot food. When I came out of the bathroom the woman was waiting for me.

"O-*niisan* (elder brother)," she began, "I suppose you know that today is O-Bon, so naturally we haven't got any meat."

"That's all right," I said, brightly, "I didn't expect meat."

"We haven't got any fish either."

"Ah . . . " (less brightly).

"And there's no cooked rice—except for the graves. And we haven't boiled any vegetables. And the shops were all closed so we didn't buy fruit. In fact, there isn't anything at all."

The woman beamed up at me cheerfully. I grinned the grin of the thoroughly desperate.

"But we've got a few pickles and a drop of sakè, so if you'd like to sit with my son and me . . . "

I spent the evening sitting in the living room with the woman and her twenty-year-old son, eating tiny pickles out of a tiny dish, drinking steaming hot cups of "First Grandchild" till the bottle was finished, and when the bottle was finished, we opened another. Later on, we sang the song of Mamurogawa.

I am a plum flower of Mamurogawa,
you are a nightingale of Shinjo.
You do not wait for my flower to bloom;
you come while I'm still in bud.

95

I dreamed a dream, I dreamed a dream,
I dreamed of us and of our wedding;
our marriage cups were full and flowing;
we raised them—and I woke.

From time to time I heard an old man muttering and laughing to himself in the room next door. Once or twice the woman got up and took a jug of sakè into the room, and when she did this the sound of the old man's laughter grew louder. Then she would come back, closing the door quietly behind her, and the laughter would settle into a gurgle again. Who was it, I wondered? Her husband in his cups? Or some dead ancestor come back to watch a half-starved foreigner eat tiny vegetables out of a tiny dish?

This was O-Bon. The real O-Bon. There is nothing like it in the cities. The people of Tokyo may visit the odd grave, but they still demand their hamburger steaks and knock back their whiskeys-and-water. Mamurogawa was a different world. I felt curiously content as I crawled into my futon that night, and the thought of O-Bon in the northern mountains warmed my stomach even though it was empty.

4

Summer Lights,
Summer Shadows

A WIND BLEW through the gorge of the Mogami River, whitening the choppy water as it swirled in midstream. The water swirled one way, the wind blew the other, buffeting the long thin tourist boats that skimmed down the rapids toward the city of Sakata.

The seventeenth-century poet Basho Matsuo came wandering down this same windy gorge on the northern journey he described in *Oku no Hosomichi* (The Narrow Road to the End of the World). Basho is considered one of the supreme masters of *haiku*—poems consisting of a bare seventeen syllables that seek to evoke a mood or tone through the fleeting juxtaposition of images and sounds. The trouble is that when you start trying to translate haiku into English, their surface simplicity can cause them to resemble the captions in somebody's snapshot album:

> *Swelled by early summer rain,*
> *swiftly flows Mogami River.*

The boatmen, sitting hunched over the outboard motors that power their craft through the slicks of the current, celebrate their profession with the same simplicity. A loudspeaker in the stern of the boat sends their old work song echoing through the riverside drive-ins where it competes with the taped Hawaiian guitars; and the tourists in the boats, fortified against the wind with whiskey, sit cooing, clapping, and attempting to sing the chorus:

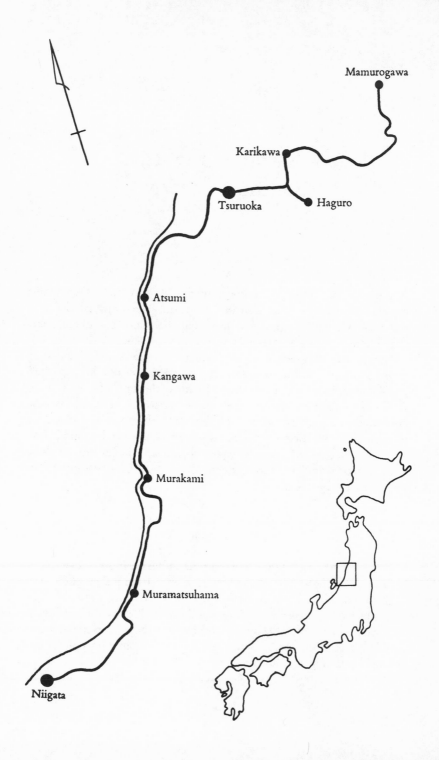

Mamurogawa

Karikawa

Tsuruoka ● Haguro

Atsumi

Kangawa

Murakami

Muramatsuhama

Niigata

Look after yourself while I'm in Sakata.
Mind you don't catch influenza.
Enya-ee! Enya-ee-to!
Enya-kora! Makase!

As the valley widened down to the plain the wind blew stronger, raking the rice in long supple waves. To the north the peak of Mount Chokai was awash with clouds that scurried past it like waifs from an ogre. I sat on a grass bank oiling my boots and was tormented by children.

"Hey, yoo! Hey, yoo! Ziss iz a penn! Jap'neze boy! Goooh! Goooh! Wass yah naymu? Wass yah naymu?"

"Look," I said wearily, "why don't you all go for a nice long swim in the rapids?"

A hush fell over the children while their stunned little minds tackled the unimaginable: the thing could speak intelligible language. They came a step closer.

"You speak Japanese?"

"Not a word," I said in Japanese. "You'd better get an interpreter."

I screwed the cap on my tin of oil and stuffed it back inside my pack.

"Would you like to play catchball?"

"Sorry, I've got to go."

"Would you like to meet a married woman?"

"Next time round."

I laced my boots and trudged off down the bank, pondering my answers to both those questions.

Outside the little resort of Kusanagi the moored boats tossed in the narrowed river. The boatmen sprawled smoking on the boathouse ramps or readied their outboard motors for the slow chug back upstream. The last of the afternoon pleasure craft came gliding into sight round the final bend, the passengers singing in the August chill, the boatman patting the wooden tiller.

. . . bear me no grudge, but blame the wind.
Enya-kora! Makase!

The wind shunted me up the long main street of the little town of Karikawa, spinning the yellowed paper lanterns that hung in the gateways of almost all the houses. Above the lanterns, tied to the

99

gateposts, bundles of pampas grass and bush clover whipped this way and that, whirring and crackling, and outside the little supermarket a man was setting up a taiko drum.

It was the first night of the Dance of the Dead. The woman at the ryokan brought me a pounded rice cake covered with green and purple beanpaste. When dark had fallen I left the ryokan and clumped through the empty streets in a pair of geta that scraped the skin off my heels. The rattling lanterns were all alight and the furry pampas grass stropped the gateposts in the darkness. There was no one on the streets, and the absence of any light but the pale jerking lanterns lent an eeriness to the rustle of the leaves and the hollow clack of my geta.

In a quarter of an hour I had found the gravelly car park where the dancing was to take place, with its squat wooden tower and its strings of pink lights madly bouncing. Most small-town Bon dances take place in school playgrounds or in the spaces in front of public buildings. Here, as usual, a little tower had been set up in the middle of the dancing area and hung with red and white festival cloths that twisted and flapped in the northern wind. The tower houses the source of the music, whether live or recorded, and the two small makeshift taiko tied to the rail at the top of this one were hardly larger than saucepan lids. Children clambered up and down the tower ladder and took turns banging the taiko, but the sound they produced was inaudible above the hideously amplified noise of The Ventures playing "Jingle Bell Rock."

I crunched about the gravel round the edge of the car park, wincing in my geta and looking for a beer stall. The teenagers of the town were gyrating in neat lines while their kimonoed parents stood winking approval. Two little primary school girls performed a complex bit of hip-swiveling choreography with their faces buried in candyfloss (there was a candyfloss stall but it sold no beer). At eight, just as I had made up my mind to go in search of a more fluid celebration, the rock music stopped. The teenagers and their kimonoed parents formed two concentric circles round the tower, a ten-ton needle thumped into a record groove, the loudspeakers crackled with static, and the first bars of "*Dewa Sanzan Ondo,*" outtwanging The Ventures by about fifty phons, ushered in for the little town of Karikawa its annual flirtation with the ghosts.

In less than a minute the circles were in their stride, the inner circle rehearsed and proficient, the outer circle ragged and unconcerned.

The two little candyfloss girls had switched universes and were now locked into their niche among the older dancers, hands in the air, bodies bending with the ancient motions of the rice planter, two steps forward, one step back, clap, as the circles turned about the tower and the two teenage taiko players labored to make themselves heard above the amplified wails.

The wind from Haguro refreshes,
the Harai River cleanses the heart.
The Harai River! Fine place!
Sing for its prosperity!

There was still no beer so I limped about with my hands in my pockets, wincing as the geta shredded my blisters and humming the song of the Awa Dance of Shikoku, which contains a cautionary lyric:

You're a fool if you dance,
you're a fool if you watch the dancing,
so you might as well dance.

"Dance," grinned a young man in a U.C.L.A. sweater.
"I'm the fool who watches," I winced cockily.
But he took me by the shoulders in a friendly way and steered me towards two large ugly girls in livid orange and pink kimonos.
"*Bijin* (beautiful women)," he announced. "Real Yamagata *bijin*. Stand between them and let me take your photograph."
I stood between them, smiling gravely, while the young man exposed half a roll of film. The record ended, the needle swung back to thump down in the same groove, and within two bars the iron maidens had collared me. The one in the orange kimono gripped an elbow, the one in the pink kimono gripped a wrist. They were clearly a tag team.
"Dance," they suggested, applying an armlock.
"Dance," grinned the young man, cocking his camera.
"Dance," yelled a man in a blue yukata. "What's the matter with you? Got corns?"
"I'm the fool who watches," I cackled in panic, but my cackles were drowned by a merry explosion of saxophones.

101

The snow melts on Mount Gassan
and flows into the Bonji River.
The Bonji River! Fine place!
Screech for its prosperity!

I danced for about forty minutes, trying to avoid the larger pebbles which sent shooting pains up my legs as far as my groin. The camera flashes always seemed to catch me at the most desperate moments, and the grin I had fixed on my face by the end of it all must have looked, on Fujicolor, like the grin on a death's-head.

At nine, the iron maidens drifted back to their dungeons, and I collapsed into a neighboring *akachochin* with the young tormentor in his U.C.L.A. sweater and his friend, Mr. Cho, who had been dragged away from a snuggly Yamagata *bijin* to talk English to the foreigner. Mr. Cho had spent two years in Edinburgh, so we were set at each other like seals in a circus ring, nodding our little balloon of language from one nose to the other.

"Ah, so you have been hitchhiking."

"No, I've been walking."

"Yes, yes, yes. And what a beautiful country is Japan to walk in. But have you found it easy to obtain rides?"

"I haven't had any rides."

"Oh, come, come, come."

"I've walked."

"Yes, yes. But what about the *longer* distances?"

"Perhaps you haven't understood me . . ."

"Yes, yes, yes. How marvelous to be British! I *love* the British. I *love* British English. I *love love love* it. I love the British *madly,* and I especially love the *beautiful beautiful* people of Edinburgh."

"I'm glad to hear it."

"But how *far* have you hitchhiked?"

In the ryokan, the wind blew open the old casement window in my room and I got up to close it. Outside, in the dark streets, the rustle and howl of it sounded alive, or like the dead in search of another dance. The casement window flew open again and I turned over, moaning in the futon, and slept with the midsummer wind at my ears.

Twelve kilometers south of Karikawa stands Mount Haguro, the most accessible of the Three Holy Mountains of Dewa. The mountains —Haguro, Gassan, and Yudono—are revered both by Shinto worshipers and by a particularly esoteric sect of Buddhism, and they have been a place of pilgrimage since at least the seventh century. They are still visited regularly by groups of what the official guidebook to the area calls "mountaineering ascetics" and are the haunt of colorful "mountain priests" who blow conches for picture postcards, as well as the abode of three major gods: Tsukiyomi-no-Mikoto (Lord Reading-the-Moon), Ideha-no-Mikoto (Lord Trough-in-the-Waves), and Oyamatsumi-no-Mikoto (Lord God-of-the-High-Mountain), who chooses to live in a waterfall. The entire area—some three hundred square kilometers—is sacred. There are shrines and temples dotted about the slopes, but they merely confirm the sanctity of the land. It is not in the shrines and temples that the gods live, but in the mountains themselves.

You reach the summit of Mount Haguro by climbing a stone causeway that consists, so the guidebook says, of 2,446 steps. The causeway rises steeply, and many of the steps are narrower than the sole of an ordinary shoe, so the climb with boots and full pack was slow and sometimes precarious. Halfway up, it grew too precarious, and I stood my pack against one of the giant cypress trees that tower over the narrow steps and continued up unhampered. In the little glades beside the causeway the sun shone hot, and as the climb grew still steeper the rich Shonai Plain unfolded far below me, lime green with rice. Beyond the plain, lifeless in the summer haze, the Sea of Japan lay blue and silver—the first sea I had glimpsed for fourteen days.

The pilgrims and sightseers carried walking sticks that they had bought in the souvenir shops by the car park. They wore straw hats to protect them from the August sun, and in the glades by the causeway they stopped, as I did, to spoon down mounds of melon-flavored ice that was shredded from large sweating blocks with iron handwheels. Between the narrow stones of the causeway black moss grew, and the towering cypresses cast pools of deep shade.

The Dewa Shrine on the summit of Mount Haguro is an airy complex of thatched wooden buildings. The smaller buildings are gnarled and carved with intricate dragons, while the main shrine has scarlet walls and a brown roof of solid rice straw. There are straw sakè barrels piled high against the walls, for the old gods know the value of booze;

and nearby there is a sumo wrestling ring, for they know the value of guts and muscle too.

The bell on its straw rope rattled and clanged as crowds of pilgrims poked the gods awake so that the gods could watch them clapping their hands and tossing their coins into the coin troughs. Red-clad shrine maidens with apple cheeks sat bouncing and chatting behind their stalls, selling little embroidered bags for charms and fortune papers for twenty yen. Those pilgrims with twenty yen to spare stood chortling over their fortune papers, then carefully refolded them into thin white strips and tied them to the branches of trees in the shrine compound. After a week of heavy pilgrimage the trees are laden as though with snow.

Behind one of the smaller buildings a priest sat writing names on wooden grave sticks. When the ink was dry he planted the sticks in neat rows like the pales of a fence. The old stone graves were dressed as people. One wore an apron printed with strawberries, another a kimono, another a shawl. The smaller graves wore pants and vests, a Donald Duck T-shirt, a baseball cap. In the afternoon wind that blows down from Gassan the long blue carp streamers fluttered untidily and gray incense smoke tormented the priest with a fit of coughing.

My rucksack was where I had left it. In the glades the sun still shone, and the green ice furred my tongue with a sharp dry tingle. One or two of the mountaineering ascetics courted worldly adventure:

"Look at it! Look at it! A gaijin! It's a gaijin! See what it does when you say 'hurro' to it."

From the height of the causeway the small island of Awashima lay a pale blue-gray on the distant sea, and I felt a strong urge to be down the holy mountain and lolling in the cool unholy water. Across the flat rice fields I caught, too, my first glimpse of the TV masts and bowling alleys of the city of Tsuruoka. The bowling alleys were topped with giant red skittles that towered over the squat little houses like the cypresses over the Haguro steps.

Down on the plain a great concrete torii gate straddled the holy highway, and the tiny shop I stopped to have a beer in sold clocks and watches as well. The night's dancing and the day's pilgrimage had left my legs so shaky that I thought seriously about lying down to sleep for the night on the narrow grass verge of one of the paddy fields. But the TV masts seemed closer, the bowling skittles redder, and so I shrugged off the spell the summer gods had cast and trudged, very tired, the last ten kilometers into the old castle town that was my day's destination.

At a ryokan I washed my clothes, and a chuckling woman showed me how to climb up onto the washroom sink, squeeze through the window with the washing in my arms, and tightrope-walk across a rooftop ladder in order to reach the drying platform, where we admired each other's acrobatics and threaded my wet jeans onto a bamboo pole.

The only other guest at the ryokan that night sold dental instruments for a firm in Sendai, so we sat in the living room together and discussed the advantages of Doctor Beech's dentist's chair. Later, we discussed the dancers of Kyoto, who are famous throughout Japan for their grace and beauty, and the dental man insisted that they were all recruited in Tsuruoka. All, without exception, came from Tsuruoka, and so, he assured me, did a lot of dentists' wives.

At nine, the woman of the ryokan brought us a dish of sliced apples, and the dental man told me about his son.

"My son's fifteen. A boy scout. He's out camping this week for one of his badges. Up in the mountains. All by himself. It's hard for a lad, but it'll do him good. The first night I drove up and took him a chicken. The chicken was alive and he didn't know what to do with it. I said nothing, I just stood there and watched him. He told me over and over that he didn't want to kill the chicken, but I said nothing, and eventually he wrapped it in a newspaper and snapped its neck. The second night I took him a live eel and a diagram of how to cut it up.

"He's not a bright boy. He cried for a while when he killed both creatures. He wanted to tell me something, but I came away before he could speak. I'm rather worried about his future.

"He's not much good with an abacus, even though I've told him it's one of the basic skills. Reading, writing, and the abacus. We make two thirds of the electronic calculators in the world, and four out of five Japanese shopkeepers still use an abacus. My son's a disappointment. He made a mess of the eel."

When he rose to go to bed, the dental man bowed very low at the door of the living room and told me how much he had learned from me that evening.

"I wish my son could have met you, but I'm afraid it would have been a waste of your time—a man like you with an education. My son's fifteen. He'll come to nothing."

105

Big Ben chimes woke me at six. They came out of a loudspeaker three yards from my window, and when twenty minutes of amplified physical jerks had properly toned up the neighborhood, a woman's voice began shrieking advertisements for cabarets and mahjong parlors. In the living room I mended my belt with a needle and thread and drank two cups of instant coffee while a priest in the next room chanted Buddhist sutras for the mother who sat swaying, with her eyes closed, in the shade by the door.

"Don't your feet ache?" they wondered as they gathered to see me off. "When our feet ache like that up here in the north, we generally say *koee...na.*"

"I see."

"Go on, say it."

"*Koee...na.*"

The priest's laugh was especially shrill. I could still hear it as I waved from the traffic lights.

≫⊱

Willow trees line the old green streams that crisscross the streets of Tsuruoka, and the streams are walled like the castle moats they once were. The day was immensely hot, with the humidity of gathering rain. In twenty minutes my clothes were soaked, and before I was even out of the city I stopped to cool off in the Chido Museum and dripped my way round a fine collection of ornamented *bandori*—the backpacks used by country people for humping firewood, vegetables, and kids. The most elaborate of these were the *iwai-bandori,* designed for carrying wedding trousseaus, and the colors and patterns reminded me of the Navajo rugs I had once seen in New Mexico. (Speaking of the Navajo, I have often wondered why people who strive to depict the Japanese as quaint have never resorted to the Red Indian ploy. The written character for "moon," for instance, is the same as the written character for "month," so the Japanese, like the Hollywood redskins, speak of things happening "many moons ago." To my knowledge, no one—not even the most frantic quaintifier—has ever translated the expression that way, but the quaintifying industry is alive and kicking, and if the Japanese would only start wearing feathers on their heads the oversight could quickly be expunged.)

In the grounds of the museum stood several "old" buildings—a

106

town hall (1881), a police station (1884)—so revered for having survived a century that they had been lugged from their original sites and painstakingly reconstructed. There was also a fine old three-story farmhouse. It had a warm thatched roof and high paper windows, and on the timber floors of its second and third stories the old silkworm trays and frames stood intact. This solid old farmhouse had been trundled plank by plank from a little mountain village some sixteen kilometers outside Tsuruoka, and was now fenced off behind a turnstile earning money for the proprietors of the Chido Museum. I wondered what the villagers had had to say, and whether they had put on their war paint.

The humidity intensified, and by midday the sky was a dense mass of cloud. On Highway 7 the Hole in One golf range was littered like a chicken farm with little white blobs, and the terrace was stacked with imitation-leather golf bags and crowded with imitation golfers. The low hills that separate the Shonai Plain from the Sea of Japan were gray with drizzle, and when I finally came face to face with the sea I could barely distinguish it from the louring sky. Still, on the first empty beach I came to I peeled off my clothes and swam out into the rain. The last sea I had swum in had been in the north of Aomori on a scorching hot thirty-first of July. Now, on the seventeenth of August, two festivals, three hot springs, one youth hostel, five minshukus, eleven ryokans, scores of beers, and 442 kilometers further south, I renewed my communion with the sea by floating in it for ten shivery minutes and catching a cramp.

On a little promontory the ugly eight-story Hotel Thunder presided over the gloom of the coast. The thin beaches were pocked and empty, and the trees on the outcrops of rock hung limp and shredded by the northeast wind. The roofs of the coastal villages were black or gray or muddy brown. There were none of the primary colors of Hokkaido, and whereas the villages of the plains spread over acres and those of the mountains are strung out for up to a mile along twisting roads, the villages of the Yamagata coast stand huddled and tight like stragglers in a storm.

Some of the little harbors I passed were situated on the inland side of the highway, so that the fishing boats chugged under the growling traffic and anchored behind the thick concrete piles. The road ran high through rocky tunnels, crossing and recrossing the railway line, then slumping back down to the level of the sea where, on one dreary beach,

107

half a dozen children were lighting jumping jacks that fizzled out after the first crack.

Dusk came on fast and at half past six it was night. In the village of Atsumi the woman at the ryokan door stood twisting her apron about in her fists.

"Are there any rooms free?" I asked with an encouraging smile.

"Well, yes, there are, but we haven't got any beds. We sleep on mattresses on the floor."

"Yes, I know," I said. "I've lived in Japan for seven years."

"And you won't be able to eat the food."

"Why, what's the matter with it?"

"It's fish."

"I like fish."

"But it's *raw* fish."

"Look, I've lived in Japan for seven years. My wife's Japanese. I like raw fish."

"But I don't think we've got any knives and forks."

"Look . . ."

"And you can't use chopsticks."

"Of course I can. I've lived in Japan for . . ."

"But it's a tatami-mat room and there aren't any armchairs."

"Look . . ."

"And there's no shower in the bathroom. It's an *o-furo*."

"I use chopsticks at home. I sit on tatami. I eat raw fish. I use an o-furo. I've lived in Japan for seven years. That's nearly a quarter of my life. My wife . . ."

"Yes," moaned the woman, "but we can't speak English."

"I don't suppose that will bother us," I sighed. "We've been speaking Japanese for the last five minutes."

From my room in the ryokan at Atsumi I watched the night mist come down on the sea. The rain had stopped, and on the distant water the pale, bobbing lights of the fishermen were like the glimmers of the departing dead.

꙳

The horizon was light but the morning sea was wild. The waves crashed high on the pebble beaches, flicking the long strands of seaweed like whips. Three middle-aged women pedaled past me on bicycles, dressed in shiny black skin-diving suits and carrying children's water wings that were covered with printed teddy bears and flowers. Wives in scarves and rubber aprons fished for shellfish in the rocky shallows, peering through square glass-bottomed boxes that the sea did its best to snatch out of their hands.

At noon on the fifty-first day of my journey I crossed the prefectural boundary from Yamagata into Niigata, and thus passed out of Tohoku and into the "Middle Region" of Japan called Chubu. Nothing but a road sign marked the passing, though once, long ago, here at this boundary, armed warriors guarded a barrier gate to prevent the shogun's enemies from escaping north along the narrow coast road into country where they would be lost forever.

The houses of the first Niigata villages were roofed with strips of bare gray wood, and the strips were held down by stones that were green with moss. In the tiny harbors fishermen scraped paint off the white, flaking hulls of their boats, and on a drive-in wall an advertisement for menswear showed a Coldstream guardsman in a bearskin saying "Well Come in Your Elegant Heart." I slept for an hour on a sand dune, then climbed a flight of old stone steps to a graveyard where the trees had been stripped of their bark by the wind and the Bon tables were gone from the graves.

But at the village of Kangawa that night they were dancing. Four red demons with clubs made of baseball bats, a snow queen covered in silver cooking foil, a black nylon crow, three coal miners with lamps, a robot with a body of cardboard boxes—all these danced in the small school playground, round the car whose battery powered the microphone into which a bent old woman was singing. Her only accompaniment was one taiko drum and the scattered clapping of the dancers as they smacked into each other's backs, tripped over their sandals, and tapped each other's noses with their fans.

The night was hot. In the minshuku the woman who had danced and clapped and driven off the children when they started making faces at me plumped down at the table in her tight green shorts and peeled us a couple of tangerines.

"I was born in this house in Kangawa and I was three when my parents took me south and we settled for a few years on the island of Shikoku. We lived in Shikoku till I was eleven. It hardly snows at all there and we used to go out and make little snowmen and cry when they had melted away by evening. I remember when I came back and

109

saw the snow here for the first time. I thought the end of the world had come. This Niigata coast is part of the Snow Country. The people of Shikoku wouldn't know how to survive a month of winter if they came to live up here.

"It was forty years ago when we came back to Kangawa and I've lived in this house ever since. You can see Awashima island from the station. You can see a little white village on the coast there. It looks so pretty. I've always wanted to go, and it's less than an hour on the boat, but I've never been. I've never been to Sado.

"I've got five children, all grown up. One lives up the coast in Atsumi. Two have gone to live in Niigata and two have moved to Tokyo. They always come back for the beginning of O-Bon, but they never stay to see the dance. I suppose it's not worth staying really. They've got better things to do in the cities."

The woman looked at me and laughed.

"I mean, it's nothing at all, is it—the masks and the prizes and the fancy dress. Everyone in the village gets some sort of a prize. It's nothing at all. It's silly."

Her face was still flushed with the dancing. She had laughed and danced for an hour in the little playground, and I had thought how much she was enjoying herself.

"Anyway," she said, "my sons and daughters will all be back again next year."

She had folded the tangerine peel into the shape of a star and begun toying with the white strips of pith on the tabletop. I slept in an annex next to the railway line. The freight trains rumbled past all night, and the night express to Tokyo roared down at one o'clock with the lights dimmed and people fast asleep in it.

On either side of Kangawa the coast has been turned into a prefectural park, and the next morning, August nineteenth, I continued my journey through it. Like much of the Japanese coast, it is craggy and green. The jagged promontories are riddled with caves, and on the sandy beaches between the rocks stand signboards that proclaim the coast *Nippon Ichi*—the Best in Japan. The narrow road to the city of Murakami runs through tunnels hewn out of the naked cliffs, propped up with raw black timbers, and the *Nippon Ichi* signs stand half-buried in

110

the piles of beer cans and broken bottles that Japanese visitors seem not to see. It is a marvelous gift, the ability to treat the inconvenient as though it wasn't there. Beside a mound of stinking rubbish so huge that it had spilled out of three large trashcans a middle-aged couple stood taking snapshots, saying:

"Isn't it pretty!"

"Isn't it fine!"

At twelve I ducked into a restaurant, but although the place had been freshly cleaned and a "MENEW" was clearly posted on the wall, I stood for five minutes shouting my head off and not a soul came. In the end I bought some apples and a can of beer and sat on the beach peering out over the pink detergent containers at the gray-green hills of distant Awashima, wishing I, too, had a pair of blinkers.

The patches of blue that flecked the sky widened into lakes by afternoon, and by evening the sun was out and glinting on the pine trees. The hills were coming to an end. From the last bend in the high cliff road I could see, beyond Murakami and the huge hotels of the neighboring spa, the long, flat plain of Niigata, and in the far, far distance the rust brown haze that clothed the city of Niigata itself.

I tramped down past a "Steak House," a "Pizza House," and a "Garden Barbeque," and found a ryokan near Murakami station where a tall, stately old gentleman showed me up to a room on the second floor. The single object of decoration in the room was a framed copy of a painting depicting the bareheaded Emperor Hirohito instructing his war cabinet to surrender to the Americans.

After I had taken a bath and eaten dinner, I sat with the old gentleman in his living room and watched a television drama. The credits at the end of the drama caught his attention.

"What is a *direkutaa?*" he asked me.

"It's an English word—'director,'" I explained. "In Japanese you'd say *kantoku.*"

"Then why don't they say *kantoku?* It's supposed to be a Japanese program."

The news came on.

"And what is a *kyampeen?*"

"It's another English word—'campaign.' It means *undo.*"

"And what is a *konsensasu?*"

"A 'consensus.' *Goi.*"

The old man sighed and shook his head.

111

"It's getting to the point," he muttered, "where to understand Japanese television you need to be a gaijin."

All night the emperor glared down at his cap, and in the morning the old gentleman gave me two peaches and his wife gave me a little parcel of riceballs wrapped in wafer-thin bamboo.

"A gaijin stayed here four years ago," she told me. "What a problem that was! He couldn't speak Japanese."

"They should have had him on television," sniffed her husband, who was not in the best of spirits.

Among the pine groves outside Murakami someone was practicing the shamisen. The high plucked notes came pattering over the shush of white surf beyond the pines. For the twenty-nine kilometers to the bathing beach called Muramatsuhama the little coast road smelled of nothing but pines. Through the limbs of the trees on the right lay the sea, frothy and blue in the morning sunlight; and to the left the distant peaks of the Snow Country, of Yamagata and the mountains of Echigo. I sat and ate my peaches on the stone steps of a tiny graveyard. The graves were green and hidden among the trees, and no sooner had I finished the peaches than a woman who was working in a neighboring field brought me seven ripe tomatoes cupped in her apron.

"I shall never eat seven."

She smiled and said nothing, and I left five of the tomatoes on an ancient grave.

In the eaves of a grocer's shop along the way some swallows had built a nest. Two baby swallows squawked loudly for food while their mother whizzed in and out with beakfuls of worms and their father sat twittering benignly on the lampshade. I asked the old woman who ran the shop whether there were any minshukus at Muramatsuhama.

"Oh, lots," she said.

There were none whatsoever and, to celebrate this, the first of three toenails fell off.

Dusk began to fall. The only promising building I could see was a drive-in which, when I reached it, turned out to be closed. I stood and watched the sky grow lemon-colored over the sea, wondering whether there was any point in trudging on along the same empty road. A car stopped. A young man in a Dallas Cowboys T-shirt leaned out of the window and asked, "Where go?"

"Niigata," I said.

There was a pause and I could see his mouth and mind both straining to come up with something in English, so I strolled over to the car, nodded in a friendly way, and said, "It's all right. We can speak in Japanese . . ."

The young man ignored this and sat glaring at the steering wheel while his teeth tormented his lips and tongue. Finally he barked, "Go with car."

"No," I said in Japanese. "You see, I'm on a walking trip. I don't want a lift, but I would be grateful if you could tell me whether there are any ryokans or minshukus near here."

The young man glared at me out of the corner of his eye, hissed softly through his teeth, and drummed on the steering wheel with his fingers.

"*Yappari* (just what I expected)," he muttered.

"I take it you don't live round here," I said brightly. He sighed and punched the dashboard clock.

In the back seat his girlfriend crawled out from under a shawl and rubbed her eyes. The young man climbed briskly out of the car and skipped round to where I was standing in the road.

"Niigata . . . Niigata . . ." he began, and then, his English failing him, "*toi . . . toi . . .* (it's a long way)."

He commenced a pantomime of walking, pumping his elbows, hoisting one foot heavily after the other, and breathing like a bellows.

"Niigata . . . *toi*. Go with car."

"It's really very kind of you," I said, again in Japanese, "but I can't accept, and anyway, you seem to be going in the other direction. What I want is . . ."

He went on miming. "Niigata . . . *toi . . . toi . . . toi . . .*"

His girlfriend wound down the rear window and said, "*Ne . . .*"

"What?"

"He seems to be speaking Japanese."

"*Baka na!* (Don't be silly!)"

And the pantomime continued. "Go . . . with . . . car. . . . Go . . . with . . . car. . . ."

There was nothing I could do but say goodbye. As I trudged off I heard the car door slam with a force that might have buckled its hinges.

The sky was a wash of pale tangerine, streaked through with lines that might have been drawn with lipstick. The stillness and silence were as pleasing as they were rare, and I sauntered down toward the beach, where three senior high school boys were making holes in the walls of the women's changing shed with flick knives.

"Hello," I said. "Do you live round here?"

They stopped making holes and giggled.

"Can you tell me if there are any minshukus?"

They giggled again, and the tallest shrugged his shoulders.

"Or ryokans?"

The tallest said, "Don't know," and laughed, and they went back to their carpentry.

The sun set in a mushroom cloud of gold. Far down the coast the red-and-white pylons of the port of Niigata were clearly visible, still thirty-eight kilometers—a long day—away. I could have turned inland onto Highway 7 and chanced my luck at one of the small towns, but the sparkle of the evening sea was like a magnet and the sand of the beach looked soft and dry. Two summer shelters stood on the sand, one roofed with corrugated iron, the other with straw. I took off my pack under the straw-roofed shelter, laid out my groundsheet and sleeping bag, and sat watching the last glow fade out of the sky and the pricks of light flicker on in the distant city. When the schoolboys left, the beach was deserted. Two or three old fishing boats had been drawn up on rollers and their nets had been spread on poles to dry. Without people, the nets and the boats and the shelters had a looming presence all their own, and when the stars came out and the moon rose, it was as though they shone on a private city. There was not a breath of wind and the lapping of the sea was so faint as to be almost soundless. I crawled into my sleeping bag and for the second time on this long summer journey I settled down to sleep on an open beach.

And for the second time, out of a sky in which the moon and stars were clear as crystal, it pissed with rain. I couldn't believe it. The straw roof held it off for about eight seconds and then gave up. I scrambled out of my sleeping bag improvising a dissertation on ethnic architecture, and trundled armfuls of my sopping belongings across to the iron-roofed shelter. It took three dashes, and as I threw the last of my stuff down onto the dry sand, the rain stopped as absurdly as it had begun. In the dark of the shelter three or four glowing cigarette ends were suddenly extinguished and the smokers, whoever they were, disappeared before I had time to blink.

The groundsheet was sticky with sand. I hung it up with the fishing nets, changed into a dry shirt, and crawled back into my damp sleeping bag. Water dripped from the corrugated iron and a breeze sprang up. It was five to nine. At nine a loudspeaker ten yards from my head began to broadcast a tape loop of dance music and two families with small squawling children came down onto the moonlit beach to set off fireworks. The fireworks lasted an hour, the dance music an hour longer. At twelve, three young men on motorcycles came zooming over the damp sand, gunning their engines and shouting at the tops of their voices. For twenty minutes they raced up and down the beach, passing within three yards of my feet. At twenty past twelve, the most daring of them decided to race through the shelter where I was lying, but by leaping up, screaming, and frantically flapping my arms at his headlamp, I managed to spare the doctors at Niigata Hospital the inconvenience of conducting a midnight postmortem.

"Sorry," yelled the motorcyclists as they roared away.

At five-thirty, when I opened my eyes, the beach was lined with shadowy fishermen who had crept before dawn into my private city and stood now with their backs to me in silent occupation. It was Sunday. I swam for ten minutes, but the water was far too cold for comfort and the fishermen stared at me with such undisguised astonishment that I thought, if I didn't get out fairly soon, the doctors in the psychiatric unit might still have an early call to answer.

At eight I found a grocer's shop open and drank a liter of milk, while the Sunday morning baseball teams paraded up and down the street and three fat girls ogled me from behind a telegraph pole.

I had managed to walk most of the eighty-odd kilometers from the Yamagata boundary without touching a major road, but the quiet sobriety of the seacoast was about to give way to the pranks of civilization. At midday I emerged from the sandy back lanes onto Highway 7, black with diesel fumes, loud with horns, and littered with headless frogs. At the "LesuTo Hausu NipPon," an establishment whose sign was printed in Roman letters, I slumped across a table watching a man in a white shirt embroidered "Magic Moment Beauty Parlor" sit sucking a strawberry milkshake. His girlfriend, whose shirt said "Contact Puck," nursed a plastic carrier bag on which Snoopy was asking, pertinently, "Did you ever have one of those lives when nothing goes right?" I ate lunch at My Happy Noodle Takeno, resisted the lure of a Scotch Pub called Chur Chill, and before long was passing a Medical Books shop in which the most prominent items were *Playboy* and a magazine called *Erotopia*. Inside the shop three junior high school girls gazed in fascination at a rack of bondage monthlies and thumbed through an instruction manual called *Fuck*. At half past three I crossed the girdered bridge that spans the wide Agano River and tramped into the great port city of Niigata.

The first thing that hit me was the smell of the drains. Ahead of me loomed a mass of brown-gray high-rises and I trudged toward them holding my breath. The vending machine that dispensed canned beer had a recorded voice to thank me for my patronage, and the man whose shop I stopped in to buy a peach congratulated me on having large feet. Across the railway track the smell of the drains grew fainter, and the scent of deodorant that wafted out of the Hotel Rich banished it completely.

Near the station I found a street of cheap-looking ryokans and was hobbling up and down deciding which to try when an old man in a white vest came out onto the street and made the decision for me.

"Here you are. Come on. This is a nice place."

Before I could reach the entrance hall, he was joined by two women in flowery dresses.

"Father! What are you doing? Father! It's a gaijin!"

The old man dug a pair of spectacles out of his back pocket, put them on, and peered at me for several seconds.

"It won't matter," he announced at length. "He won't want to eat here. We'll tell him it's fish."

"Father!"

"He can go to a restaurant where they have knives and forks."

"But suppose he wants his own bath . . ."

"Or coffee . . ."

"Or a bed . . ."

I heaved my pack onto the floor of the entrance hall, sat down on the step and closed my eyes.

"It's been a long day," I said, carefully.

"Oh, dear," said the older woman, shuffling her feet.

I took off my boots. Two small piles of sand spilled out onto the concrete floor. There was sand in my hair and two holes in my shirt.

"I suppose it's all right . . ."

"I would like to eat here," I said.

The old man started to say something, but the younger woman took him by the arm and steered him into the room next door.

"I'm a bit weary," I said.

My socks were wet through and the smell of them filled the entrance hall.

"It's fish . . ."

"Yes, yes. I'm a bit weary."

The older woman picked up my rucksack, saying nothing.

I stood up, stiff in every joint, and followed her upstairs.

An old Japanese proverb observes that there are four truly terrifying things in the world: earthquakes, thunder, fires, and fathers. In the old folk tales, thunder was ascribed to horned demons dancing on drums in the clouds and sneaking down to steal children's navels. Now that it has been reduced to a mere electrical discharge it has naturally lost much of its awesomeness and, like the lakes that were once the haunts of dragons, it can be measured, recorded, and punched into a computer. Fires are still a major hazard, for although the buildings in city centers tend nowadays to be made of concrete, in the suburbs and in the countryside the commonest building material is still wood. What's more, the extreme congestion in suburban residential areas has meant that the little wooden buildings are packed so closely together that a spark in one can ignite half a dozen, and there have been many instances where the twisting narrowness of suburban streets has prevented modern fire engines from reaching a blaze in time to avert a tragedy. Fathers, of course, have changed with the times. Fathers in modern Tokyo spend two hours standing on crowded trains each morning, nine hours fiddling about at an office, three hours knocking back whiskeys-and-water while bar hostesses tell them how manly they are, and two hours standing on crowded trains each night. They are far too preoccupied to be terrifying. But earthquakes are as fearful as ever.

On the sixteenth of June, 1964, a submarine earthquake measuring 7.5 on the Richter scale occurred near Awashima island, sixty kilometers north of Niigata city. Although the earthquake was directly responsible for only twenty-six deaths and fewer than two thousand houses destroyed, it provided telling evidence that the real dangers of an earthquake arise not so much from the jolting itself as from the natural and domestic consequences.

The first natural consequence of the Niigata earthquake was a tidal wave that hit the city at a height of five meters, flooding 10,500 houses and causing damage to dozens of other towns along the coast. The second consequence was a disastrous rise in the water table along both sides of the estuary of the Shinano River, the other river upon which Niigata stands. The land here had been reclaimed from the sea some three hundred years earlier by the simple process of quickening silting with bucketfuls of sand; but as the land shook, the subterranean water percolated to the surface. Ironically, the lighter wooden buildings floated and survived, while of the reinforced concrete structures in the city, more than a fifth were ruined. A third consequence was a major fire in a large oil refinery caused by crude oil sloshing about and being sparked by static electricity. The fire consumed ninety-seven oil tanks, a company dormitory and shops, 290 neighboring houses, and burned for a fortnight.

Perhaps the most sobering lesson of the Niigata earthquake was its total disregard for human "progress." The Bandai Bridge across the Shinano River had been built in 1929 and was considered a crude affair. Its concrete piles had been pronounced too heavy for the soft, sandy riverbed on which they stood, and its rigid, load-bearing construction, it was feared, would snap in a major tremor. By contrast, the brand new Great Bridge of Enlightened Peace, which had been opened to the public only fifteen days before the quake, was designed by experts to be earthquake-proof. It had neat, slim piles of tubular steel and was constructed independently of its supports so as to withstand the strains of shaking. The Bandai Bridge survived intact; the Great Bridge of Enlightened Peace collapsed.

Today, the buildings on the east bank of the river are conspicuously new. There are restaurants, department stores, plazas, arcades, and a vast shopping complex known locally as Bandai City. But if you cross the Bandai Bridge and stroll through the streets to the west of the river you are quickly among the narrow shops, the two-story houses that learned to float, the temples, and the dark, inviting little bars with their red paper lanterns swinging outside them. It is here, in the maze of these older streets, that the Niigata carnival is most delighting.

Like the city itself, the Niigata carnival is a striking mixture of the old and the new. The floats that trundle through the narrow streets with their portable shrines and tubs of sakè on them are preceded by an American-style marching band in red dragoon tunics. The carnival controllers who walk beside the floats wear pale blue-and-yellow kimonos. In their right hands they carry paper fans to direct the floats; in their left hands they carry walkie-talkie radios to direct each other. At every street corner the policemen, who astonishingly permit traffic to cross the procession, blow their whistles and wave their arms in blithe independence of the traffic lights. The result is that drivers, having no idea whether they are supposed to obey the whistles, arms, lights, or paper fans, end up obeying none of them, the floats slowly jam themselves into an immovable line of buses and trucks, and the entire event begins to resemble the aftermath of a major natural disaster.

The pavements were so crowded on the fifty-fifth afternoon of my journey that movement along them was out of the question. Since early morning, people had been camping on plastic mats at the side of the road, but by the time the procession had reached their mats, several hundred trouser legs were blocking their view, and so the campers were forced to stand with the other spectators in ranks five deep across the pavement. The thousands of amateur photographers were more mobile, darting from side to side of the road, eliciting blasts from policemen's whistles, cracks on the head from violently flapped fans, shouts from irate taxi drivers, and long deep wails from the horns of buses that grew louder and more desperate as the disaster progressed, till eventually the scores of taiko drums were audible only if you were standing next to them.

On one of the floats sat Miss Niigata, a pretty girl in a long pink dress, perched on a throne with a crown on her head, smiling radiantly and waving at the crowds. Photographers climbed onto her float to snap her, policemen blew their whistles at her, taxi drivers suggested novel ways of broadening her education, and pimply youths serenaded her at the tops of their voices. Nothing disturbed her. She would continue to smile just as serenely should an earthquake strike, should the street catch fire, should her terrifying father sneak up and steal her navel. She was still smiling thirty minutes later and her float was still as hopelessly stuck.

By evening the streets were quiet again. August was three-quarters over and the summer festivals were coming to an end. The taikos and the lanterns were disappearing, and the people in the mountain villages were preparing to cut their rice. Farmers were going back to their

119

fields, city workers were going back to their cities, Miss Niigata had gone back, serene, to her father, and the dead were asleep for another year.

The Niigata carnival ends with fireworks. I watched them from below the Bandai Bridge. There were no drums now, no whistles, no horns—only the shouts of children and the crack of the fireworks as they exploded high over the dark river.

"Look, it's a star!"

"Look, it's the sun!"

Bright bunches of color splashed onto the night sky and slowly fell in rains of fire to vanish in the black water under the bridge. The stars and the suns were green and gold, and the last firework of all was a willow tree.

⚔ 5 ⚔

The Back of Japan

IN THE SAND DUNES that stretch from Niigata to the sea the villagers
had planted watermelons. There was no soil that I could see, and they
had ploughed the thin sand of the dunes into furrows where the dark
melons lay rotting. When the wind blew, it troubled the melons and
they lolled like drugged heads. The wind sucked the light sand into the
air and flicked sharp grit into my eyes so that I had to crouch by the
side of the empty path and try to clear them with a towel. Three times
the path through the dunes forked without warning and ended in a
stringy tangle of barbed wire. My map was a mess of lanes that seemed
not to exist, but I followed the distant whistle of a train and, in the
late afternoon, came out of the dunes to find myself on a paved road in
front of a ryokan that looked completely deserted. In the entrance hall
the morning paper lay untouched, and the wind riffled it as I held open
the door.

"Hello. Is anyone there . . . ?"

Nothing, no sound, not even the usual telltale rattle from the
kitchen.

"Hello. . . . Excuse me . . ."

No sound from outside the ryokan either, as though a sleeping
sickness had come down with the end of summer. I shouted for two
minutes into the silent building before a small dumpy woman slid
open the door of her parlor and stood breathing heavily with her
back against the doorpost.

"I'd like to stay . . ."

She shook her head.

". . . if there are any rooms free."

121

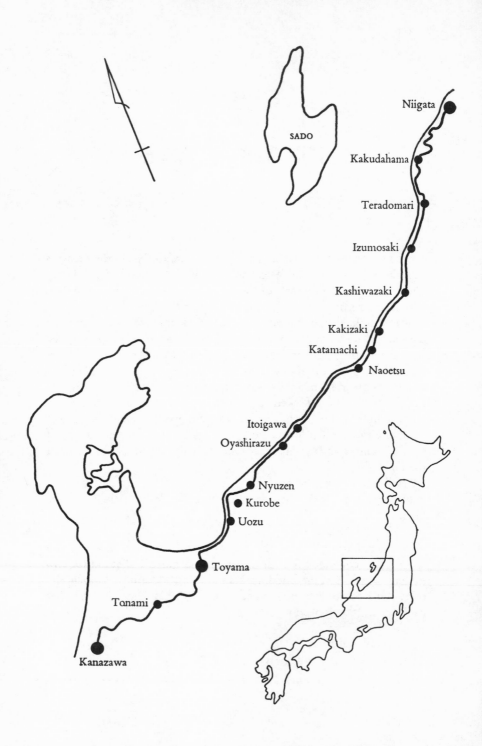

SADO

Niigata

Kakudahama

Teradomari

Izumosaki

Kashiwazaki

Kakizaki

Katamachi

Naoetsu

Itoigawa

Oyashirazu

Nyuzen

Kurobe

Uozu

Toyama

Tonami

Kanazawa

"I'm sorry, we're full."

She bent down and picked up the unread morning paper. The stillness of the building around her was broken only by the ticking of a clock in the parlor. She turned the newspaper over in her hands and blinked.

"Full."

"I see. Is there anywhere else?"

"Kakudahama."

"How far is that?"

"Ten . . . fifteen minutes' walk."

I closed the front door very quietly so as not to disturb the innkeeper's peace and walked down through the dumbstruck village. The map showed bold straight roads where only desolate paths wound into the dunes, and I took my bearings from the distant sea. The little bathing beach of Kakudahama was eight kilometers away. It took me an hour and a half to reach it, cutting back across the darkening swathe of waste sand, ploughed and dotted with innkeepers' heads.

Of the twenty or thirty plywood minshukus that lined the beach only three had lights on. The sun had set behind the minshukus and they stood still and battened like boxes. In one of the three lighted buildings an old couple squatted, tormented by flies, eating their dinner in the middle of a vast, empty room that had been built for a summer full of bathers. One corner of the room housed a dusty souvenir stand where a bundle of unsold children's windmills spun raggedly in the draft that lifted the matting as I gingerly slid open the door.

"Yes, of course you can stay, only all we've got is the trout we caught in the river this morning, but it's nice trout, and some squid from Sado if you can eat that. From Sado island. I'll be glad to cook it for you. And some rice. And some tea. And there's beer, of course, and sakè if you like that. We're on our own. There's only the two of us and I'm afraid my husband's rather hard of hearing. There's two guests coming from Tokyo the day after tomorrow that have booked and we've put in the register. They'll stay a night and then we'll close. Most of us have closed now and gone back to the village to spend the winter. It's up the coast, not much of a village. The old ones do no work in the winter. They sit and drink tea and watch the young ones fish. We'll close down on Saturday. I'll cook your trout. It's been a short summer, hasn't it?"

The breeze dropped and in the heat of the night I slept with the

windows open onto the sea and woke up in horror to discover that
the mosquito coil had gone out.

The next morning, after a swim and a shower, I began to walk along
the *Shiisaido Rain* (Seaside Line), a toll road through what the guidebook describes as the Sado-Yahiko Quasi-National Park. From the
height of the toll road the beaches below looked gray and bare this
twenty-fourth of August, devoid of any trace of holidaymaking. Rows
of the same thin plywood shacks, shuttered and boarded, lined each
small bay. Yet the day was fine. The only clouds were the cream-
white halo that capped Mount Kimpoku on distant Sado. The light
August breeze in the pine groves teased out their fragrance and sent
it scurrying with me up toward the low hills. Ahead of me a car
stopped and an irate-looking man climbed out and began to scoop a
space for me on his cluttered back seat.

"It's all right," I called out. "I prefer to walk."

He looked at me as though I were mad, as though no one in his right
mind could possibly want to *walk* along a route singled out for its
scenic attractions.

At lunchtime young mothers with babies strapped to their backs
fetched their sons and daughters home from school on motor scooters.

"Mummy, what's a gaijin doing here?"

"I expect he's come for the culture."

On the outskirts of the town of Teradomari two small black-and-
white kittens sat shivering by the roadside, their bellies distended,
wailing at the cars. The car cemeteries gave way to shiny car showrooms, and near the town center the tenants of a block of flats called
Colony Niigata, from which the two dying kittens were probably
abandoned, sat on their balconies drinking orangeade and watching a
fisherman's family trying to maneuver their heavy old boat along the
dusty main street. The boat creaked as it swung from side to side while
the young men cursed it and hauled it on chains, the women scuttled
round from stern to bow with the wooden logs on which they were
trying to roll it, the old men smacked the logs with mallets, and the
Niigata Colonists grinned down at the antics of these oilskinned bump-
kins and fiddled with the dials of their transistor radios.

Ever since encountering the Japan Sea in Yamagata I had been weighing its reputation, a reputation for grayness and gloom which long ago earned this coast the name that still derides it: *Ura Nihon*, or the Back of Japan. (In fact, the name is considered so derisive that you are not allowed to utter it on NHK, the national broadcasting network.)

Strictly speaking, the coastal strip from Niigata to Fukui is part of the Chubu ("Middle") District, a geographical division that stretches across the full width of Japan to include much of the industrial sprawl that has ravaged the Pacific side of the country. The Pacific coast is the most densely populated, the most commercially important, the blackest, noisiest, smoggiest, unhealthiest, most ruinously developed area in the country. The *shinkansen*, the famous "bullet train," provides glimpses of it between Tokyo and Hakata—a seemingly unending belt of gray oil tanks, of docks, of factories that cloak Mount Fuji with dust and curtain the islands of the Inland Sea. The cities of the Pacific coast sprawl one into another: Tokyo indistinguishable from Kawasaki, Kawasaki from Yokohama, Osaka from Kobe.

In comparison, the Japan Sea coast is a backwoods. True, it has its industrial centers: Niigata is one of the largest, and in a few days' time I would pass through the city of Naoetsu with its sprawling steel and fertilizer plants. But these are nothing compared to the Pacific squalor, and a part of its reputation for gloomy isolation must stem from this area's tardiness in "modernizing."

A greater part, though, stems from pure geography, for the Japan Sea coast was never on the main route to anywhere. The chief artery of communication between the old imperial court in Kyoto and the seat of real power in Kamakura—and later Edo (Tokyo)—was the Pacific-coast highway called the Tokaido. That was the great trunk road of history, an inspiration to writers, painters, and adventurers, and for eight hundred years the spinal cord of Japanese civilization. The Japan Sea coast was a world away from it on the other side of the mountain range that slices through central Honshu and is now called (since it was so christened by a German missionary) the Japan Alps. So inaccessible was this backward, benighted *Ura Nihon* that people were sent here as a punishment. The offshore island of Sado—the largest of Japan's many minor islands—was notorious from the twelfth century as a place of exile, and its rocky shores and misty valleys have furnished a prison for some of the glummest characters in Japanese history.

Mongaku was one—a sort of twelfth-century Japanese Rasputin. He

125

began his career by lusting after his cousin and killing her by mistake (he had meant to kill her husband), for which piece of carelessness he shaved his head, became a monk, and religiously persuaded the powerful general Yoritomo to wage all-out war against his rivals at court. Yoritomo was successful, and for a while Mongaku enjoyed the fruits of victory. But, alas, not content with provoking mere war, he went on to hatch a plot against the emperor Gotoba, and when his protector Yoritomo died in 1199, Mongaku was whisked off to Sado, where he fretted away the rest of a glum life.

The other famous clergyman to suffer in Sado was the militant evangelist Nichiren, less a Rasputin than a thirteenth-century Ian Paisley. Nichiren insisted on a firm bond between church and state—so long as it was his church, and his alone, that the state paid any attention to. So vehemently did Nichiren denounce all other Buddhist sects (he once exclaimed that the government would have done better to execute the "heretic" priests than the emissaries of Kublai Khan) that he was packed off to Sado in 1271, where he passed two glum years in a mud hut and suffered from chronic diarrhea.

The highest-ranking exile was the emperor Juntoku, sent to Sado in 1221 for attempting to overthrow the military regents. He spent 20 years there, died on a hunger strike, and had 650 years to wait before he was officially reinstated. The founder of the Noh theater, Zeami Motokiyo, lived eight of the last years of his life in Sado. The courtier Hino Suketomo, who had tried to raise an army on behalf of the powerless emperor Godaigo, was shipped to Sado in 1324 and assassinated there by the glum governor. And as late as the mid-nineteenth century a penal colony was working the dreary Sado gold mines.

The afternoon grew overcast. I sat on the beach at Teradomari—the beach from which all these exiles had set sail—and stared across at the gray mounds of the island, remembering my walks there, the meadows and caves and the lingering snows of Mount Kimpoku in May, and thinking of my own seven-year exile in Tokyo.

> Ah, toward Sado
> the trees and the grass bend.
> Ar'ya ar'ya ar'ya sa.

Near Izumosaki a bent old woman was scrubbing out a dusty little wayside shrine and lighting candles. The houses in the villages had been battered by the wind and salt to a uniform gray-brown. They were fenced off from the sea by gray bamboo palisades, the tops of which were rough and frayed, and the houses were so patched and weatherblown that they looked as if they had been camouflaged for an invasion. Between the oily, littered beaches the sea pounded on high stone walls and in the first shower of rain I went for a swim and cut my foot on a broken whiskey bottle.

The shops in the town of Izumosaki displayed four or five sticks of baked flyblown fish in each of their windows and little else. Down the coast towards Kashiwazaki a solitary gas rig straddled a small patch of rain-pocked sea, and in one tiny village an incongruous Hotel Japan loured over its own private bit of beach where three young girls paddled aimlessly about under torn, wind-whipped umbrellas.

"What are you doing, *arubaito?*" asked a toothless woman pushing a wheelbarrow. (*Arubaito* is the German word *arbeit,* which the Japanese have commandeered to mean a part-time job.) The rain had blown over and I was sitting on a beer crate under the awning of a grocer's shop.

"No, I'm not doing *arubaito*. I'm having a rest."

The woman stopped, and the three dogs that were following her lurched, yapping and sniffing, into the grocer's rubbish bins.

"You speak good *hyojungo* (orthodox Japanese). Where did you learn it?"

"I live in Tokyo."

"Ah!"

The woman brushed away a bluebottle that was caught in her head-scarf.

"I was born in Tokyo. In Toyo-cho. I bet you don't know where that is."

"I bet I do. I had a friend who owned a futon shop there. We used to go drinking at a folk-song bar in Asakusa."

The woman's mouth dropped open so wide I thought she was trying to catch the bluebottle.

"*Maa! Asakusa! Natsukashii!* (Ah! Asakusa! That brings back memories!) I haven't heard anyone talk about Asakusa for more than seventeen years. That's how long I've lived here. Seventeen years and four months. Asakusa, ah! Have you seen the Sanja Festival?"

"All three days of it."

"*Maaaa! Natsukashii!* And the log-rolling festival on the Sumida River? And the old Tokyo firemen's dances . . . ?"

She pulled back her headscarf and grinned me a toothless grin that was half rueful, half delight.

"My husband comes from Kashiwazaki though."

"And you've never been back to Tokyo?"

"Never. Not once."

She shifted from foot to foot and I patted one of the dogs that was trying to scrape an empty sausage skin out from under the crate I was sitting on.

"Asakusa, ahhh . . . !"

"Don't you like it here?"

She nodded once, perfunctorily.

"I like it." And she looked at the sea as though it had just material-ized. "Oh, I like it. Kashiwazaki's all right . . ."

She called to the dogs and lifted her barrow, smiling the same wide toothless smile.

"Yes . . . oh, yes . . . and you knew Asakusa . . ."

The exile walked on with her barrow and dogs.

Above the city of Kashiwazaki a layer of mist sliced Mount Yone-yama in half like an orange. Sado had disappeared, hidden in the rain clouds, and the column of smoke from the city rose to merge with the dense pall of the sky. On an empty beach a solitary painter sat, daubing his canvas with the grays of cloud, the brown-gray of the smoke, the white-gray of the mist, the pink-gray of the buildings. Nearer Kashi-wazaki, suited "salarymen" lay asleep in their cars by the sides of the roads. The pavements were roofed against snow, and in the gloom of the late August afternoon the neon lights on the undersides of the roofs had been turned on to brighten the window displays: a row of stone monuments, a kimono on a rack, an incense burner for six hundred yen, a picture of the Bay City Rollers for a thousand.

I looked for a quiet ryokan in the back streets. The first had a road gang digging outside it, and I had already taken a room in the second when I discovered that it backed onto a saw mill.

At dinner in the little dining room the flabby woman who ran the ryokan talked to me incessantly, while the only other guest, a middle-aged businessman, addressed one or two comments to her and to the ~~ ~~ had clearly made up his mind to ignore my existence.

"Where were the old Sado gold mines?" he wondered.

"I don't know, I'm sure," said the woman. "I've never been."

"Perhaps," he reflected, "they were somewhere near Ogi."

"They were just outside Aikawa," I said.

"Ogi," decided the man. "They were probably in Ogi." And he imparted this information to the grandfather clock.

"An American couple stayed here last month," the woman confided when the businessman had gone. (That could account for the lavatory slippers being tied together with two feet of string.) "They were a nice enough couple, but they couldn't say a word. They'd been over to Sado, which is more than I have."

"Were you born in this town?"

"I was born in this house."

"And you've stayed here all your life?"

"What choice did I have?" The woman got up and began clearing away the dinner trays. "Who in their right mind would stay here if they had a choice?"

In the morning, at six, the sawmill woke me. I had slept with the windows open all night and the damp in the air had laid a chill on my clothes. Everyone agreed it had been a short summer.

✄

The road began to climb toward the bridges of the Yoneyama Pass. Far below, on the beach at Kujiranami (Beach of Whale Waves), a solitary honeymoon couple waded slowly out into the sea, scooped up water to splash each other, then waded on again, separately, out toward the rocks. Despite the huge banks of clouds in the sky, the day was stiflingly hot, and the slow climb up through the foothills had the sweat pouring off me in a quarter of an hour. The foothills fanned down to the coast like a scallop shell, and the road crossed the furrows on two long suspension bridges. The bridges swung and sang in the wind and shook like paper when a truck growled across them.

> *The clouds pile up over Yoneyama.*
> *Before long there will be a shower:*
> *hiss of rain, slash of lightning,*
> *in our ears the thunder rumbles.*

129

But the rain clouds drifted over toward Sado and the roar of the trucks was the only thunder. Along the highway, rows of small shacks advertised fresh crab, but they were locked and shuttered. I overtook a tramp going south for the winter. Under his arms he carried two large parcels wrapped in army surplus blankets and a black umbrella that had lost most of its ribs. His face was old, the color of nutmeg, and his hair and beard were short and steely gray. I said good morning but he stared straight ahead of him until I was several yards past, and then he spat.

Well into the twentieth century this stretch of coast was the haunt of the *goze*—blind wandering shamisen players who trudged through the villages of the old province of Echigo, from wedding to wedding, from festival to festival, begging food and lodging in return for a song. All were women (though the shamisen is an instrument traditionally taken up by the blind of both sexes), and most were members of a strictly hierarchical society that organized them into small dependent bands. The younger and more ambitious of the *goze* might supplement their pittance of an income by selling their bodies at the village fairs, though if this were known to the society, they would quickly find themselves stripped of companionship and forced to wander through the Back of Japan alone, with only a stick and their songs to survive on.

I sat on a sea wall toying with a beer can. The tramp passed me, staring at the road. I kept him in sight for half an hour, but at Kakizaki he was gone.

And on the one sandy street at Kakizaki three lions were performing a shaking dance. Their masks were lacquered red and gold, their manes were made of straw, and the snap of their jaws was like whipcracks. The lions had draped themselves with colored sheets, and their baseball shoes scuffed up the sand when they swung, holding the heavy masks to their shoulders with both hands. Two dusty priests blew wooden flutes and a third smacked a taiko strapped to a wheelbarrow. They processed slowly up the street towards the village shrine followed by six or seven awe-struck children, till a dancing lion noticed me and began to giggle through the jaws of his mask.

I drank a beer at the grocer's shop, and the grocer's little son fetched his toys to show me: a robot with guided missiles for arms, a bright red Porsche, and a stuffed gorilla.

"I see, and what does the robot do?"

"Drives the Porsche."

"And do you know where gorillas live?"

130

"In the zoo."

When I left Kakizaki a lacquered demon with a ten-inch nose was running up and down the street chasing people into their houses and being particularly frightful to teenage girls. I nodded good afternoon to him as I passed and his red nose shook with laughter.

Though the weather forecast had predicted drizzle, there were patches of blue in the late afternoon sky, and the clammy heat of the day began to evaporate as evening came on and the sea paled. I found a ryokan at the little town of Katamachi where the bathroom wallpaper depicted antique horse-drawn carriages with advertisements on them for "Whitbread," "Rothmans of Pall Mall," and "Hobley and Sons, High Class Bakers, Buckhurst Hill." In the dining room the decor was equally traditional: it consisted of a plastic chandelier and a large mirror with "A Present from Kashiwazaki" printed across it. Over dinner I became friendly with a truck driver from Yamagata, and we decided to stroll back and have a look at the hot spring resort that I had passed a kilometer before entering the town.

"Of course, it ain't a real hot spring," said the truck driver, "but that don't matter. We ain't after a bath." And he nudged me in the ribs.

The proper way to approach hot springs, he told me, was not to go to restaurants or bars because they always charged twice what they were worth. The proper thing to do was to find a ryokan.

"But we've already got a ryokan," I pointed out.

"Ah, but that's a ryokan for stayin' in. What we're after is a ryokan for *playin'* in." And he nudged me again.

The bargaining that took place at the ryokan door was unlike anything I had ever seen in Japan (where bargaining and tipping are almost unknown), and within three minutes, to my utter astonishment, we had settled on an hourly rate for a room that was half what the woman had first demanded. As we trooped behind her up the narrow stairs, my friend the truck driver gave her bottom a sharp smack.

In the room he did the same with the fifty-year-old maid who had brought our beer. She responded at once by grabbing his crotch with both hands, and he fell down shrieking onto a pile of cushions.

"Your health." We drank. He flashed me a wink.

"You're going to have to take me to the lavatory," he told the maid. The maid heaved herself to her feet, opened the door, and conducted the truck driver out into the passage. When they came back about ten

131

minutes later, the truck driver was limping and the maid was carrying a dish of dried octopus. The truck driver flopped down onto the frayed tatami and massaged his groin. The maid settled herself on one of the cushions, drank a beer, and took charge of the conversation.

She didn't like the truck driver, she announced. She knew she wouldn't like him when she first clapped eyes on him. She couldn't make out what I was doing in his company, a nice boy like me. A nice big boy like me, with nice blue eyes, who ought to have more sense.

The truck driver grinned me a pained, waggish grin.

In fact, if it wasn't for me being with him, she'd have packed him off at once and no mistake. Nasty fellow. She didn't like him at all. But she liked me, she said. In fact she loved me, she said.

The truck driver stuck out his tongue, and the fifty-year-old maid, who had matt black teeth and was inching her skirt up towards her suspenders, thrust her legs out straight in front of her to reveal a pink flowered petticoat covered with what I hoped were beer stains. The truck driver raised his right fist, his thumb between his middle and index fingers, and cackled. The maid smoothed out her stained petticoat, glared across the table at him, and topped up my glass.

Yes, it was entirely possible that she loved me, she thought, but there were a few things that needed clearing up. For instance, she didn't know how I put up with truck drivers. Particularly this one. He had an abominable accent and, what's more, she reckoned he wouldn't pay the bill. In fact, she thought I ought to be careful going about with the likes of truck drivers from Yamagata, because it could end up costing me a lot of money. And that would be a shame because I had such fine white skin. She could see that, she said, even though my face was brown. Wouldn't I roll up my sleeve for a minute? That's right. There, what did she tell me. Lovely white skin. Whiter than a girl's. And she laid her dark fifty-year-old arm beside mine and sucked air thoughtfully through her gums.

Oh, I ought to know more about the ways of the world than to go about with truck drivers. You couldn't trust them. They were only out for what they could get. She would show me what she meant. She would bring the bill this minute. In fact, she should have brought it a quarter of an hour ago, because she'd had enough. More than enough. If I liked, she would write us separate bills and then I wouldn't need to

132

worry. What's more, I could stay and have another beer, but as for this lout from Aomori, she didn't think there was any possibility of putting up with his behavior for five more seconds.

She brought two bills. The truck driver sniffed and paid them both. I fetched out my wallet and pushed it across the table at him and he grinned at the maid and pushed it back. I took out three thousand yen and thrust it into his sleeve. He fished it out, snarled at the maid, and stuffed it down the back of my neck.

The maid sat stony-faced, smoothing out her petticoat, and the woman who owned the ryokan came up from downstairs and said she was terribly sorry but there were two traveling salesmen with a dozen suitcases who had turned up quite unexpectedly, and since this was the only room she had to spare, she hoped we wouldn't mind, and what a terrible pity, and she trusted we would come back again when we had the leisure.

The truck driver ignored the maid. He bade the owner goodnight in exquisitely polite Japanese, gave her bottom a resounding smack on the way down the stairs, and we cemented our friendship by sitting on the oily beach at the end of the street singing the rudest songs we could remember.

Three little boys were tormenting a kitten in the main street of Kata-machi as I walked along it next morning. They were throwing it up into the air as high as they could and spinning it so that it turned head over paws and fell squawling and mewing onto the pavement. I told them to stop it. They looked at each other and burst out laughing.

"It's cruel," I growled at them from across the road, and the owner of the garage next door wandered out to chuckle at the gaijin speaking Japanese.

An old man on a bicycle stopped me to ask for a light.
"I'm afraid I don't smoke," I said.
His head jerked up and he stared at me very close.
"Aren't you a gaijin?"
"Yes, I am."
"I'm terribly sorry, it never occurred to me . . ."
And he pedaled off, still apologizing.

133

In a grocer's shop a four-year-old child was screaming and pummeling his mother in a tantrum.

"Shh," warned his mother, "the gaijin's watching."

And I walked out of the town hissing under my breath. The red-lacquered demon with the ten-inch nose stood a better chance of melting into the landscape than I did, besides which he got to chase teenage girls. The celebrity afforded by blue eyes weighed heavily on me as I trudged towards a thick rust-brown cloud that I took to be a fog rolled in from the sea, but which turned out to be the city of Naoetsu.

Naoetsu is described in the official guidebook as "one of the flourishing industrial centers on the Japan Sea coast." It is so flourishing that from a distance of four kilometers you can't see it. As you get closer the mechanics of its disguise become apparent. The chimneys of the Nippon Stainless factory and the Mitsubishi petrochemical complexes pump a solid stream of choking brown smoke into the Sunday afternoon sky. The dock is full of cranes and filthy little tramp steamers, and a continuous trickle of dust filters down from the snow roofs that ward off nature from the pavements. Naoetsu has the distinction of being the only city in Japan whose beer shops I raced by without a second blink. I had a vision of petrochemical yeast dissolving most of my vital organs which were then replaced by a stainless steel liver and an injection-molded Mitsubishi stomach. On the billboards of petrol stations gigantic bikini-clad women profered cans of motor oil at thirsty motorists. I fled Naoetsu in top gear and didn't look back at it till forty minutes later by which time it had disappeared.

The towns and villages along this last stretch of the Niigata coast were strung out in thin lines, squeezed between the dark sea on one side and the rapidly encroaching mountains on the other. The streets were narrow, the shopfronts open, and some had an oddly Middle Eastern air, an air of life lived squatting in doorways or in the one or two square yards in front of home. The harbors were empty. At one point the sea looked inviting enough for me to scramble down onto a squalid little spit of sand and pick my way over the beer bottles for a swim. When I came out of the water my legs were black with oil. I sat on a rock and rubbed them with a towel, wincing at a blond-haired, blue-eyed kewpie doll that lay blackened and decapitated at the line of the tide.

From the hills the city of Itoigawa looked disconcertingly like a mini-Naoetsu, though the fact that I could see it from the hills at all lent me hope. It also lent me the courage to have a drink there, and so my after-dinner stroll took me to a little bar called *Sango* (Coral) where I was privileged to sit next to the Masked Marauder, a professional wrestler with a pigtail and a Playboy shirt, and his much more savage-looking pinstriped manager, who snarled whenever I tried to start a conversation. The mama-san flitted from one to the other of us, congratulating us all on being so unusual; and when the Marauder and his manager left, two drunk old navy veterans came in and set about teaching me the marching song of the kamikaze pilots:

> *You, sir, and I, sir,*
> *are cherry blossoms of a kind, sir,*
> *blooming in the garden of the naval academy.*
> *And if we bloom, sir,*
> *we are ready, too, to fall, sir.*
> *Let us fall in splendor for the sake of the*
> *country.*

The first hour of my march on the morning of August thirtieth took me through the sprawling Asano cement works, a vast dusty maze that occupies an area about a third the size of the whole of Itoigawa. Mounds of grit clogged both sides of the river, all the way down to the distant docks where small bright yellow cement mixers were being loaded onto cement-colored ships. The shallow river slopped thinly over the pebbles, and occasionally, between the chutes and the piles of slag, a little patch of cultivated rice lay dull and caked with powdered cement. The gray day was tinged brown by the smoke of factory chimneys, and Highway 8, when I finally found it again, was thick with dust and the fumes of cement trucks.

But to the west the foothills of the Hida mountains abutted steeply onto the sea, and as the road swung out to meet the coast, the belt of factories came abruptly to an end. With the sea lapping tamely on the shingle below me, I climbed the narrow highway, roofed with iron against rockfalls and snow, and entered the little prefectural park that commemorates the dangers of the Oyashirazu-Koshirazu beach.

Oyashirazu means "parent abandoned," Koshirazu means "child abandoned." The names are reminders of the hazards that travelers faced before the road was cut into the cliffs, when the only passage along this stretch of coast was across the thin strip of shingle at the tideline. In heavy weather huge breakers pound the shingle, and a traveler stranded beneath these cliffs would have to cling for his life to the battered rocks and pray that he was not sucked off them and drowned. This happened so frequently, the story goes, that at the first sign of a quickening wind, you forgot your parents, you forgot your children, and thought only of scrambling on before the waves grew too high to pass.

The cliff road was opened in 1883, and the danger from the waves was overcome. But the road is fraught with its own dangers. It is far too narrow for the diesel trucks that now chuff up it yard by yard, far too tortuous for the speed at which the tourists screech round it in their luminous orange Cedrics. To the solitary walker, shunted off the road by all the trucks, honked at by every Cedric that passes, the beach below beckons like a haven.

The village of Oyashirazu has been completely bypassed by a newer stretch of highway. The drivers roar by without even noticing it, and the ryokan and the little restaurant in the village are closed. I stopped for lunch at the Lesthouse Nihonkai and was treated to "Stupid Cupid," "Crazy Love," and "Happy Birthday Sweet Sixteen" broadcast over the restaurant's loudspeaker system at a volume that would have prompted any stranded traveler who valued his eardrums to duck under the waves in order to preserve them. Eventually, lunch abandoned, Lesthouse abandoned, I rounded the last descending curves of the highway, passed the black-roofed houses of the last village in Niigata, and with the sun squinting hazily through the afternoon clouds, I crossed the prefectural boundary and emerged from a filthy, mile-long tunnel onto the flat coastal plain of Toyama. Straw-hatted women pedaled their bicycles, children marched trimly home from their schools, a grandfather with a fuzzy-haired baby strapped to his back stood by the side of the highway eating toast and jam, and in the green, close-packed, watery fields the rice slowly ripened.

Perhaps the first thing you notice about Toyama is its gravestones. Those of Niigata were ragged and black. They perched in clumps on the edges of clifftops and seemed on the point of crumbling into the sea. The gravestones of Toyama are huge and elaborate, each one erect on its own stone plinth with its own flight of steps leading up to it like a cenotaph. They are flanked by lanterns and stone letterboxes into which mourners can respectfully post their business cards. There are trimmed flowers in the polished stone vases, incense smoking in the incense burners, and the Chinese characters on the graves have been chiseled by craftsmen. Graves like this clearly cost a small fortune, but few families in Toyama seem to begrudge the expense.

On the quiet coastal road, away from the highway, the houses stood tidy and scrubbed. Their black slates shone, their little yards were neatly fenced, and their lawns were dotted with plaster storks. At Nyuzen the Nyuzen Lions' Club had equipped each bus shelter with a dustpan and brush. The cars of the local driving school buzzed neatly about, all a uniform rose-pink, and the Western-style toilets in the coffee shops I stopped in had fluffy seat covers and silent flushes. Toyama is one of the smallest prefectures I passed through on my journey. It ranks thirty-third in the country in size (out of a total of forty-seven), yet its per capita income is the seventeenth highest—and, for a prefecture stuck here at the Back of Japan, that is a remarkable achievement.

"It's because we work," crowed a busy shopkeeper, "and we've got no time for people who don't. We've got a nice little prefecture here, a nice little life. And by the way"—eyeing my rucksack—"what do *you* do for a living?"

The highway curved further away to the south. Beyond it Mount Tateyama was hidden in haze. To the north, the sea was a brilliant cornflower blue, a thin ribbon above flat sparkling fields that, on this last day of August, mellowed towards harvest.

But on the banks of the Kurobe River stood a cluster of thumping factories that made granite chips, and the outskirts of the city of Kurobe were dominated by a plant that turned out aluminum window frames and zippers. The largest buildings in the city itself were the plant's three massive housing complexes, with the company's initials— Y.K.K.—on their roofs in letters so high they could be read for miles. On the streets of the city the telegraph poles bore Y.K.K. advertisements, and Y.K.K. buses shuttled snoozing employees from company workshops to company restaurants to company gymnasiums to company beds.

Was it haze that hid Mount Tateyama, I wondered, or was it a whiff of company smog? Or was it smoke from the company fire that seemed to be smoldering just outside the factory? Five red fire engines came hurtling down the narrow road with firemen in asbestos armor clinging to their ladders. I could see them only indistinctly as they converged on the bubble of smoke across the plain, but their sirens shattered the quiet for miles, and the haze round Tateyama, when I really looked, had a definite charred-brown tinge to it. The poet Basho once remarked that it is "fun" not to see holy mountains when you have been looking forward to seeing them, so I zipped Mount Tateyama and its fires out of my mind and tramped at dusk into the small city of Uozu.

"Look, it's a Frenchman!" said one little boy to his schoolfriends with an assurance that worried me for several days.

The ryokan I found was full upstairs, but if I didn't mind sleeping downstairs in the room next to the carp pond, I was welcome to sample its hospitality. I didn't mind a bit. The carp were entertaining; their feeding time was the same as mine. As I watched them from the veranda outside my room, gobbling pink pellets like submarine pigs, the woman of the ryokan brought me a slab of *korimochi*—white, hard, hammered rice cake, studded with beans, hung up for a month, then roasted over glowing charcoal.

"You've missed the Bon dance, but you'd hardly have noticed it. It's not worth watching any more. We used to have a very good Bon dance till ten years ago when they took away the town square for a bus terminal and built the elevated railway. There's nowhere we can dance now, but you can't complain. The railway's made life so much more convenient . . ."

After dinner I went out for a walk along the dark streets of the city and watched people pissing and emptying their teapots into a little stream that flowed down to the harbor. When I got back to the ryokan the guests were in an uproar. Oh Sadaharu, the Yomiuri Giants' Taiwanese first baseman, had just equaled Hank Aaron's American major league record of 755 career home runs and was to be awarded the title of National Hero.

"What a magnificent Japanese!" yelled the salesmen in the room next door.

Quite a compliment for a Chinaman, I thought.

By the side of the road an old man in a straw boater sat carving rough stone statues of Jizo, the Buddhist guardian of travelers, children, and pregnant women. Along country lanes the figure of Jizo is often a commoner sight than road signs. You come across him, too, at the sites of traffic accidents, and on the anniversary of an accident he is preened and pampered like a summer grave. The sea was divided into neat squares by floats, and beyond the floats white fishing boats shimmered in the morning haze. In one small harbor a newish monument depicted the Goddess of Mercy balancing herself on the head of a floundered whale. The whale had flopped over onto its side, and it was impossible to say whether the goddess was blessing it or trampling it to death.

At noon on this first day of September I swam near the estuary of the Joganji River. The beach was fine and relatively unlittered, but the water was cloudy and had an odd, sweet, unsalty taste that reminded me of rotting cabbage.

"You shouldn't have swum," clucked the middle-aged woman in the ice-cream shop just past the bridge. "Not this late in the summer. In August everyone cleans their houses for O-Bon and they tip most of their rubbish into the river. It's an old custom, but nowadays, with more houses and more rubbish to tip, it's getting to be a real nuisance. When the wind blows in from the sea you can smell it. A sweet smell . . ."

"Like rotting cabbage . . ."

"Or squashed fruit or compost. You know what I mean."

I said I did. She made me a strawberry ice.

"The daughter of the family next door is in America. She's studying English there for a year. They've given her a million yen. Do you think that'll be enough?"

I said it depended on her tastes.

"Oh, but Toyama people are very thrifty. We know the value of money all right. Families from Toyama were among the first to emigrate to Hawaii and Brazil. Always trying to improve ourselves, we are; on the lookout for a better life. My eldest son's a barber in Tokyo—a proper barber, American-style. He earns three million yen a year. My second son works in a dairy. He earns two and a half million yen with bonuses. We've got three hundred and ninety square meters of land, and we're thinking of buying another hundred and sixty."

I asked why Toyama people wanted to emigrate.

"It's such a little prefecture, you see, and there's a long history of moving away. People who didn't emigrate would generally go to Osaka or Tokyo to find work. Today almost everyone goes to Tokyo, and when they come back you can tell it by their accents. But moving abroad must have been such a wrench. I can't imagine doing it myself. There are so many Japanese things I'd miss. I'd miss the four seasons like anything. They don't have four seasons abroad, do they?"

I paid my bill and shouldered my pack.

"Anyway," said the woman, "you're too young to worry about work. You've got college to get through first, I expect."

I turned inland feeling remarkably frisky. It must have been the strawberry ice.

Halfway through the suburbs of Toyama I went into a coffee shop, and before I had time to sit down at a table, one of the customers said, "Ah, an American."

No, I sighed to the hushed shop, I was not an American. There were other kinds of foreigners in the world, and some of them even found their way to Toyama.

Instantly, conversation about me bubbled, but it was a conversation from which I was totally excluded.

"He's wearing boots."

"He's got a sleeping bag."

"And he's looking at a map. What d'you reckon he's up to?"

"It looks like he's walking into Toyama."

"Doesn't he know there's a bus?"

Once or twice I was asked a question.

"Where are you going?"

"Kyushu, eventually."

"What, through Tottori?"

"No, through Hiroshima."

And the questioner would promptly turn his back on me while my answers were relayed round the shop.

"He's going to Kyushu. He's not going through Tottori. He's going through Hiroshima."

"Why?"

"I don't know."

"Wouldn't it be quicker through Tottori?"

"He might not know that, being an American."

On my way out a man caught me by the elbow.

"Where do you come from?"

"England."

140

"Do they speak English there?"

"Some of them do."

The man leaned back in his chair and studied me.

"Well, I've heard that in English they use the word 'another.' They use it quite often. What does it mean?"

I explained as best I could, with a couple of examples. The man turned and nodded to his companion.

"There, what did I tell you? He speaks Japanese. I can't imagine where he learned it."

✳

The city of Toyama is nationally famous for the manufacture of patent medicines, usually sold door to door by elderly enthusiasts in small wooden chests (the medicines, not the enthusiasts), and these chests become part of the household furniture. The preparation and sale of the medicines, called *kampoyaku* (Chinese concoctions), bear all the signs of a small-scale cottage industry, but the entrepreneurial genius of the people of Toyama has parlayed this unlikely source of fortune into a business with an annual wholesale value of more than 190 billion yen. The city's oldest and best-known *kampoyaku* manufacturer is Kokando, and I arranged to pay them a visit.

The Kokando factory—opened in 1876 and rebuilt shortly after the war—stands in the southern sector of Toyama near the old tram stop named after it. The girl who showed me round spoke slowly and precisely and with the solemnity of a preacher who has the undivided attention of a disarmed infidel.

"Before the war our ninety-nine medicines—the widest range of *kampoyaku* in Japan—were manufactured and packed entirely by hand. Nowadays, of course, we use machines, but the traditions and processes remain the same, and the recipes continue to derive from those which were imparted to Lord Maeda in the seventeenth century.

"The botanical ingredients include Korean ginseng (a very expensive kind of carrot) and the roots of the Indian ginkgo tree. But more highly prized are the items we obtain from the internal organs of animals. There is, for example, the dried glandular fluid of the male musk deer, drawn off during the rutting season and employed in the manufacture of a powerful stimulant. Originally, in order to obtain this

141

fluid, it was unfortunately necessary to slaughter the deer, but now-adays, thanks to the development of new methods, it can be obtained humanely through plastic tubes. Then there is the bile of the Japanese bear, a pain killer and an agent in the reduction of fevers. The secretion from the poison gland of the Chinese toad is mainly used in the treat-ment of heart diseases, though it, too, kills pain with remarkable efficacy. And gallstones produced in the bladders of cows are a restora-tive and an antidote to several toxic substances."

The girl bestowed on me a reverent smile, and we stopped to watch two young women in nurse's uniforms, whose faces were entirely hidden behind gauze masks, sorting through a trough full of tiny yellow capsules.

"They are checking them for shape," the girl explained, "and their job is so terribly taxing on the eyes that they must change shifts every thirty minutes."

"What's in the capsules?" I asked.

"Oh, vitamins—and one or two other things," said the girl with studied nonchalance, and I followed her down the length of the ma-chine shop, where white-clad women were operating little conveyor belts in a hush that reminded me of Remembrance Sunday. The only sounds were the faint click and patter of the neat gray machines and the occasional sigh of an elderly employee poised in her mask over a tray of colored tablets—or perhaps, out of sight of the casual visitor, over a cauldron of steaming Chinese toads.

The names of some of Kokando's products were as fascinating to me as the ingredients. What was in Six God Pills, I wondered, or Real Mother Powder or Woman Reliever? Those with "English" names were equally intriguing. What did "Mashin A" cure, and why would one want a dose of "World Hap"?

Before leaving, I was given a small brown bottle of chilled liquid to drink. I learned from the label that it was made from asparagus, which, considering the range of possible free samples, was something of a letdown. However, it also contained royal jelly, and the label recommended it in glowing English for "sport, driving, mountain-climbing, working, and being beautiful." I swallowed it in a gulp, bowed solemnly to my guide, and went to get a haircut.

The young woman in the hairdresser's wore the same nurse's smock and white gauze mask as the employees of Kokando. She washed my hair, cut it, dried it, gave me a fierce massage, pounded my skull, vibrated my spine and thighs with a mechanical vibrator, shaved my chin and cheeks, my forehead, the tops of my eyebrows and the space between my eyes, cleaned my ears with padded sticks, and trimmed the hair from the insides of my nostrils. A missionary who came in once or twice, she remarked, had exactly the same sort of nose that I had. *Takai* (high) was her word for it, and she smeared it lavishly with skin cream.

Walking back through Toyama in the late afternoon, it was impossible not to detect the glint of affluence. The shop windows were crammed with Hanae Mori fashions, the main streets had names like Sunflower Boulevard, and when I went to draw some money from a large post office, no one thought to ask me for identification. Crossing from Niigata to Toyama had reminded me a little of crossing from Yugoslavia to Austria: from a land of calloused laborers to one where slightly obese people consume cream pastries and have safe-deposit boxes in air-conditioned banks. Opinion polls now regularly announce that something like ninety percent of Japanese people regard themselves as belonging to "the middle class," and I expect the percentage in Toyama is even higher. I paid a lot of money for a dinner of sweet prawns and went to bed early in my middle-class ryokan with its vase of plastic flowers and its coin TV. There were no mosquitoes or wind to wake me and I slept the sleep of the solvent.

On the way out of Toyama the haze that had been hugging the city lifted, and in the lulling heat a range of blue-gray mountains stood faintly visible to the south. I was quickly out of the center of the city, striding through the flat suburbs where small green rice fields lay sandwiched between single-story shops and cupboard-sized beauty parlors. The signs of affluence grew fewer—one of the last was the "New World Coffee and Dance"—and as I started to climb toward the thickly wooded western hills, a low ripple of thunder snaked sluggishly from end to end of the basin.

Throughout the morning the clouds mounted and the light changed as though through a set of filters, till by midday the sky had turned a bright salmon pink. Ten minutes later the rain began, not in drops but in a sudden belting torrent. The thunder slammed from cloud bank to cloud bank, and small livid spears of lightning crackled down through the salmon pink sky.

No wonder the Japanese think foreigners are odd. A car screeched to a halt twenty yards ahead of me, and the driver rolled the window down and beckoned to me frantically through the blinding rain.

"Come on! Quick!"

I sloshed up to the car as he flung the passenger door open, and grinned sheepishly in at him.

"It's all right," I said. "I'd prefer to walk."

He did reply, but it was inaudible above the rain, and his jaw had dropped so far that he had a bit of trouble articulating.

No other cars stopped; they probably couldn't see me. No houses appeared, no shelters to rest in. A long way further on I found a little drive-in and sat there for two hours soaked to the skin, drinking beer and waiting for the storm to pass. The owner was a pleasant man, and when I had finished my second bottle, he opened a third without any prompting and brought it over to my table where we sat and drank it together. Outside, the storm raged in fits and starts. In the lulls the owner would run out into the car park and spend a minute staring up at the sky. Then he would come back and sit down at the table and give me a confidential weather report.

"Sky's clearing a bit to the south, but a lot more clouds blowing up from the northwest."

A fresh sheet of rain clattered down to rattle the drive-in windows.

"There," grinned the owner, opening a fourth beer, "what did I tell you?"

At one point a little boy, about five or six years old, came out of a back room, pulled down his knickers, and pissed on the drive-in floor just by the cash register. The owner shrugged and topped up my glass, his wife fetched a mop, and the three other customers continued to slurp their noodle soup.

"Apologize to the gaijin," the mother insisted, but the child had already sauntered away.

The storm never blew itself out that day. There were respites when I launched off in frantic top gear, praying that the rain would hold off till the next grocer's shop, but the further I went into the sodden hills the sparser the grocer's shops became, and although the thunder

144

had grown more distant, the rain, when it fell, was as sharp and slashing as before. Near the crest of the hills a bedraggled young man in a mackintosh who had set up a fruit stall by the roadside came splashing across under an umbrella to give me a bunch of grapes.

"Car break down?" he asked, nodding at my wringing-wet hair and clothes. No doubt about it. Foreigners are mad.

Outside the little city of Tonami the thin swollen thread of the River Sho was rushing and swirling between slick gravel banks. The ryokan could not, they said, provide a meal, so I had to dash out again along the teeming streets in yukata and geta that were both too small for me, trying to prevent the wind from swiping the ryokan's umbrella, till I found a small restaurant that served rice and fish. And there, at ten minutes and six seconds past seven on this stormy Saturday evening, I witnessed in glowing color on the restaurant's TV the event for which 120,000,000 people had spent three days holding their breath.

Poor Oh Sadaharu. Ever since he had equaled Hank Aaron's home-run record the pressure on him to surpass it had been escalating at fever pace. Crowds had been camping out at the Giants' stadium in Tokyo, tickets were fetching twenty times their stadium prices, TV cameras were zooming in on Oh as he sat on the team bench biting his nails, to the total exclusion of the batter at the plate, and—more incredibly than any of this—games were actually being televised until they ended. (The normal procedure on Japanese commercial television, where every program, including the news, corresponds in length to the amount of cash an advertiser has paid, is to cut games off when the sponsor changes—usually around the middle of the eighth inning with the score tied, two runners on base, two outs, and a full count.) But tonight the tensed nation was rewarded for its vigil. In the bottom of the third inning of a game against the Yakult Swallows, a visibly relieved Oh cracked the run that cracked the record.

There were a few who moaned, and some of these appeared on the same TV channel later in the evening to point out, for example, that baseball stadiums were smaller in Japan, that the pitching was weaker, and other traitorous notions. One even had the gall to suggest that the pitching tonight had been positively friendly. But all these barbs were rapidly sheathed when the Prime Minister's Office confirmed that Oh was now officially a National Hero. The mud-spattered young fan who had retrieved the historic ball broke down in tears on the late night news, and the camera invaded a wedding reception to interview the bride and groom.

"Ten minutes and six seconds past seven!" marveled the groom. "Why, that's exactly the moment we were taking our vows!"

"You may have missed the game," commiserated the interviewer, "but I know you'll never forget your wedding anniversary—September third—what a day—the day Oh hit Number 756!"

The storm had passed by morning and the air was hot and humid— the sort of morning you would expect after the electrical activity of thunder and bat. Crickets in the hedgerows were singing louder, and the rice seemed to be ripening faster. Across the plain to the south the new expressway curled off to the horizon, while my older road meandered up toward the low blue mountains. There was little traffic: the expressway had siphoned it off, leaving the villages on the plain to wilt and fade. At midday I stopped for a lunch of raw fish, and the tubby woman who ran the restaurant kept running in and out of the dining room saying, "Are you sure you can eat it? Are you sure you won't leave it?"

The afternoon was still; the air grew hotter. I walked on up through the dark green woods, past tall trees lush and silent after the storm, till at two o'clock on the sixty-eighth day of my walk I reached the crest of the hills and crossed the prefectural boundary from Toyama into Ishikawa. The rocks that lined the high, deserted road were smothered with moss, damp and dark, and this lent to the first few miles of the new prefecture a coolness and age that the coastal plains had lacked.

In the higher fields the harvest had already begun. Stumps of lopped rice poked up like broken teeth, and between them the mud-brown water gleamed. Cut, bound stalks had been stacked into thin ricks that lined the fences along the road and occupied the corners of the small stepped paddy fields. By the side of the road a young couple sat sketching the harvest, tracing the lines of the blue mountains to the south and peopling their sketches with imaginary figures—or real ones like the old man in his incongruously spotless white shirt who was carrying a pair of heavy buckets on a pole across his dark tanned neck.

A few of the farms owned miniature combines, so neat and small they looked like Tonka Toys. But for the most part the harvest was being gathered by hand, and it is really only in places like this—these tiny terraced paddies at the Back of Japan—that you realize how little the technology and industry for which the nation has gained a world-wide reputation has lightened the working life of rural families. The Japanese have found ways of incorporating calculators into wrist-watches, digital clocks into electric razors, and video cassette recorders into microwave ovens; and the old man still grits his teeth and grunts as he swings the buckets across his back, and the women shuffle forward, ankle-deep in mud, their backs hardening over the years till in their sixties they can no longer stand up straight, and cut their rice with little six-inch scythes.

Once out of the hills and under the expressway, I was swiftly enmeshed in the "other" Japan: the car cemeteries, the new car showrooms, the repair shops, and the petrol stations, all flashily confirming that the only worthwhile purpose in life is the sale, maintenance, and burial of motor transport. A pinball parlor called Golden Balls set the seal on my reentry into civilization, and just before five in the afternoon, having crossed the neck of the Noto Peninsula in two hurried days, I tramped into the historic city of Kanazawa.

The historic city of Kanazawa is well used to visitors. It is one of the most frequented tourist centers on the Japan Sea side of the country. In Kanazawa you can see the ruined walls of a sixteenth-century castle, an ancient gateway, a university, temples, shrines, houses that once belonged to samurai, two Kentucky Fried Chicken outlets, and a shop that serves thirty-four varieties of doughnut. In the underground shopping arcades taped birds twitter, and between the Mode Shop and the Mistress Shop a small queue of people waits patiently to use the *terefon kyapusuru* ("telephone capsule"). Street signs abound in English and Russian (Irkutsk is one of Kanazawa's six sister cities), and many of these street signs direct you toward this proud town's chief attraction: a landscape garden called Kenrokuen, which, the official guidebook notes, is "one of the three most beautiful gardens in Japan."

The name Kenrokuen means Park of the Six Virtues. These six virtues, the guidebook explains, are its size, its peace, its strength, its age, the impressive view one can obtain from it of the city, and its careful blending of natural objects such as ponds, trees, streams, and stones.

It is certainly large. When one thinks of Japanese landscape gardens,

147

one tends to think in miniature—of the tiny rock or moss gardens that nest inside Kyoto temples. Kenrokuen is far larger than these, and while the temple gardens are meant strictly for contemplation, you can stroll along the pathways of Kenrokuen as you would through an English park. The garden is built on elevated ground, so the view it affords of the city is not a bad one. A European might not consider Kenrokuen old. It was laid out in 1822, and in Europe there are parks and gardens that predate it by several centuries. But here in Japan, where fires and earthquakes so frequently ravish the cities, and where, consequently, many of the most famous landmarks have had to be rebuilt in modern times, anything that has stood for a hundred years can claim to be venerably "old."

You can experience a little of Kenrokuen's peace by looking at the photographs in the guidebook. The ponds are unruffled as they mirror the cherry blossoms or the deep blue irises that crowd the paths in early summer. Above the largest pond stands a little teahouse where Lord Maeda, the daimyo of Kanazawa, might have sat on an evening in late September improvising poems about the autumn moon. In a sense, the guidebook is right about age, for here again, as in the gardens of Kakunodate, age is a matter of sensation, not of years. The stones, the moss, the dark rocks that look as if they have grown inch by slow inch in their places—these impart to the garden its feeling of timelessness, and this in turn inspires in the viewer a sense of peace.

There are no people in the guidebook photographs. I assume they were taken in the early morning before the garden is open to the public. (In fact, there is a small society in Kanazawa whose members regularly visit Kenrokuen in the early mornings so that they can sample the tranquility that the guidebook photographs convey.) When the garden opens and the public arrives, the feeling you experience is not quite the same.

I went to see Kenrokuen on a fine Monday afternoon. Children screamed, young men shouted, businessmen drank and staggered about, cameras clicked, babies cried, thousands of people followed dozens of guides along the paths between the unruffled ponds and the long-suffering trees. Each guide carried a flag in one hand, so that her charges would not lose themselves in the crush, and a portable loudspeaker in the other hand, through which she furnished the explanations so essential to the appreciation of natural beauty. The older tourists listened to the guides and stayed so close to their heels that they seemed to be on leashes. The younger tourists listened to the transistor radios they carried slung across their shoulders:

I want you, baby.
I want you, ba-a-by.

"And now, everybody, if you will step a little closer—please be careful not to snap the bushes—you see before you the symbol of Kenrokuen—the stone lantern known as the Lantern of the Koto Bridge."

The tourists aim their cameras and a little boy spits bubble gum at a carp.

"This ancient granite lantern on its beautifully arched legs is the most celebrated object in the garden. It is designed to instill in us the same sense of peace as when we listen to the gentle plucking of a harp."

Anata wa sexy.
Anata wa sex-y-y-y.

"The lantern was made two hundred years ago—so you can see how extremely ancient it is—and the twelfth Lord Maeda placed it here beside his favorite pond, the Pond of Mist. The paths are rather crowded today, so please take care that your children don't fall in."

Click, click. "Aaah!" Click, click. Splash!

"Poets have written poems about this lantern . . ."

Click.

"Painters have painted it . . ."

Click.

"Photographers have photographed it . . ."

Click, click, click, click, click.

"And you can buy plastic replicas of it in the souvenir shops by the bus stop, some conveniently attached to ashtrays. And now, if you will kindly come this way—hurry up, please, the bus leaves in three and a half minutes—we will admire the famous and venerable pine, said to have been grown from a seed of the great tree in Omi that lived for a thousand years."

It took me what seemed like a thousand years to find the gate. The crush was so thick that I could hardly see the path in front of me, and the loudspeakers and radios on either side of my head were seriously numbing my sense of direction.

"Look at the gaijin! Look at the gaijin!" the children screeched from among the trees.

"Hey, yooo! American boy!" the young men cackled from behind Lord Maeda's teahouse.

In the shop by the gate I bought a guidebook, and I sat in a little restaurant near the garden, drinking tea and looking at the color photographs. Size. Peace. Strength. Age. The Pond of Mist. The Lantern of the Koto Bridge. In spring the cherry blossoms are thick as clouds. In winter the lantern wears a cap of snow.

"How peaceful!" I thought, as I sipped my tea. "How calm! How quiet! How Japanese!"

≈ 6 ≈

Buddha and the
Floating Bridge of Heaven

ON THE CURB of the main road out of Kanazawa a dozen or so mourners fresh from a funeral stood fidgeting in loose black suits around a
hearse. The hearse was a long maroon-brown limousine on which a
marvelous folly of black and gold lacquer had been constructed to
resemble a portable shrine. The driver bowed solemnly to the mourners, who plucked bits of invisible fluff off their suits and then sprinkled
pinches of salt over themselves before lapsing into a large two-story
restaurant for lunch. They looked like an outing of tired crows, sitting
at the long wooden table of the restaurant eating their pork cutlets in
complete silence while the color television set in the corner blared an
advertisement for a "new sexy" brassiere called Top Feel.

I had had enough of main roads and cities. The Cafe Terrace Love
Love (the menu included Love Love Pudding) brought that home to
me with a wallop, so straight after lunch I turned sharp across the railway tracks onto the old coast road that the Hokuriku Expressway had
left puddingless and empty. It was a scorching hot day. The cement
piles of the expressway shut the sea off like the bars of a prison, but
between them I could glimpse it close and blue. The narrow streets of
the one or two little villages I passed through on this flat coastal strip
were silent and packed with solid black shadows, but the heat bounced
wickedly off the open tar road. In the sky real crows flapped, rasping
to each other, surveying the stubble in the fields that had been cut,
while gray wisps of smoke trailed up from the pale fires burning autumn husks.

151

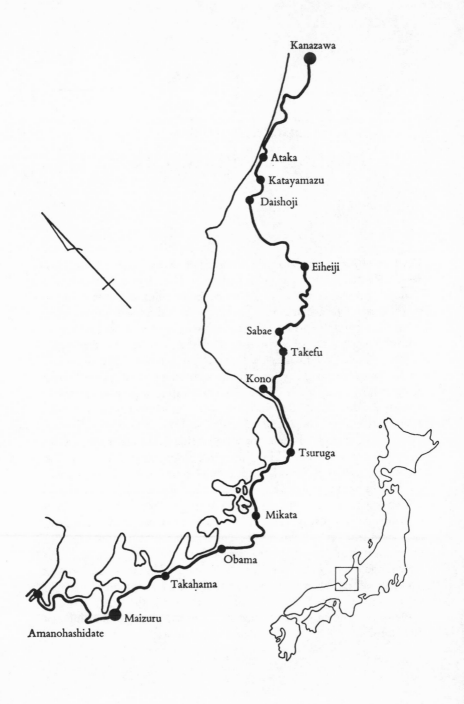

Kanazawa

Ataka

Katayamazu

Daishoji

Eiheiji

Sabae

Takefu

Kono

Tsuruga

Mikata

Obama

Takahama

Maizuru

Amanohashidate

Far, far to the southwest, very faint through the haze, the bluish-pink peak of Mount Hakusan rode above the grayer smoke of a string of small factories. Some of the fields were still unharvested, flowing and golden in the hot wind from the sea, and the husk smoke skittered like kite streamers across them, while the factory smoke mounted in stolid verticals, as impervious to wind as to season.

The road turned into a path and the path into a narrow meandering track between paddies, so that I had to keep an eye on landmarks: the piles of the expressway, Hakusan, the tantalizing ocean. I stopped for a beer in a little restaurant near a small-town station that was as deserted as the shadowy villages. The man who owned the restaurant had been born in the north of Honshu and told me he had worked all over Japan, in department stores and factories, driving trucks, laundering overalls, saving up for fifteen years to build this tiny shop that can barely have earned him a bachelor's living.

"But it's near the sea and the fields and that's what counts. There's so much of this country I haven't seen, and—my goodness—here you are walking the length of it! I see no point in going abroad, myself. What's the use of swanking about Hawaii and Guam when you've seen no more of your own country than the place you were born and the inside of an office? If I had my life to live again, I'd spend a year of it in each of the forty-seven prefectures—getting to know them all, their people and their ways. It's too late now, and I've a business to run, but if I ever have kids I'll make sure they see at least as much of Japan as I have."

He made me a free cup of coffee "for the road," and when I left the restaurant and set off along the track that had turned once again into an avenue, the crows were still flapping noisily over the stubble, but the sparkle had gone from the afternoon sea.

That night I was the only guest in a ryokan where the screens, as I sat eating dinner, opened onto a perfect moonlit garden. The old woman who owned the ryokan, and who was dressed in an exquisite chrysanthemum kimono, had brought her budgerigar to watch me eat, and throughout the meal he ran backwards and forwards across my shoulders, staring in lunatic fascination at each piece of red fish I slipped into my mouth. His name was Piko, the old woman told me. And what was my name? Aran-san? Ah, Aran Deron? No? Well, never mind, I was just as handsome as Aran Deron. And was I French, too? And did all Frenchmen write such lovely Japanese as Aran-san had written in her register? Would Aran-san not like some sakè? And could she not fill Aran-san's rice bowl again? It was such a pleasure to have a friend to talk to, wasn't it, Piko-san? Piko-san was sure it was. And would Aran-san mind if Piko-san stayed to watch him drink? Piko-san loved to watch his friends do that.

The old woman knelt on the cushion next to me and poured my sakè, cup after cup of it, smiling and chatting till I grew drowsy. She spoke to the budgerigar and to me with exactly the same measured politeness, and in the end we both ran out of replies. A breeze sprang up and the old woman moved away to draw the screens across the moon. I shut my eyes for a second and opened them half an hour later, sprawled out on the tatami mats with my feet under the table, my thin summer kimono wide open at the front, revealing my thighs and chest and belly and penis. The old woman was kneeling, talking quietly to her budgerigar, glancing across at me from the other side of the room where she had gone, a long while ago, to close the screens.

Would Aran-san like any more sakè? She could heat it for him in a trice if he did. No? Ah, well then, perhaps, since he was tired, he would like her to leave him and let him go to sleep. Piko-san could help his old granny lay out the mattress for Aran-san, who was really much too weary to talk any more. What a nice talk we had, though, didn't we, Aran-san? How fast the time goes when you're with a friend.

I watched the old woman silently clear away the dinner plates and lay my mattress out on the tatami, well away from the screens so that no drafts would disturb me. I sat up and pulled the cotton kimono around me while she knelt in the middle of the room and carefully lit the green mosquito coil. The budgerigar sat on her shoulder and watched, absorbed, as the blue ribbon of smoke swam up toward the ceiling.

"Say goodnight to Aran-san."

"Goodnight, Piko-san," I said.

The old woman quietly turned out the light and, with her friend, disappeared down the dark passage toward her kitchen.

The morning of September seventh, the seventy-first morning of my walk, was another baking hot one, and these Ishikawa roads were behaving oddly—continuing for several kilometers broad and tree-lined between smart little ball-valve factories and neat green lawns, then trailing off into thin rubble tracks, then suddenly broad and surfaced again. There was absolutely no traffic. The little village of Ataka, where I stopped to ask directions, seemed as empty as a ghost town, and I had to rattle the doors of three shops before I found one open. In the dark, dusty cool of the shop, a tall old man with white hair and no teeth treated me to a lecture on village history, while a fighter plane screamed low over the rooftops, circled tightly out to sea, then screamed back round the same circuit like a toy plane on a wire.

"That's the trouble," the old man said, growling up at the ceiling from which small specks of dust were flaking down onto his bananas. "The commercial jets we could put up with; there's only half a dozen a day. But these blasted Self-Defense Force training flights—take-offs and landings and what have you—can you wonder people move away, and the ones that don't stay locked up indoors? In fine weather it goes on from morning till night. It's enough to make you pray for a storm."

Where was the airport, I asked, looking at my map.

"About three kilometers down the road. There was an airfield there during the war. Then the Americans came and chewed it up with bull-dozers, and we were all allowed to farm the land. Everyone grew plots of rice there, me included, and we got a couple of fair harvests out of it. But as soon as this Self-Defense lark started, the government— the *Japanese* government, mind you—came and took the land away again with not so much as a please or thank you, so today we've got cracked eardrums instead of suppers."

The old man gave me the directions I wanted to the site of the Ataka barrier gate. He also gave me a withering scowl.

"What on earth d'you want to go and see that for?"

"I'm interested in history."

He squinted down at the little cassette recorder that I carried in a pouch on my belt for making notes.

"You a writer, then?" he asked, perceptively (someone else had thought it was a digital brandy flask). Yes, I told him, I had written a few things.

"Well, just you remember this," he said, getting up off his stool for the conclusion of his lecture, so that he stood a good deal taller than I did: "A country is like a sheet of paper; it's got two sides. On one side there's a lot of fancy lettering—that's the side that gets flaunted about in public. But there's always a reverse side to a piece of paper—a side that might have ugly doodlings on it, or bits of graffiti, or goodness knows what. If you're going to write about a country, make good and sure you write about both sides."

With this admonition swimming in my head, I crossed the narrow Ataka River and clumped down through a grove of silent pine trees to the welcoming, one-sided sea.

> The dune at Ataka where the pine trees stand,
>   amid which—
> How clear! This ancient barrier gate!

That poem was written in 1933, and the poet was, quite properly, exercising her fancy. There is no barrier gate, nor was there one then. In the eight hundred years since the shogun Yoritomo is supposed to have set up a barrier here, the sea has eaten a good half kilometer into the coast, and the gate, if it ever existed in physical form, is now a mass of barnacles. But the site is that of one of the best-known incidents in Japanese legend—an incident celebrated in the popular Kabuki play *Kanjincho* (The Subscription List). It is worth summarizing the plot of this play for the example it contains of the tension between duty (*giri*) and humanity (*ninjo*), a tension that some maintain still forms the basis of much Japanese thought and behavior.

The shogun's younger brother, Yoshitsune, a victim of fraternal jealousy, fled the capital in 1187 and made for the far north. To prevent his escape, the shogun commanded the setting up of barrier gates in all the provinces. Yoshitsune was fortunate in having as a retainer a man of prodigious wit and strength called Benkei. (The relationship between Yoshitsune and Benkei is similar to that between their contemporaries Robin Hood and Little John, and, interestingly, legend has them meet in the same way—on a bridge where they fight each other to establish superiority. In the English story Little John wins but sees in his adversary a leader worth following. This would never do in Japan, where feudal propriety requires the lord to hold all the trump cards, so Yoshitsune gains the victory, turning Benkei's subservience into a nice uncomplicated norm.)

In order to pass the Ataka barrier, Benkei and the other retainers have disguised themselves as *yamabushi*, or "mountain priests," fierce Buddhist mendicants who went about armed with iron-tipped staves.

Yoshitsune, at Benkei's suggestion, is inconspicuously dressed as their bearer and brings up the rear. But the guardian of the gate, a samurai called Togashi, has been forewarned of Benkei's ruse and has made up his mind to kill all *yamabushi* on sight, so when the fugitives approach the barrier, their plight is more serious than they realize.

Benkei confronts Togashi with the story that they are collecting donations for the restoration of a great temple and Togashi abruptly demands to see his list of subscribers. Benkei, of course, has no such list, but he calmly draws a blank scroll from his pack, holds it close to his face so that Togashi cannot read it, and brilliantly improvises the sort of elaborate formal preamble that such a document would require. Togashi's suspicions are aroused, however, and he sneaks a glimpse of the blank scroll, which plunges him straight into the *giri*-versus-*ninjo* dilemma. Benkei is lying, and Togashi's duty demands that he kill or take them all prisoner. But, as a man, he cannot help admiring the fearless way in which Benkei is conducting himself; so instead of ordering their arrest, he cross-examines Benkei on the garments, habits, and beliefs of *yamabushi*. Benkei, whose father was a priest and who has taken religious orders himself, answers all the questions faultlessly, displaying an astonishing knowledge of Buddhist arcana. Togashi is so overawed that he gives permission for the fugitives to march through the barrier, which they begin to do. But then the disguised Yoshitsune is pointed out to him, and the conflict between admiration and duty flares up once again. Togashi orders the bearer to halt.

Benkei now delivers his masterstroke. Pretending to be angry that the bearer's sluggish pace has caused them to be delayed again, he seizes a staff and beats Yoshitsune, threatening to kill him. Togashi is aghast. Raising a hand against one's lord is an unpardonable sin, and if the bearer really is Yoshitsune, then by all the codes of feudal behavior Benkei has no recourse but suicide. So moved is Togashi that he swiftly restrains Benkei and sends the whole party on its way.

As soon as Togashi is out of sight Benkei grovels apologetically before Yoshitsune, who nobly forgives him for saving his life and then priggishly recites the tale of his own woes, especially the persecution he has suffered at the hands of his brother, to whom he was completely loyal, thus rounding out the theme of fidelity and disgrace. Finally Togashi reappears and offers Benkei some sakè, which he consumes in massive doses out of the lid of a tub. He then performs a lively dance

157

while the members of his party steal away, having "trodden on the tail of a tiger."

The Greeks wouldn't have seen a play in it at all. Shakespeare might have turned it into an entertaining episode (a bit like Gad's Hill probably), though his attention would no doubt have focused on Togashi, the complex man of divided loyalties, caught between the worlds of responsibility and moral courage. But for the Japanese dramatist and his audience, the real hero of the affair is Benkei, a figure of simple-minded devotion, taking his life into his hands for a lord who displays far less wit and invention than he does. His heroic stature is enhanced by the fact that he drinks like a fish and is uncommonly clever with words.

At the cash desk of the little Ataka museum the custodian yawned and drowsed, while an endless tape droned out the tale of the subscription list to the ears of a bronze Togashi and Benkei, who stood immortalized on a large plinth outside the shuttered "rest house." The noodle shops and restaurants were all closed, including the Tea Room Sydney. Plywood cutouts of the three Kabuki characters, with holes for sightseers to poke their faces through, had been set up in front of a big hooded camera; but there were no sightseers, no cameraman, no movement or sound whatever—only the endless drone of the tape and the soft wash of the patient sea that, eight hundred years into the future, will have found all these lovely new monuments to lavish barnacles on.

It began to rain as I was tramping through the nearby hot spring resort of Katayamazu, but none of the huge Western-style hotels (The Grand Hotel, The Kaga Plaza) looked inviting enough for me to want to spend the night in them. Nor did the flashy little boutiques, nor the neon strip joints, nor the Adult Shop Venus entice me on this stormy afternoon; though it was nice to think of Yoshitsune and his friends emerging from their perils at the Ataka barrier to find all these entertainments waiting for them: honey traps more sticky than the shogun could devise.

I trudged on into the city of Daishoji, where the woman who ran the ryokan I stayed at delivered opinions on the weather with the air of a professional meteorologist.

"It's not going to rain today," she promised as I left her looking up at the sky next morning. Parts of the streets had dried out in the night but the wind was still high and the clouds dark and ugly. Within five minutes of the woman's forecast great spots of rain had begun to come down again—first a drizzle, then a downpour—and this was to prove the most memorable rain of a long rainy summer.

In April the cherry blossoms open and fall; in June the steady rains come, coating the shoes in the shoe cupboard with white mold. In October the maples turn startling crimson; in the winter months, on the Japan Sea coast, the snow lies so deep that in the mountain villages people must burrow about like moles. Japan is a land of vivid seasons, glowing, cruel, blessed, or cursed. Autumn brings the fiery leaves and it also brings typhoons.

The worst typhoon of the year was Typhoon 9. The Americans christened it Babe, but in Japan it was called the Okinoerabu Typhoon after the small island, 350 kilometers south of the southernmost tip of Kyushu, where towards midnight on September ninth it caused the lowest atmospheric pressure ever recorded in the Japanese islands (907.3 millibars). The eye of Typhoon 9 never came closer than that to the mainland. It was spawned eight thousand kilometers away in the South Pacific and finally blew itself out in China after striking land near the mouth of the Yangtze River. But its claws had a ferocious reach. In Japan Typhoon 9 sparked fifty-seven landslides, killed one person and injured scores, closed four hundred roads, buried or blew down five thousand houses and flooded three thousand more. It dumped rain in torrents all over the country. In poor little Okinoerabu, at its height, an incredible 1.37 inches fell in the space of ten minutes, while the wind screeched through the treetops at more than 196 feet a second.

Here, as I crossed the prefectural boundary from Ishikawa into Fukui on the morning of the eighth, the wind loosened rooftiles, overturned bicycles, and spun plastic detergent containers in wild pink dances across the teeming roads. The rain ran down my face like little rivers, and in the streaming chill of it my bones ached. There was nowhere to shelter, nothing to do but to trudge on singing songs to myself that I could barely hear above the noise the wind made. In the rain and wind of Typhoon 9 I climbed the thirty-six kilometers of twisting mountain roads that lead to the great Zen temple of Eiheiji.

It was dark when I reached the gate of the temple and too late to stay there as a guest. The government lodging house was full, and the man at the desk looked stunned when I interrupted his careful explanation of how to get to the youth hostel and told him I would rather stay at a ryokan.

"Do you mean a *Japanese* ryokan . . . ?"

But there were no ryokans of any kind to be had that night. It was *shiizun ofu* (off season), the man explained, and they would all be either closed or reluctant to take anything short of a busload. In the end I found a room above one of the small souvenir shops that crowded the road to the temple gate, and collapsed gratefully onto the floor of it. Drenched, cold, and very tired, I hung my dripping clothes over an electric fire to dry them and lay down to sleep as soon as dinner was over. The wind still roared and the rain beat upon the windows of my room as though they were taiko drums. All night the claws of the typhoon ripped at the shuttered streets, at the six-hundred-year-old cedar trees, and at the carved wooden gates and thin paper screens of Eiheiji, the Temple of Eternal Peace.

By morning the claws had worn themselves blunt and a quieter, gentler rain was falling. In the gentler rain, as I strolled round Eiheiji, the roofs of the temple shone like old silver, and the green moss in the cluttered gardens looked preened and vibrant and freshly alive. Eiheiji is a vast, beautiful temple, its rooms and halls connected to each other by corridors and long flights of covered wooden steps. Black-robed monks with shaven heads and trainee monks in loose black jackets and trousers sauntered through the corridors and halls with little smirks on their scrubbed faces, ignoring the tourists who were being ushered about, shuffling and whispering; and as the rain still fell, the rustle of robes, the ring of curious fingers brushing a gong, the patter of slippered feet on the cold, smooth boards or the shush of silk *tabi* socks over soft straw matting—all rose and fell in volume like the gasps of air in a bamboo flute and left in their wake a greater silence than before.

The churches of Europe—the great ones—soar up in dizzying verticals at the sky. Eiheiji hugs the contours of the earth. When the sun strikes the stained-glass windows of a cathedral they explode in primary colors like a carousel. But the colors of Eiheiji are earth colors—the somber greens of the garden, the browns and grays of smooth polished wood and slate, the soft gold color of old tatami. The builders of the Christian churches of Europe—churches in which a religion of humility is preached—seem often boastful, often to be saying to us: "Now, look here, this is the House of God. It is here—*here*—not over the road with those dingy Presbyterians but here in *this* church that God dwells." The builders of Eiheiji were a lot less strident: "Oh, God dwells in our temple, if you like. But then, he dwells in everything else as well—in clods of earth, in the eyes of the blind, in the pebbles of the seashore as well as in our shrines."

The landscape of the mountains,
the sound of streams—
all are the body and voice of Buddha.

Eiheiji was founded in the middle of the thirteenth century by the author of that poem, a priest named Dogen. Dogen had spent four of his most formative years in China, being trained in Zen at Mount T'ien-t'ung, and because the Chinese are a practical people, his revelations, when they came, were of a practical kind. Dogen did not look for spirits in the air or worship an arcane, invisible Buddha who moved only in mysterious ways. "The truth is everywhere," he insisted. "The truth is where we are. One small step separates earth from heaven."

Despite the comparative sobriety of its architecture, Zen often seems to inspire in its adherents a supercilious attitude to the rest of mankind; an attitude that delights in one-upmanship, in riddles, puzzles, and the power of extraordinary experience. But Dogen maintained that in order to grasp the meaning of existence it was not necessary for a person to be unusually clever or to spend his life doing remarkable things. Simply by "sitting still and doing nothing" a man could discover what there was to be learned about life. Prayer and ritual were important to Dogen, but not much more so than cooking or sweeping the yard. All functions of the body, including the most basic, became, in the temple he founded, limbs of Zen. The toilet in Eiheiji contains an altar to Ususama Myo-o (The Guardian of the Impure), and together with the bath and the meditation hall, it is one of the three places in the temple where speech is forbidden and where a particularly strict code of contemplative behavior is observed by everyone who enters. It was Dogen's intention to make of Zen not an abstract philosophy, but a practice. The advice he gave his meditating disciples was blunt, straightforward, and mind-wrenchingly practical:

161

Think of not thinking.
How do you think of not thinking?
By not thinking.

The rain had stopped when I left Eiheiji and began the long descent of the mountain. Blue dragonflies danced over the grass by the roadside and parched brown grasshoppers with lemon-colored wings flitted with soft clicks from stalk to stalk. I imagined the dragonflies dancing around Dogen on his trips to and from the temple, and his seeing in them, as he saw in all things, an endlessly renewable shard of the Buddha.

Then, as I walked, I noticed that several of the dragonflies had stopped dancing and were beating their wings against the dirt. I bent to look at them and I saw at once that all the dragonflies were dying. There was not a soul on the road and no sound but the click of the lemon-winged grasshoppers. I watched the dragonflies for a while as they shook in this heat that had come after the typhoon. Then I stood up and walked down the mountain, across the highway and the shady river, and on into the meadows of Fukui.

That afternoon I felt more drained than at any other time on this four-month journey. It was not a depression exactly, nor one of the passing spells of frustration that I had grown so used to dealing with, but a deep emptiness not rooted in anything that I could readily explain or shrug away. I tramped on through the harvest wondering why it was I felt like this. Because the summer was ending? Because dragonflies die? Because I knew, as I had known for years, that I did not have the strength or the patience to sit for so much as an hour and think of not thinking?

The sun came out near the town of Sabae and shone on the trees, still green and wonderfully fresh from the rain. It shone on the brown faces of village women who smiled at me on their way home from the fields. It shone on the golden heads of rice that were waiting for the women to come and cut them. The holiness of living things can scoop a terrible hollow in a pilgrim's stomach. Blake would have got along well with Dogen.

The rain had done my legs no good. As I sat oiling my boots in the entrance hall of the ryokan at Sabae I felt I ought to be oiling my knee joints, they were so stiff. After breakfast I had opened the little closet where my clothes were hanging and the sour smell of them had filled the room. Typhoon 9 had veered off toward Korea—to the special delight of the announcer on the morning news—and the hot sun that it had brought in its wake was a merciless procurer of stinks.

The traffic between Sabae and the little city of Takefu had been siphoned off by a bypass, and the older road I walked along was narrow and nearly empty. Farmers were threshing their rice in sheds between small thumping machine shops, and the complete Takefu city baseball team sped by on bicycles, shouting and waving to me and knocking one another into the gutter.

I was struck more than once by the coarseness of Fukui manners, particularly the manners of working men, or perhaps it was simply that their remarks were more to the point than I had grown accustomed to:

"Where do you think you're going, then?"

"Why? Doesn't this road lead anywhere?"

" 'Course it leads somewhere. Don't all roads?"

"Well, I'm aiming to get out onto the coast eventually."

"Huh!" (Spits.)

"Isn't this the way?"

"That's the way if that's where you're going. Don't stand about, then. Go on, hop it!"

It seemed a very un-Japanese style of conversation, if you believe what you read in in-flight magazines, and the bluntness of Fukui workers had obviously rubbed off on a lot of the kids, too:

"Ugh! Look, it's a funny gaijin! Oi, America! Oi, America!"

No, I said solemnly, I was not America.

"What then? France?"

No, I wasn't France.

One little girl, in a single-handed attempt to introduce a note of civility into the exchange, said, "Excuse me, then, Mr. Gaijin, but where do you come from?"

England, I told her.

"Ugh! England!" chorused the boys.

"I know *everything* about England," crowed one particularly cocky little horror who had elbowed and shoved the polite girl out of the way.

"Oh yes? Well, what's the capital?"

"Don't know, but I can speak English conversation."

"Go on, then."

"Yes no yes no yes no yes no."

And I had to put up with several minutes of this chant before the kids eventually grew tired of me and went off to strangle cats or something.

I ran into another group of schoolboys just after I emerged from the quiet roads onto the highway, but these didn't say anything to me directly. Instead, they marched in single file behind me, giggling and sniggering and speaking to each other in funny foreign accents. I turned round finally and told them it was rude to treat people like circus freaks, but the tallest of them simply repeated my words in the same nonsensical nasal voice while the others fell about laughing.

More trials were furnished by the highway itself. Eight or nine kilometers beyond Takefu it vanished into the murk of the Takefu tunnel, and this proved one of the worst nightmares of the entire four-month tramp. There seemed no way round it, so I plunged into the tunnel with my little pocket torch to wave at oncoming traffic. I don't know whether the drivers saw the torch or not, but they paid it no attention whatever, and in the ten minutes it took me to struggle through that 835-meter-long sewer pipe I was squashed flat against the wall a dozen times and almost had my shirt ripped off my back by the spikes and hooks of six or seven thundering diesel trucks. Worse than this and the ear-wrenching noise was the fact that halfway through the tunnel I ran out of oxygen. It was the filthiest place I could remember being in. The circle of rusty daylight at the end of it looked like the bottom of a stopped-up lavatory bowl, and the closer I got to the air again the more unbreathable it appeared. I emerged finally, choking, spitting, one side of my body covered with soot and slime from the tunnel wall, my mouth as dry as a dung brick, and found I had to sit for nearly a quarter of an hour on the grass verge by the highway to recover my breath, by which time it had begun to rain.

It was still raining at five o'clock that afternoon when, having turned off the highway at the end of a stiff and miserable day, I trudged down four kilometers of steep cliff road into the little seaside village of Kono.

They saw me through the kitchen window of the first ryokan—which is always a sign of complications to come—and even before I had opened the door they were whispering to each other and bobbing frantically out of sight. The whispering stopped when I called out from the entrance hall, and a woman edged sideways out of the kitchen and stood staring at me with her thumb in her mouth.

"Do you have any rooms free?"

She shook her head.

"What, none at all?"

She glanced back into the kitchen and shook her head again.

"You mean you're closed?"

She shook her head.

"You're full?"

She nodded, her thumb still in her mouth. We stood and looked at each other with pained expressions on our faces.

"Well, in that case I wonder if you'd let me have some matches?"

The woman fished into her apron pocket and gave me a box of the ryokan's matches. I walked down the village street to a little yellow public telephone and dialed the number on the matchbox. It wasn't even necessary to disguise my voice.

"Hello, do you have any rooms free?"

"Yes, how many of you are there? We're . . ."

I replaced the receiver very gently, dropped the matches into a dustbin, and walked on down the street to the second ryokan.

Here I got something like the same response (they weren't full, they said, they were just having the weekend off), and at the third ryokan, where the door between the entrance hall and the living room stood wide open, the woman didn't even bother to get up off the tatami mats or to wrench her eyes away from her TV screen.

"Sorry, we're not accepting guests."

"Is there anywhere else?"

"You'd better go and find out, hadn't you?"

She was such a perfect embodiment of Fukui manners that I expect if she had been on her feet, she would have slammed the door in my face. As it was, she left me to do the slamming (as hard as I could with a pack on) and then splash across the muddy road in the rain to the fourth and last ryokan in the village, where, before the woman could tell me that the building had been condemned or something, I briefly outlined what had happened at the other places, pointed out that there was nowhere else I could possibly stay, told her that I was writing an

165

article on hospitality in Fukui Prefecture for (I named an influential weekly magazine) and hinted that if this last refuge were denied me I might devote a couple of paragraphs to her personally.

I got a room. It wasn't bad either. I managed to wash my clothes before dinner and the food was plentiful and the price quite cheap. But my indignation took a long time subsiding and I spent part of the evening (there were no bars in the blasted place either) composing a letter to the mayor of Kono, which I tore up and stuffed into an ashtray the following morning.

For most of the next day, and the day after that, Highway 8 was unavoidable. It hugged the heavily indented coast as far as Tsuruga, climbing to sharp promontories from which, in the baking hot September sun, I had dazzling views of the surrounding countryside—a narrow, spearlike fiord below, the smooth hump of the Tsuruga peninsula, and beyond the furthest fingers of land, miles to the west, the mountains of Kyoto. Traffic was always a menace on highways, but never more so than on twisting climbs like these. Trucks would overtake each other on the wrong side, blast me with their horns, pump thick black diesel fumes into my face, and often force me off into the grass as they roared by two abreast. I was glad not to be buried in one of the little graveyards that lay scattered along the side of this highway, where any attempt to Rest in Peace would have been like trying to sleep through Armageddon. It's just as well the Japanese cremate their dead; if they left complete skeletons lying about in ground as wracked and jolted as this, you'd hear them rattling like ruptured gearboxes.

In the fields that lay a little way back from the road the harvest was in full swing, and where the last rice had been stacked and the stubble flattened, farm families sat picnicking in wide-brimmed hats. The weather that had come in the wake of Typhoon 9 was hotter than any I could remember since the first blistering days out of Cape Soya. It was a waste of time washing shirts and jeans; a quarter of an hour after setting out they were drenched in sweat, dark and itchy, till by evening they smelled as though they'd never seen soap powder since the day they were stitched.

I came to another tunnel, this time mercifully skirted by a narrow track that wound away down the side of a cliff and was deserted except for spiders and bees. I trudged along it, peeling cobwebs apart that might have hung undisturbed for years, till I reached a tiny fishing village, completely invisible from the highway, where I discovered to my surprise that a toll road was being constructed along the base of the cliffs. The old man who ran the grocer's shop expressed surprise too.

"Yes, it's making quite a dent in the landscape. The 'Kono Seaside Highway' they're planning to call it. It's for city people to drive along on weekends, and in summer I expect it'll be quite pleasant. In fact," he grinned and nodded at one of the construction workers who had come in with a towel round his head for a lollipop, "they did all the surveying for it in the summer, didn't they? They had a good time, those engineers with their theodo-what-d'you-call-its and their tin helmets. I don't think a single one of them has any notion of what the sea does to this coast in winter. I tell you what: you won't catch me anywhere near that road when the wind starts rising. The waves'll pick the cars straight off of it. They're going to charge people a toll for the privilege of drowning!"

I spent a quiet night in the city of Tsuruga, and the following morning I tried, as I did each day before setting out, to transcribe the comments I had confided to my cassette recorder into the stiffbound notebook that now contained 120 pages of microscopic script. But this morning of the seventy-fifth day of my walk, my hand was shaking so badly that I had to put off the job until evening. Perhaps the heavy rains had left their mark on more than just the joints of my knees, or perhaps I was simply more tired than I realized. I stopped in at a coffee shop within thirty minutes of leaving the ryokan and sat there with my eyes closed for an hour, while traffic rumbled by outside the window and the Beach Boys sang about the good vibrations. Only when I got up to leave the shop did I realize that the man in the tam-o'-shanter eating fried noodles and jam on toast in alternate mouthfuls was not part of some typhoon-induced dream.

If the hospitality of the ryokans in Kono and the smirks and taunts of kids on the road had left me with a less than sunny impression of the natives of Fukui Prefecture, at least the landscape offered no cause for complaint. I had swapped Highway 8 for Highway 27, which was a much less hectic, bone-jarring affair, and from its high, pine-hidden shoulders I could see the black-tiled roofs of scattered seaside villages, the haze rising off the azure sea, and in the late afternoon, directly ahead of me, five small lakes sparkling silver and gold in the glow of the descending sun. The valley that contained the lakes was a lush lime green against the greeny black of the surrounding hills, and as I walked into the little town of Mikata, past a supermarket where a loudspeaker was broadcasting "I'd Like to Get You on a Slow Boat to China," a little boy with a Union Jack on his T-shirt said "Bye-bye" so incredibly politely that I stopped to congratulate him on his choice of flag.

The ryokan I stayed in that night was an unusual one. Instead of providing the normal dinner of four or five small dishes and varying them from day to day, it specialized, rather as a high-class restaurant might, in two local delicacies—broiled carp and grilled eel. Before I took a bath, the very attractive twenty-three-year-old daughter of the ryokan went with me for a stroll in the elegant garden, where we watched the black carp swimming about in their pond and netted the one I was to dine on. Later on, in the bathroom, I noticed a black carp staring glumly at me from out of a glass tank set into the wall. It struck me as a perverse idea to have the dinner survey the diner like this, and although I couldn't absolutely swear it was the same fish, I spent less time wallowing in the tub than I might have if the tank had contained a couple of tiddlers.

But there was another reason for skipping smartly back to my room: the daughter had promised to serve me dinner. We sat with the screens ajar, she in a sleek dark dress, me in the ryokan's extra-large yukata, and talked for a long time about how she had gone to Tokyo the previous year to appear on a TV quiz show. She had planned to become an actress, she told me, and had spent four months in Kyoto giving it a whirl, but she hadn't enjoyed the work very much and decided finally that she preferred to live here, near the sea and the Mikata lakes. We drank a good few cups of sakè as I crunched eel bones and nibbled my carp, and by the time the girl had cleared away the dishes, had seated herself again on the soft cushion opposite me, and resumed the story of her life in a voice that grew more melodious the more sakè I sipped, I had begun to sense the possibility of a tasty sequel to a tasty eel.

Woe to that eel (if woe can be to anything already swallowed in small mouthfuls)! Or, much more probably, woe to that carp (since I am convinced now it was the occupant of the bathroom tank that

I had been blithely dipping in mustard sauce)! Because that half-digested creature chose this extremely critical moment—this delicate, irretrievable moment of deciding how to maneuver a mattress out of a wall cupboard without appearing overly forward—to have his own back with a vengeance.

"Isn't it quiet," I murmured to the girl and farted louder than I have ever farted in my life. The girl dissolved in helpless giggles and disappeared rapidly in the direction of her sitting room. I hurled my own mattress down onto the tatami. Her brother served me breakfast.

A tattered signboard outside a padlocked restaurant showed a road that wound up into the coastal cliffs, then petered out into a row of red dots, then vanished altogether. A man in a fishing-tackle shop confirmed that the cliff road had grown impassable through lack of use, so I continued trudging disconsolately along the oily inland sweep of Highway 27. The summer heat of the last few days had partly evaporated in the night, and dark clouds were building along the ridges of the hills. I passed a young tramp with long hair and a beard carrying a cloth-wrapped bundle and a dented copper kettle, and like all the other tramps I met on my journey, he grimly ignored my existence. A woman pulling a cart loaded with straw came slowly up the other side of the road and stopped to yank back her headscarf and stare at me. And as I stood consulting my map at a point where it looked as though I could finally get off the highway, a car drew up, the driver wound his window down and said in English, "Where go?"

"Obama," I replied, not looking up from my map.

He was half a minute piecing together his second English sentence, and when he had done this, he said, very carefully, "Where go?"

"Obama," I sighed and folded up my map.

The driver frowned at me, pointed straight down the highway, and said, "Obama. Obama. Obama."

"Yes," I replied in Japanese, "but I'm walking, so I'd rather get off the highway, you see. Anyway, I can read a map quite well and I know exactly where I am."

The effect of this on the driver was remarkable. It was as though each Japanese word I uttered were a gob of spittle in his face. His forehead puckered into furrows, his lips tightened, his eyes narrowed, he wound up the window and roared away, leaving me to turn wearily onto a quiet road that crossed a short, sluggish river.

The road ran parallel to the river, skirting a filthy little granite-chip factory, passing fields where men sat perched sedately on tractor seats while women followed behind them doing the donkey work of stooping and stacking. In the distance the radio mast in the little city of Obama grew spectrally visible against the gray of the sky and the cloudy coastal hills. At half past four a strong wind began to blow in from the sea, and as I recrossed the river into the outskirts of the city, large solitary drops of rain started to splash down onto the pavement.

That night I had a dinner of barbequed liver in a little restaurant at the top of an iron fire escape. The owner and his wife were both Koreans, and when by eight o'clock it seemed likely that I was going to be their only customer, the owner—a jolly, big-boned man—decided to close up shop for the evening and we went out together to have a few beers.

Both the owner and his wife had been born in Japan—the children of Koreans brought over just before the war to work as forced labor in the naval yards and mines—but neither had been granted Japanese citizenship (their parents were "subjects," not "citizens"), although the wife no longer spoke a word of Korean and the owner had not spoken it for twenty-odd years. There are something like 670,000 Koreans living in Japan at present, the majority of whom were born here and know no other language or way of life. Yet most of these must renew their residence permits every three years and carry their alien registration cards about with them, or risk being sent "home" to a country they may never have seen.

The owner told me he didn't think he would have wanted Japanese nationality anyway. He appeared happy enough with his situation, though a bit sheepish about forgetting his parents' language. He had a daughter who had never learned Korean, and neither he nor his wife was capable of teaching her. At first he had wanted to send her to a Korean school, but the nearest was in Fukui city, two and a half hours away by train, so she attended an ordinary local school instead, where she was completely indistinguishable from any of her classmates— except for the card she carried in her bag, with its photograph and fingerprint.

On the way out of Obama next morning I stopped to watch five young men perform a dance on a grubby piece of wasteland between

170

a petrol station and a barber's shop. Each of the dancers wore a red-and-green tunic and a long blond straw wig, and each held a pole with a white tassel on either end, which he swung in arcs like a spear. This performance—I discovered from the barber, who had left his customer half-shaved to come out and watch it—marked the opening of the two-day Hoze Matsuri (or Ceremony of Release), the city's annual autumn festival. The accompaniment to the dancing was provided by a large taiko drum and six small saucerlike gongs; and the seven or eight spectators who followed the dancers from site to site clapped solemnly in time to the tinkles and thumps. I looked round for any hint as to why this unlikely spot should have been chosen for a dance, and saw it finally—a tiny unpainted shedlike shrine perched inaccessibly on a wooded slope behind a hoarding that advertised Toyota Motors. Whatever god resided there would certainly need a fair bit of entertaining to compensate for the dreariness of his surroundings. I suspect even Dogen would have had a hard time detecting the body of Buddha in a sump.

The highway rejoined the coast at Obama, and after a couple of hours of heavy tramping I clambered down a grassy bank and had a glorious swim in a beautifully empty lagoonlike bay. The sea was so warm that I wished it cooler, and as I floated on my stomach gazing down through the foggy green water, a jellyfish drifted lazily by my head and made a brief, tingling foray across my face.

Sitting toweling myself in a little restaurant above the bay, I chatted to the old man who ran it. He was busy trying to puzzle out how his new electric cash register worked, and in between mouthfuls of fried rice I told him about the jellyfish.

"That's quite out of the question," he said with authority.

"But I saw it. I can still feel the tingling on my face."

The old man pointed across at a calendar.

"You see," he said as though to a child, "the jellyfish season ended yesterday."

Further along the coast the inlets were all walled with concrete, and in the largest of them a dredging operation was in full swing: engine growling, crane creaking, slamming and banging that put an end to any thoughts of another swim. At Takahama I slipped off the highway and wandered down toward the lighthouse, where I found a government lodging house and decided to stay the night. The plump old woman whose job it was to serve me dinner told me an American had

171

stayed there a month ago. He had wanted toast and coffee for breakfast and had been most upset that they only had rice.

"Can *you* eat rice?" she asked suspiciously—not Do you want it or
Do you like it, but *Can* you eat it, as though it were a skill.

In the bath I watched a happy father bathe his two little laughing
daughters and then turn his soapy towel over to them while they took
it in turns to scrub his back. It rained during the night, and a wild wind
slammed the sea against the dark rocks by the lighthouse. In the morning the beach was deserted except for three men who had driven their
car down onto the pebbly sand and were peeling on black rubber skin-
diving suits, eyeing the loud spray as a turkey might an axe. In the tiny
park outside the lodging house fallen leaves flapped noisily along the
ground and beer cans bounced and rolled about the paths. I trudged
back toward the highway and passed three women washing underpants
and vests in a swollen stream by the side of the road. The stream looked
none too clean to me, and in a land where five-cycle washing machines
are commonplace, it appeared, that blustery first morning of autumn,
that a time warp had trapped this sliver of the coast.

September fifteenth is Respect for the Aged Day, one of Japan's twelve
national holidays. By midmorning the wind had blown most of the
straggling storm clouds away, and in the subdued breeze flocks of
white cumulus drifted lazily over the hills casting round blimplike
shadows. Most of the drive-ins I passed were closed for the holiday.
Near one—the Oasis—a ragged little procession of dark-suited men
picked its way up a hillside behind a brown-robed priest. One man
carried a white wooden *sotoba* stick of the kind that are planted in clusters behind a grave; another carried a bunch of wilting yellow flowers.

At midday I emerged from the low hills that separate Fukui from
rural Kyoto. My march through the Chubu District of Japan was finished—a march of just over seven hundred kilometers that had begun
twenty-eight days before when I crossed the prefectural boundary
from Yamagata to Niigata. I was now starting a brisk seven-day stroll
through the northwestern reaches of the Kinki ("Near the Capital")
District, so called because, from the earliest times to the 1860s, the imperial hub of the nation lay not far south of here—in the Yamato area

around Nara, in Asuka, in Nara itself, and finally, for almost eleven centuries, in Kyoto, whose name means simply "capital city."

The first villages I came to on the Kyoto coast contained some of the finest thatched shops I had seen on my journey. If it had not been for the vending machines outside them selling instant "Cup Noodle" they might have seemed finer. As I approached the large port city of Maizuru the shops turned glass and concrete again, noodle dispensers gave way to denim jackets lavishly embroidered with English texts—"Let's Go Dance, Kitty or Jimmy" (always wise to hedge your bets)—and as I tramped into the city I was surprised to see a large brown snake swimming nonchalantly along in a ditch.

Since 1901 Maizuru has been a major Japanese naval base. It is situated on a perfectly sheltered bay, approached from the sea by a long narrow channel that forks into two anchorages some seven kilometers apart. In the eastern anchorage, on this bright Respect for the Aged Day, lay three destroyers, two minesweepers, and four gleaming torpedo boats, all flying the Japanese naval ensign, as well as a rusty Panamanian freighter and two Liberian tankers in dry dock. Four little boys stood in a line by a bus stop pissing at all these ships through the wire netting, while their kimonoed grandmother, weighed down with carrier bags, looked on in satisfaction.

On a school sports field fringed with refreshment tents a fancy dress carnival was in progress. Five fat middle-aged men dressed as bumble-bees were performing a desultory conga, their yellow-and-black bellies wobbling like blancmanges and their paper wings catching each other in the eye. In another part of the field eight younger men were prancing up and down with large cardboard penises tied between their legs—perhaps a sign of Respect for the Aged. I stopped to drink some lemon-ade but quickly attracted more frothing children than the bumblebees and penises combined, so I emptied the paper cup in two gulps and plodded off down the highway.

Because its twin anchorages are so far apart, the city is divided into two sectors, East Maizuru and West Maizuru, and these are separated on the landward side by eight kilometers of road and a curved, unlit tunnel. Emerging from this tunnel at about four o'clock in the after-noon, I was forced to leap onto the grass verge by a car that came screeching up the slope toward the tunnel entrance at about twice the speed limit. As the car approached, the driver gave me four loud blasts on his two-tone horn, stuck his head out of the open window, and yelled "Gaijin! Gaijin! Gaijin!" at the top of his voice. I barely had time to glimpse his laughing face before the car had swept past me into the tunnel, slammed on its brakes as the driver saw the curve, spun with a sickening squeal of rubber across the road, and smacked into the tunnel wall.

I stood on the grass verge open-mouthed. Another car was racing up the slope after the first and I did the only thing I could think of to stop it, which was to wave my arms at it like a demented windmill. The driver stared, grinned, muttered something to his giggling passenger, and shot by me into the tunnel. A split second later there was another nerve-grating screech of brakes and the sound, amplified by the tunnel echoes, of two Liberian tankers colliding.

I struggled out of my pack and had begun running back into the tunnel when a motorcyclist came up the slope at a sensible speed and I managed to stop him and explain what had happened. He suggested that I find a phone and call the police while he—being Japanese and so more obviously sane—stand there and flag down oncoming drivers. I shouldered my pack and sped off down the road in top gear till I came to a yard where an old man was loading crates of beer onto a little delivery truck.

"Can I use your phone?" I panted.

"Why, what's up?"

"It's an emergency!"

The old man picked his teeth.

"What sort of an emergency?"

I explained the accident.

"Who d'you want to phone?"

"The police, of course."

The old man spat out his toothpick and puffed out his chest in what struck me as a well-rehearsed impersonation of Kojak.

"I'll do it," he growled. "I can do it in Japanese."

And he rolled off airily across the yard while I turned away toward West Maizuru mouthing Swahili, a language I do not speak.

Five minutes later two police cars and a wailing ambulance roared by me heading for the tunnel. It took me three quarters of an hour to reach the center of West Maizuru and during this tramp it occurred to me that, since I was the only witness to the accident, I ought to make a proper report of it. So I marched full of public spirit into the first Swahili-speaking police box I came to.

"You know that accident . . . ," I began.

The younger of the two policemen in the box stood picking bits of lint off his cuffs and the older one sat gazing at the ceiling, tapping a pencil on his gray metal desk.

"What accident is that, then?"

"In the tunnel about fifty minutes ago. Two cars. I was the only witness."

The younger policeman took control.

"I expect they'll be dealing with that at the main station."

"I thought I'd better make a report."

"Thank you."

"So here I am."

"Yes, well, they'll know more about it at the main station."

"Do you think I should go there?"

"You can if you like."

The older policeman stopped tapping his pencil and started to twirl it like a little baton.

"Whereabouts is the main station?"

The directions involved half the buses in Maizuru.

"Can't I walk?"

"It's much too far."

"Well, wouldn't it be possible to phone from here?"

"No," interrupted the older policeman, "I don't think that will be necessary. Why don't you just forget about it? I'm sure they'll have all the details they need."

A bit peeved that my sense of public spirit had been so bluntly nipped in the bud, I asked about a place to spend the night and with this the policemen seemed on firmer ground. But over dinner I was nagged by a nasty thought. Suppose the driver of the first car had been charged with dangerous driving—as he certainly ought to be. He might have made me a part of his defense: "There was this gaijin, you see . . . a real one . . . and he was dancing through the tunnel wearing a cardboard penis. . . ." So I obtained from the ryokan's telephone directory the address of the main West Maizuru police station and went there as soon as I had finished eating.

The policemen on duty had just finished eating too—there was a

175

pile of unwashed noodle bowls on one of the desks—and as I strolled in through the glass doors a TV commentator was announcing that the count on Oh Sadaharu was one strike and one ball.

"I've come about that accident."

One strike, two balls.

The two policemen at the desk glanced briefly away from the TV set and one nudged the other.

"That accident in the tunnel . . ."

The nudged policeman stood up, straightened his tunic, and ambled over to the counter where I was standing.

"I think I was the only person who saw it, you see, so I thought I'd better come and tell you what happened."

"Tunnel?"

"Between East and West Maizuru. About four o'clock."

"Oh, yes. That tunnel."

"There was an accident there."

"How do you know?"

"I saw it. I'm the only witness."

The policeman drummed his fingers on the counter.

"You'd better talk to the officer in charge. Oi! Ono!" he called. "Come out here a minute, will you?"

And the youngest policeman I had so far had to deal with poked his head round a door on the other side of the room with a single yellow noodle still dangling from the corner of his mouth.

"Here's a foreigner who saw that accident in the tunnel."

One strike, three balls.

Officer Ono swallowed his noodle and came briskly over to the counter, buttoning his tunic. The other policeman ambled back to the TV set where the catcher and pitcher were conferring. I explained to Officer Ono what had happened at the tunnel, and he wrote down everything I said very carefully on a sheet of ruled paper. I estimated the car's speed and drew a diagram of its erratic swerve into the tunnel wall. Then I told him what I thought had caused the accident.

"The driver was looking at me, you see, and yelling 'Gaijin! Gaijin! Gaijin!' at the top of his voice."

Officer Ono put down the pencil he had been making his notes with and looked across at the other two policemen, who were distracted from the TV screen long enough to glance from me to him and

176

chuckle. I finished with the part about the motorcyclist and the phone call.

"Yes," said Officer Ono, who had not written any of the last part down, "that confirms what the other witnesses told us."

The pitching coach had strolled across to the mound, and one of the seated policemen took this opportunity to bark a quick order at Officer Ono, who blinked, thanked me, and made straight for his door.

"Don't you need my name and address or anything?"

"No, I don't think that will be necessary."

"I see. That's all, then, is it?"

"Yes, indeed. Goodnight and thank you very much."

I never found out whether Oh reached first base or behind which tree the other witnesses had been lurking, but the incident has a post-script. When I returned to Tokyo at the end of my journey, I wrote to the police in West Maizuru to ask whether anyone had been seriously injured in the accident, and I received a postcard from Officer Nino-miya of the Traffic Division, which said in part:

"Thank you very much for your recent polite inquiry. We checked our records at once and discovered that no injury was reported. The driver of the car was eighteen." His name and full address followed. "Two of his friends were with him in the car but, being young and strong in body, they came to no harm. All of the officers here at the station would like to express their profound thanks for the utmost cooperation you rendered on that occasion. Please do not fail to drop in and see us when you are next in our vicinity."

Respect for the Aged Day ended with me dropping in elsewhere for a sizable beer and the Hiroshima Carp beating the Yomiuri Giants 4–3.

⟩⟨

I left Maizuru, striding through the suburbs where elderly women sold vegetables off the pavements and Russian sailors tried on cheap woolen jackets in the cramped, dark shops on the highway. Then I turned north along the bank of a deep, full-flowing river, and just before coming out on the seacoast again I passed under a railway bridge that, a moment before, an orange-painted train had crossed. I stood and watched the train cross the bridge and felt a strong com-

177

pulsion to stride into the next little station I came to, buy a ticket, and rejoin human life. It wasn't that I felt more than usually tired, though I had had a week of insomniac nights, lying awake from two to five each morning watching the dawn creep into some unfamiliar sky. Simply, there was a homeliness about the rattling train; an everyday taken-for-granted matter-of-factness that contrasted brazenly with the ridiculous aches in muscles that I was still only just discovering I had.

Beyond the railway arch I could see the sea crashing in heavy white breakers on a beach, and above the last of the bare estuary fields kites wheeled, uttering their strange high-pitched mew as they searched for small creatures made homeless by the harvest.

I had become obsessed with distance, and I noted every day's total in neat script in my diary, adding it to the week's and the month's and the journey's. This was my eightieth day on the road and the previous night I had logged 1,997 kilometers. When I reached Sapporo I thought I had done something respectable, and at Hakodate I thought I had done something uncommon. At Niigata I thought I had done something admirable, and at Kanazawa something remarkable. At Maizuru I thought I had done something astonishing, and I expected to reach Shimonoseki feeling that I had done something incredible. But watching this little train rattle across its bridge while the kites wheeled and the breakers crashed, I wondered whether I would reach Cape Sata knowing I had done something mad.

Amanohashidate—the Floating Bridge of Heaven—is a narrow sandbar about three and a half kilometers long which stretches across the Bay of Miyazu, enclosing half of it like a lagoon. Just as Kenrokuen in Kanazawa is one of the Three Most Beautiful Landscape Gardens in Japan, so Amanohashidate is considered one of the Three Most Beautiful Scenic Places. The habit of counting and classifying things is deeply ingrained among the guardians of Japan's natural assets, as the explanatory English signboard at the southern end of Amanohashidate makes particularly clear. The main section of the sandbar, it records, is 2,425 meters long and has an area of 130,484 square meters. At its greatest width it is 149 meters across and at its slimmest 19. The "investigation" of 1934 revealed that there were 3,990 pine trees on it, while a second "investigation" in May 1950 showed that this number had risen to 4,522. Such investigations, then, not only content minor government officials but, on the evidence of these statistics, excite the pine trees too. The signboard also advises that the "distance necessary time on foot" from the small revolving bridge at the southern tip of the bar to Kasamatsu Park at the northern end is exactly sixty minutes, and so I set out jauntily along the sandy track that on this sunny September day was splattered with the shadows of the busily pro-creating pines.

Few people, it seems, walk the length of the sandbar. At Chionji temple, near the southern end, a group of tourists had just broken off their prayers at the urgent beck of several bullhorns and had rushed down the old temple steps and boarded a boat for a sightseeing cruise. That is certainly a better way of appreciating the sandbar as a whole than to walk along it, where only the details are viewable; but it was the details that I liked most.

Whether they are procreating or not, pine trees are nicely eccentric plants, and it is not an accident that the Japanese accord ancient ones the same veneration due hermits and saints. Nor is it only ancient pines that possess a touch of human idiosyncrasy. At the narrowest, least protected point of the sandbar, where the full force of the wind cuts across it from the open sea, the trees are fiercely, tortuously bent, as though a life spent resisting the siege of gales had driven them to permanent distraction. Walking, I had the leisure to see them as in-dividual creatures rather than as globs of green lost in a larger land-scape, and perhaps because of this I left the sandbar feeling not that it was heavenly at all, but that, as with Eiheiji, its proper element was the earth. Others have clearly felt the same:

> *Ah, floating bridge!*
> *Why does the ferryman*
> *grow older?*

asked the poet Hosokawa Yusai, disappointed perhaps that, on the Bridge of Heaven, men, like pine trees, shake and bend as they age.

By tradition, the finest view of Amanohashidate is obtained neither by walking along it nor by circling it in a boat, but by climbing the hill at the northern end and looking down at it from the height of Kasamatsu Park—the Park of the Umbrella Pine. Nor, as I discovered on traipsing up to the park, do you simply stand and look at it—that would be far too earthly. What you do is climb onto one of three stone benches, stand with your back to the Bay of Miyazu, and then bend down and look at the Bridge of Heaven from between your spread thighs. This remarkable method of viewing scenery is supposed to give you the impression that the Floating Bridge is actually floating; and it is worth wondering what the person who first made that discovery was up to at the time.

Anyway, the sight of group after group of Japanese tourists going through the motions of this obligatory ritual provided me with a solid hour's entertainment. I especially liked the attempts of the girls wearing skirts to prevent the stiff sea breeze from revealing other heavenly things and the attempts of the middle-aged businessmen to keep both their dignity and their spectacles intact. Best of all I enjoyed the performance of one keen amateur photographer who, not content with simply peering at the sandbar through his thighs, exposed about half a roll of film through them too, which involved a dexterity that one had to envy. (Questions about why he didn't take his photographs the right way up and stick them in his album upside down are idle: he was having A Good Time.) He was also just about the only viewer in an hour who looked at the heavenly bridge for more than two or three seconds. Most got it over with as quickly as possible, climbing down off the benches and resuming an upright position with a great flood of relief on their faces. Some months before, the Mona Lisa had been exhibited at a Tokyo gallery and had attracted such throngs of art lovers that the time each was allowed to spend in front of it had to be carefully rationed. The gallery owners decided eventually that the optimum time for viewing the Mona Lisa was seven seconds, and this was felt by most art lovers to be satisfactory. It is not surprising, then, that two or three seconds suffice for the Bridge of Heaven. Mount Fuji generally rates five or six and the Second Coming of Christ will merit ten.

Of course I couldn't end my visit to Kasamatsu Park without testing tradition for myself, so when a break finally occurred in the long stream of people, I marched to the middle bench, stepped up onto it, bent down smartly, and looked at the sandbar through my thighs. It did a jackknife, a triple somersault, and a belly flop, though I am prepared to believe that its acrobatic talents owed as much to the three bottles of beer I had drunk as to any bodily contortions. (Later on I tried viewing the Umbrella Pine through my thighs, but it was much less frisky and looked nothing like an umbrella.)

In the early evening, back on the road, the four black chimneys of the Iwataki Power Station added their own thick clouds to the September dusk that was creeping down. One by one the lights went on in the ring of hotels round Miyazu Bay, quiet now, but soon to pack in the droves who descend annually when the leaves turn. Ahead of me, a mass of gray-blue shadows, lay the mountains of western Honshu, which I must cross in a grueling two-week trek before meeting the coast again at Hiroshima. The lights were coming on in the city of Miyazu, too, and in the last few pleasure boats of the afternoon as they made their rounds of the sandbar. Steeped in its own shadows, with the clouds darkening above it, Amanohashidate lay now like some half-exhausted Nessie—no heavenly bridge at all, but an earthbound prankster that came home each evening gratefully to roost.

7

The Thunder God's Eye

FROM ALMOST ALL the wooden worksheds along the roads of rural Kyoto came the clop and click of handlooms weaving sashes for the kimono shops of the old capital. On a small grassy plot near one of the worksheds a woman tended a bed of fat white silkworms, churning them round and round with their mulberry leaves as though she were churning cheese. I passed a small pond of carp—part ornament, part pantry—and I remembered being told by my twenty-three-year-old actress friend—gone, alas, with the wind—that the gold variety of carp is never eaten, security being a privilege of the beautiful.

Three or four of the houses in one small village were being sprayed inside and out with a foul-smelling pesticide—probably in an effort to rid them of white ants, but no doubt equally effective against the cockroaches that are the everlasting companions to the Japanese summer. Japanese literature has made much of the insect world—usually to evoke that elegant sense of pathos, called *sabi,* with which so much Japanese poetry is redolent. This is a haiku by the master, Basho:

> *The pity of it . . .*
> *beneath the helmet cries*
> *the long-horned grasshopper.*

This one is by Shohaku:

> *The pine cricket*
> *sings in vain*
> *in my house abandoned to the weeds.*

But I have never come across an elegantly pathetic cockroach, nor heard of one being celebrated in verse. To be born a *gokiburi* (even the Japanese word for the thing is spat out of the mouth with three nasty plosives) is to be born eternally despised.

The lodging I found on my eighty-first night was in a little ryokan that adjoined a dark, cramped restaurant where, despite appearances, I had one of the best dinners of my journey. Throughout it, the old man and woman who ran the place—and who seemed quite content with one customer for the evening—quizzed me about my experiences since birth, the old woman confining herself to practical matters such as how I had managed to survive the London fog (*all* Japanese people are brought up believing that the residents of London wage a perpetual battle to breathe), while the old man ventured a deeper line of inquiry that ranged from comparisons between Queen Elizabeth and the emperor to reflections on war and the price of defeat.

"No one respects the emperor nowadays—not since we Japanese lost the war. The crown prince, yes; and there is a lot of affection for Princess Michiko (the commoner the crown prince met on a tennis court and married), but not for the emperor, not since we lost. Japan is such a small country, you see—not able to sustain a loss like that."

"I should have thought Japan sustained it pretty well," I said, "judging by the prevailing economy. We used to have a joke in England during the sixties: if Japan loses another war, she'll rule the world."

"Ah," replied the old man with a sharp intake of breath, "such jokes are part of the spoils of victory. The people who make jokes like that have never known how it feels to be defeated."

The conversation turned to my walk through Japan, and the old man made a comment that I have thought about often and still don't understand:

"You're walking from Hokkaido to Kyushu. You're lucky. No Japanese could do that since we lost the war. Our spirits shrank with defeat, you see. We're not big enough for such a journey."

In the morning, over a breakfast of grilled fish and fresh green peppers, the old man brought out an old battered photo album and showed me a picture of two American girls who had stayed at his ryokan, how long ago he couldn't remember. Neither of the girls could speak Japanese, he explained, and the man in the picture with them was a local schoolteacher who had been called in as an interpreter. After breakfast the old man insisted on taking pictures of me too,

183

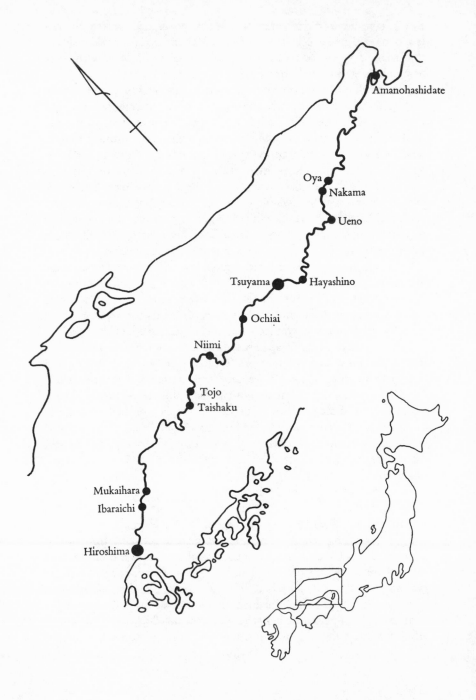

Amanohashidate

Oya
Nakama

Ueno

Tsuyama   Hayashino

Ochiai

Niimi

Tojo
Taishaku

Mukaihara

Ibaraichi

Hiroshima

standing first with him, then with the old woman, then with two grandchildren who had been summoned from a house across the street, and finally with a man who I think had come to read the gas meter.

The old woman had washed my jeans and shirt for me the previous evening, and we discovered that they were not quite dry. She was almost beside herself with dismay.

"Oh, couldn't you stay another day? You could keep your yukata on and go out for a stroll in that, and I *know* they'd be beautifully dry by tomorrow. . . ."

No, I laughed, I had to be on my way, and I pulled the damp clothes on and fastened my pack straps.

"Sign the visitors' book for us," the old man said, and as I did I noticed that I was the only guest who had signed the book all summer.

"You have a large spirit," was the old man's parting comment. "It doesn't surprise me that you won."

Though the mornings and evenings had grown cooler, there was still only a faint tinge of autumn in the hills. The narrow road—no longer a highway—rose steeply away from the already distant coast, and large tourist buses lumbered down it on their way to Amanohashidate, the drivers honking me off the curves, the passengers scuffling to gape at me through the large rear windows.

At noon that day I left Kyoto and entered the middle hills of Hyogo Prefecture. Only three prefectures in Honshu span the width of the whole island from the Japan Sea coast to the Pacific or the Inland Sea, and Hyogo is one of them. Perhaps because of this, I found it a prefecture with a comparatively rich spread of rural dialects. In Kobe, the prefectural capital, they often swear blind they can't understand a word the old women say up on the northern coast, and during the three hard days I spent trekking through Hyogo's central mountains I'm certain I encountered more oddities of language than I did on most other parts of my journey. This will surprise a lot of Japanese people, who have been taught to think of Aomori and Kagoshima, at the extreme ends of the mainland, as offering the ultimate in quirky Japanese. I have never found this: partly because Aomori is one of the prefectures I know best, but also because, in those faraway places, most people make a conscious effort, when confronted with a foreign face, to speak as straightforward a form of the language as they can. In Hyogo they simply didn't bother—which put a strain on my ears as well as on my feet.

Still the rattle of the weavers' looms echoed along the twisting roads, punctuated occasionally by the suppressed hysteria of a long triple row of battery hens. In the grocer's shops I stopped in for refreshment I was told again and again and again how small a country Japan is, and asked what military base I was from. If I was in a conversational mood, I would sometimes take the opportunity to point out that Japan is twice the size of my country, larger than all but three of the something-like-thirty countries of Europe, that Holland (from where many of Japan's original ideas about the outside world came from) is one-twentieth Japan's size, and that Switzerland (which Japanese advertisements depict as a vast, airy country with great tracts of pasture and limitless ski slopes) would fit comfortably inside the island of Kyushu. I didn't take this opportunity too often, though, because I could see that I was not believed; and if I had added that I was neither in the military nor even an American, I should have run the risk of being hounded out of the shops as an inveterate liar.

Fewer kites wheeled over the fields, for here, in these high villages, most of the rice had yet to be harvested and the rats and snakes were still hidden safe among it. The further I walked the steeper the hills grew, the thicker, darker, and smokier the woods, till late in the afternoon, just outside the little town of Oya, a car stopped and the driver directed me without any preamble to the local church.

"Church?"

"You're a Christian, aren't you?"

"No, I'm not."

"Oh well, then, better try the police box."

And with dusk already settling on the roofs and an audience of schoolboys trailing after me, I decided I was weary enough to take the driver's advice; so I located the one police box in Oya—a tiny lean-to in front of a private house—strolled into it, and introduced myself to Officer Uehara of the Hyogo Constabulary.

Officer Uehara was a short tubby man with a short tubby wife who bustled away to put the kettle on. The schoolboys had trailed me right up to the police box and were crowding round the open doorway

186

watching Officer Uehara fidget with the collar of his brown sports shirt.

"I am a Japanese policeman," he announced to start the conversation off, tapping his nose with his index finger.

"I thought you were," I said. "You're sitting in a Japanese police box."

"Yes," he agreed. "That's right. I am."

The schoolboys kicked one another.

"Show me your passport, will you, please?"

I produced once again the alien registration card that all foreign residents are obliged to carry. Officer Uehara took it gingerly in his fingers and read it through from beginning to end. He noted with approval that the photograph was recent and that the fingerprint was nice and clear.

"Do you know," he said, handing it back, "that's the first time I've ever seen one of these alien's cards. They're handy, aren't they?"

"Handy?"

"For remembering things. Your address and so on. Now, what can I do for you?" And he glared at the schoolboys who glared solemnly back at him.

I asked if he could recommend a place to stay, and after a few moments' thought, he picked up the phone and dialed a number from memory. But the ringing tone had scarcely begun when an idea occurred to him and he quietly placed the receiver back on its rest. His wife brought two bowls of tea to the table and shooed the schoolboys away from the doorway with a single imperious gesture. They were clearly far more awed by her than they were by Officer Uehara.

"Would you mind showing me the contents of your wallet?"

"Wallet?"

"Just the notes, I mean."

I counted my money out onto the table and Officer Uehara viewed it with great satisfaction.

"It's Japanese money!"

"Yes, of course."

"Well, that's a relief, isn't it?"

"I beg your pardon?"

"Quite a relief. Yes, I see. You can put it away now. Come on, I'll take you to the ryokan."

187

Which he did, but the ryokan was closed, so we strolled across the road to a second ryokan, but the owner had to go to Osaka early in the morning and was not accepting any guests.

"Have you eaten?" asked Officer Uehara as we stood at a loss outside the ryokan door.

"No, I was expecting to eat when I'd found a room."

"Tell you what," he said, rubbing his chin, "there's a minshuku at Nakama, about six kilometers up into the hills. People stay there when they go fishing in the river. It's a nice place. I'll give them a ring for you. They won't be full this time of year, but I doubt if they'll do dinner at such short notice. You can eat in the restaurant here if you like, and then I'll run you up there in the car."

"That's very kind of you, but I'll have to walk."

"Eh?"

"I'm on a walking trip, you see."

It was dark now, and the wife had switched on the light in the police box. The first evening stars glowed faintly above the low hills and Officer Uehara stood biting his lip.

"Curry rice?"

"Whatever you like."

"You can't walk, you know. It's already dark."

"I've got a pocket torch."

"It's not safe."

"I'm used to walking."

"Not in these hills. We'll eat here."

And he steered me into a small, dimly lit shop where a man with one eye was serving two teenage motorcyclists a couple of fatty pork cutlets.

"Curry rice," ordered Officer Uehara, "and a bottle of beer. He's got a passport."

But before the beer came he was biting his lip again.

"It'd be no trouble. The car, I mean. We could be there inside twenty minutes. Walking, it'll take you a couple of hours, and the road's a mess—bridges and turnings, and no lights, none at all."

"I'll find my way."

"It's not that easy."

"There's absolutely nothing to worry about."

"Please . . ."

"What?"

The curry came, with rice and beer the same temperature. Officer Uehara went into the back room to telephone the minshuku and one of the spotty motorcyclists, who had listened to our conversation with bated breath, hissed at me across the table:

"Are you a friend of Uehara's?"

"I suppose I am."

"He swears something terrible."

". . . he's got a passport and everything," came the officer's voice on the telephone, and a minute later he was back to tell me that the minshuku in the hills had a room for me.

"Look, won't you reconsider about the car? I wouldn't mind a drive, honestly . . ."

"No, really. I haven't been inside any kind of vehicle for nearly three months and I don't want to get inside one now. Besides, six kilometers is nothing when you've walked two thousand and sixty-seven."

"It's just . . ."

"What?"

"Be careful."

"What of?"

Officer Uehara was silent for a long moment, and I was spooning up the last of the curry rice when he said, softly but quite distinctly:

"Foxes."

"What?"

"Be careful of the foxes. Their spirits can bewitch you."

I looked up expecting to see a broad grin, but there was not the least trace of humor in his face.

We said goodbye at the door of the restaurant, and Officer Uehara looked sheepishly down at his feet.

"Don't think badly of us, will you?"

"What do you mean?"

"That business about the alien's card and the money and so on. Don't take it the wrong way. Remember us kindly when you think about Oya."

"Thanks for the meal."

"You're very welcome."

"And I'll take special care to avoid the foxes."

Officer Uehara's tubby face showed not the remotest flicker of a smile.

In the starlight the narrow road wound up and up into the hills, crossing dark streams on small stone bridges, winding past the last isolated buildings of the town and into the darkness of the forest. I stopped outside one lonely house and listened to a woman singing in her bathroom. The night air was warm, the stars bright silver, and by the time I reached the minshuku at Nakama the white moon had risen high over the woods.

"Welcome. Didn't see anything on the road, I suppose?"

. "Like what?"

"Animals, or anything like that?"

"Foxes?"

"I was thinking more of wild boars. The first bus in the morning often drives a crowd of them off the road. A hundred and fifty kilograms some of them are, with acceleration like a guided missile. You were all right in a car of course. Pretty scary on foot. Where did Uehara drop you?"

I never told him. But late that night, lying in my futon, I watched the shadows the moon cast on the pale paper windows of my room—moving shadows that crept from wall to wall, large as sheep, silent as the moon itself. It was dawn before I fell asleep.

The stream that people came to fish in bubbled away from the minshuku door, and the empty road followed it steeply into the hills. A red helicopter hammered low over the paddies, driving the kites and the crows away, its shadow flicking across the golden rice like a grasshopper out of some absurdly inelegant haiku. Ever more steeply the road wound and twisted, through villages whose houses were strung out along it like beads. Firewood stood stacked outside the wooden bathrooms, sometimes reaching up to the tin roofs, and in the hills high above the villages the rice crop was squashed into cramped, narrow terraces that looked more like a giant's footholds on the mountainside than arable fields.

These three days in the mountains of Hyogo—during which I covered 113 kilometers—took me up and down some of the steepest slopes of the journey. A balding young man in one of the villages I walked through told me that an NHK camera team had been there some months before to film the *inuwashi*—the rare golden eagle that is a specially protected creature in Japan. They had come loaded with cameras and tripods and had been completely unable to haul them up the vertiginous footpaths into the hills. Eventually, they had given up trying and had hired men from the local villages to lug their equipment about for them like Sherpas on a Himalayan expedition.

From the highest passes I had breathtaking views of the green deeply wooded valleys, with their sharp twists and cliffs that made it look as though a pickaxe had hacked them out of the landscape. The only eagle I came across was emblazoned on the side of a bright new loggers' truck. (Emblazoning trucks is a minor but vigorous art form in some parts of Japan.) The eagle was perched, rather precariously, on a fanciful American flag, while a bewigged geisha with a pipe in her mouth —the work of some inglorious Utamaro—adorned the other side of the truck, and two gold carp, protected by their beauty as the eagle is by the atrophied calf muscles of NHK cameramen, disported themselves on the tailboard.

Toward noon, I passed a shaved bit of mountainside that signboards told me was a ski slope, and emerged from the steepest of the hills onto Highway 29, where I found a drive-in and had a lunch of noodles while the proprietor and his family hooked fish out of a filthy dirty tank and tossed them with unsettling, secretive smiles into a tin bucket to die.

At about four o'clock I came to a part of the river that had been turned into a lake by the construction of a dam. In a dark, tiny sweet shop near the dam an old woman advised me to spend the night at the *Saikuringu Taaminaru* ("Cycling Terminal"), a hot-spring lodging house which I presume was so called because it catered to the hundreds of students who came through these hills in the summer on bikes. I recognized the turnoff to the lodging house, which I reached about an hour later, by a brightly lit electric sign glowing an effusive welcome. The place itself was about a kilometer and a half along a track that ran up into the hills, and when I arrived a large barking dog greeted me equally effusively. The doors of the lodging house were curtained and locked and it took five minutes of rattling them to rouse the white-shirted custodian, who bustled out finally to tell me that they were closed.

"But you've got a sign all lit up down on the highway."

"Yes. We always keep it lit."

"What for, for goodness' sake?"

"To make people feel welcome."

"But you're closed!"

191

"That's right."

Which was, perhaps, the most quintessentially Oriental conversation of the entire trip.

I stamped back down to the highway in the dusk in an unrelentingly British frame of mind. The sign, as I passed it, still glowed its vacuous welcome and if I had been a bother boy I would have put a boot through it. Being a man of letters, though, I contented myself with a few letters, stamping on under a risen moon and a rapidly darkening, star-flecked sky until I reached the little town of Ueno and trudged about in search of a ryokan.

At the first one I came to I opened the door and called out in a hearty voice. Beyond the open screen, in the darkened living room, I could see an elderly man in a white vest sitting opposite a Buddhist altar for the dead. I called out to him five or six times, but he simply sat staring across the small room at the photograph of a woman on the altar, flanked by flowers and misted by incense smoke that drifted like a fog through the whole building.

I crept out of the door as quietly as I could and turned away down the pitch-black street, using the pocket torch I carried for tunnels. There seemed to be no lights in the town at all, nor any shops open, and the windows of the second ryokan I found were as black and empty as their surroundings. It was very eerie, as though the whole silent township were awaiting the passing of some grim angel. Yet the man in the second ryokan welcomed me, and we sat together in his fly-spattered living room while he watched me eat a cold steak smothered with sauce out of which I picked a dead mosquito so deftly with my chopsticks that the man didn't know whether to apologize or applaud.

Halfway through the meal we were visited by a member of the Communist Party selling copies of their newspaper, *Akahata* (Red Flag). I could hear the conversation in the entrance hall as I picked a second mosquito out of my miso soup.

"I don't think much of the emperor, but we need him to preserve the traditions of our country. I don't think much of your lot either, but I'll buy a paper for the sake of democracy. I've got an English bloke eating steak in my living room. Why don't you come in and have an argument with him?"

But the party member tactfully retreated, and *Red Flag* served to mop up the spilled sauce and miso soup.

As I walked out of the town next morning I saw some very decorative election posters. One was of an elderly politician with a portable cassette recorder, thrusting a large microphone urgently forward, perhaps to elicit opinions from his constituents or perhaps to encourage them to sing. There was an even better one further on—a plump middle-aged candidate for the House of Councillors in a red-and-black striped rugby jersey running forward with a beautifully polished rugby ball under his arm and not a pomaded hair out of place. Perhaps the helicopter had something to do with elections too, for it was thudding about the sky again this morning, swooping over the streets of Ueno that were as lifeless by daylight as they had been by night.

In the next little town I trudged through it was Road Safety Day, and the town hall had mounted an exhibition of photographs of mangled cars and bicycles. Along the main street came a jeep with two town hall officials in it and a loudspeaker broadcasting a woman's voice saying, "Ladies, aren't you worried about your husbands?" I suppose this had something to do with road safety, but in a place where foxes bewitch police constables and signs welcome you effusively to places that are closed, who knows what husbands get up to?

By midafternoon I was nearing the highest point of another mountain pass. The sweat on my back was biting cold whenever I stopped, but despite the discomfort, I sat for a few minutes' rest, watching a gang of road repairers, the men lounging in the seats of their bulldozers while elderly women stooped to hand-mix cement. Then I walked on through the pass and so crossed out of Hyogo Prefecture and into Okayama. The Kinki Region had taken me a bare seven days, but they had been very hard ones. Now, on the last leg of my walk through Honshu, I was entering the Chugoku ("Middle Country") District— not to be confused with Chubu (the "Middle District," from Niigata to Fukui) nor with the Japanese word for China, which is also Chugoku (that land having been known throughout most of its history as the Middle Kingdom). "Middle" at first seems an odd thing to call this extreme western tip of the main island, until you remember that the first Japanese settlements were almost certainly in the northern half of Kyushu while the first real center of political power grew up in the Nara basin. It is midway between these two pivotal points that the Middle Country lies.

The afternoon was overcast, with a thin mist of rain on the distant peaks, and the road turned steeply down into the teeth of a strong mountain wind. The hours spent trudging up mountains like this strain

193

the muscles of your calves and thighs, while the hours spent trudging down the other sides can send strange pains shooting through your feet. Sometimes it's hard to say which is worse, and the relief you feel on reaching a summit is always short-lived. In the first village I came to in the valley, I passed a group of children on their way home from school. As often, it was impossible not to notice the difference in attitude between the sexes. First I passed two little boys who giggled their heads off and screamed back at the four girls following them, "*Gaijin da! Gaijin da!*" and ran off shouting "I rub yoo!" When the little girls passed me they simply nodded and said "*Kaerimashita,*" which in this part of Japan is the greeting that schoolchildren are taught to use when they encounter their elders. For most of the trip this had been the pattern—jeered at by boys, greeted sensibly by girls—and I found myself regretting again and again that not a single one of the election posters I had been passing bore a woman's face.

At the Japan Synthetic Rubber Company a group of cheery women hung out of the second-story windows to get a look at me, and at a grocer's shop another cheery woman rang a ryokan to book me a room.

"Shall I just tell them it's a man?" she asked a bit timidly.

"No," I said, "you'd better tell them I'm foreign."

But when she did, the woman on the other end of the line grew so flustered that I had to take the receiver and spend two minutes persuading her that I wouldn't bite her head off, and then another two minutes assuring her that this was not all some kind of elaborate joke, since she couldn't believe that anyone who spoke Japanese could possibly be something else.

"I thought you were having me on," she confessed when I finally reached her ryokan after disappointing two schoolgirls on motor scooters who had asked me to write my name in their notebooks and were visibly upset when I spoke to them in their own language.

"Make him speak English! Make him speak English!" shouted four grubby little boys who had tailed me for more than a kilometer and were now crowding into the entrance hall of the ryokan gaping; but the woman shooed them all away.

"People round here have got a passion for languages," she explained, unwrapping the beef she had rushed out to buy because no foreigner, whether Japanese-speaking or not, could possibly digest fish. She charged me an extra thousand yen for the beef, and the yukata she gave me to wear after my bath had "Japanese National Railways" printed all over it. She was, I saw, cost-conscious.

꒰

The Idemitsu Petroleum Company used to run a series of TV commercials which showed customers—or sometimes just people asking directions or caught in the rain—being welcomed to one of their petrol stations with tea and cakes and a display of friendliness not normally met with except in fairy godmothers. I used to scoff. I no longer do. As I was tramping past an Idemitsu stand next morning, a man in a peaked cap with a scar on his chin came running out to invite me in for coffee, and in order to make sure that we communicated properly, he thrust his face as close to mine as he could get it without giving me a godmotherly kiss.

"Where are you going?"

"Hayashino."

"I'll take you there in the car if you like."

"No, thanks very much. I'd like to walk."

"Ha ha ha! Well, where were you born? New York?"

"No, London."

"What part of London? Scotland or Wales?"

We sat inside the office on smart vinyl chairs while the godmotherly woman who tended the cash register bustled about making cups of instant coffee (adding powdered milk called Creap) and a petrol pump attendant in striped overalls peered shyly in at the doorway.

"Is it true that English people have only one bath a week because there's a shortage of water?"

"No, it's because they're congenitally dirty."

"You're not dirty, though. How come you're walking? Have you run out of money or what is it?"

"Are you sure you're English?" wondered the bustling godmother. "You don't look much like James Bond."

I stayed nearly an hour at the petrol station, drinking coffee and Creap and eating cakes, and before I left, the shy attendant plucked up his courage and asked me for my autograph.

"What ever do you want my autograph for?"

"For the memory," he whispered, blushing to the roots of his hair.

Far to the southwest a ribbon of traffic growled along the Chugoku

195

Expressway. A little girl on my older, narrower road skipped happily home from school with her yellow satchel on her back and was immersed in the choking black fumes of a diesel truck that she did not even appear to notice. A small gray van stopped in front of me and one of the two women in it got out and flapped round onto the pavement.

"Hello! Hello! Can you speak Japanese? You can? Phew! That's a relief! We thought we'd better stop and ask. You'd have been in trouble if you couldn't."

What kind of trouble she never said, and I didn't think it proper to ask, but she gave me a *nashi* (a hard, juicy fruit, something between an apple and a pear) to make sure that starvation would not add to my woes, and told me that it came from the seacoast to the north and that *nashi* grow best on slopes near the sea.

"You ought to go up to the coast too, you know. You'd get into less trouble up there."

Evening came on, and in the town of Hayashino, after asking at several rice and sakè shops (shops selling rice and its byproducts are ideal places to make inquiries since they are often the oldest established shops in the district), I found a beautiful seventy-year-old ryokan, full of odd, dark, stepped corridors and smoky bamboo screens, where I passed the eighty-sixth night of my journey. The only other guest was a traveling salesman who ate dinner with me and who confessed himself astonished when I made the weekly telephone call to my wife.

"Your wife? What ever for?"

"So she won't worry."

"That's funny. In my case it's exactly the opposite. I'm usually away from home about ten days a month, and if I phoned my wife she'd think there was something wrong with me."

The food was good and there was lots of it, and when we had stuffed ourselves with more *nashi,* we settled down to lie on our elbows, listening to the night sounds of Hayashino—the cry of a child, the squeak of some late shopper's bicycle, the sharp sound of the wooden clappers that in the dry season warn against fire—and in this satisfied, half-somnolent state, we ruminated on the problems of the world.

"What do you think of all these Indochinese refugees coming to Japan?" the salesman wondered.

"I thought there were hardly any coming. The government won't let them in."

"At the port of Fukuyama where I come from they've had to keep turning them away. It's a pity, and of course foreigners can't understand it. They're forever criticizing us for one thing or another. If it's not cars or dolphins or whales, it's refugees. But what can we do? We're such a tiny country, so mountainous, so overcrowded. . . ."

I reached for another of the hard, juicy *nashi* and thought about the empty tracts of land I had walked through in Hokkaido, where living has become so inconvenient, and of the deserted highlands of northern Akita, where farm workers have left paddies lying fallow and crammed their families into two-room city apartments, and of the southernmost of all the Japanese islands—islands such as Iriomote, so underpopulated that the government will build a house free for any Japanese family willing to settle there.

". . . no, foreigners simply can't understand, coming from countries where there's so much space for everyone. Sometimes I feel they don't want to understand—that they misinterpret us out of spite. I know, anyway, that I don't want to go abroad again. I've been to Hong Kong, Singapore, and Korea. I've never been to a white man's country and I don't think I could bear to go. They treat all Asians as inferiors, just as if we were blacks or Jews. We're not cold-hearted. We've just got no room to spare for anyone else, that's all."

We ruminated on the problems of the world for an hour more, but their solutions seemed as out of reach as though we had manacled each other's hands.

The day of the autumn equinox—September twenty-third—was hot and muggy. The old ryokan in Hayashino flew a Japanese flag to mark the national holiday, as did many of the houses and shops on the road that straggled beside the railway track into the city of Tsuyama. I reached the city by midafternoon after a fairly easy but sticky day, and was strolling through the covered shopping arcades looking for a quiet coffee shop when I suddenly found myself on television.

"Would you mind being interviewed?" bubbled the interviewer—unnecessarily, I thought, since the camera was already panning up and down my tatty figure. The interviewer was a nice-looking girl in a bright pink trouser suit, and the microphone she thrust at me, unlike the politician's in the poster, had a little yellow ribbon tied round it.

"What about?"

"Fashion," she said quite seriously, and for a moment it crossed my mind that I had stumbled onto some kind of candid comedy program. I was wearing—and the camera was busy scrutinizing—a pair of torn, patched jeans, filthy dirty mountain boots, a denim shirt in urgent need of a wash, a muddy blue towel wrapped round my neck, a leather belt with a blunt hunting knife attached to it, and a fourteen-kilogram backpack.

"Fashion?"

"Yes," said the interviewer. "For example, what colors do you especially favor in autumn?"

And so I stood in the arcade with its mirrored roof and silver tinseled lampposts, surrounded by gawping holiday shoppers, trying to make myself heard above the stereos outside the electric shops and the loudspeakers advertising nude cabarets, and discussed my preferences in haute couture. As soon as I told the girl my name, she insisted—as quite a lot of people did—on calling me Alain Delon.

"You're the same type," she giggled, batting her eyes.

Steady, I thought, not in front of five million people.

The interview ended on a slightly anticlimactic note, with the girl asking me to sing an English song and me excusing myself on the grounds that I had just walked two thousand two hundred and fifty kilometers and was a bit out of breath.

"What a sense of humor you English have!" she chirped, pinning a little badge on my stinking shirt, which said "Cette couleur est un parfum."

The autumn equinox drifted to a close with black-tied waiters in a very smart coffee shop serving me cups of Kilimanjaro, and me returning early to my ryokan in order to launder the quite unfashionable autumn smells out of my apparel.

The smells next morning were not so easily disposed of. They were pumping and shoveling out the drains along the street, and the whole neighborhood was pervaded by the ripe smell of the lavatory. This is a regular feature of traditional Japanese buildings, and in Tsuyama and several other towns of the region the communal drains themselves seemed to be mainly half-open ditches by the roadside covered with a few concrete or cast-iron slabs to stop walkers from falling in.

It had rained during the night and there was still rain in the air as I tramped out of the city. Quite a lot of people waved to me in the suburbs, so I suppose the fashion interview had been broadcast. As the suburbs gave way to country again I noticed that an unusually large number of monumental masons had set up their businesses along this road, and two or three of the showrooms I passed had notices urging customers to buy their graves now while stocks lasted. The other specialty of the region seemed to be *yokan* (sweets made of bean jelly), but for weight-conscious tourists a sign suggested live stag beetles as alternative souvenirs. Most of the time, the older road I was marching along ran parallel to the new expressway, and several people I stopped to talk with complained that the expressway had killed off their livelihoods. Towns like Ochiai were dying, they said. Perhaps the monumental masons had anticipated the demise.

And yet Ochiai was sprightly enough to boast a large yellow Sun Plaza shopping center and a *juku* (cram school) offering lessons in English to kids with dull brains or hyperambitious parents or the local "passion for languages." The cars on the old road were lively too, taking all the bends with the sharp squeal of tormented rubber that is a feature of just about every TV car commercial in Japan. The craze for "supercars" has led to a marked increase in speeding offenses on Japanese roads, and perhaps the masons had anticipated that, too— though I knew from my own experience at Maizuru that, so long as the drivers were "young and strong in body," they could survive the unlikeliest terrors of the highway.

A fishmonger's van from the Japan Sea coast was sending ear-splitting taped messages through the villages, bouncing them off the empty hills, as I left the half-deserted road and began the long hot afternoon's tramp over another sparsely populated mountain. The narrow winding path, sometimes barely wide enough for a single vehicle to scrape along it, threaded its way through plots of tomatoes, across three fine old rough stone bridges, past village shops whose little windows were full of plastic model construction kits, and later, as it came down into the lower valleys, through a gorge of towering limestone cliffs that spread a canopy like dusk across it. There were limestone quarries in the outskirts of the small city of Niimi, and by the time I had emerged onto Highway 180 and trudged the last hour or so along it into the city, I found that I had covered forty-three kilometers—the longest single day of the trip.

I was much too weary to relish a tramp through the back streets in search of a place to stay, so I decided to toss my fate once again into the hands of the local constabulary, and as it turned out, the Niimi police headquarters was among the first buildings I came to. I tottered into it and grinned at the two officers on duty, one in uniform with slick greasy hair, the other in plain clothes lounging against a tin filing cabinet, scratching the stubble on his chin.

I christened them afterwards the Roughie and the Smoothie, and it is hard to imagine two members of any profession offering a more perfect contrast. In addition to his greasy hair, the Smoothie had nails that were neatly pared, his uniform buttons neatly shone, the wooden desk in front of him looked as though he waxed and polished it twice an hour, and it was clear that he loathed me on sight. The Roughie wore a rumpled jacket with the lining hanging out of one of the pockets, and his hair stood up like the bristles on a shaving brush that had been gnawed halfway down to the handle by some starved nocturnal creature. It was pure good fortune that the Roughie out-ranked the Smoothie, for the Smoothie seemed capable of making life quite unpleasant for people like me without even trying.

The Roughie heaved himself off the filing cabinet and offered to ring a ryokan for me. He had a voice like a gravel chute which the ryokan owner on the other end of the line must have recognized, be-cause if he hadn't known it was a policeman phoning him, the voice could have panicked him into phoning the police. The Roughie came straight to the point.

"Look here, can you take a gaijin for about 3,500 yen? He speaks Jap-anese; we're speaking it now. He's hitchhiking from Hokkaido . . ."—he kept repeating this misinformation as though it were a crime I had confessed to, which the ryokan would overlook if they were chari-table. "Yes, I expect he eats fish all right. Chopsticks? Shouldn't be at all surprised . . ."

And the quiz went on for several minutes, while I stood there trying to pretend I was enjoying it. Finally the Roughie put the receiver back on its rest.

"They say they're full," he said, and scratched his head.

"They often say that when you tell them it's a gaijin," I explained. This remark peeved the Smoothie.

"They're concerned about the fact that you can't speak the lan-guage."

"What language are we speaking, then?"

"I mean properly. In case there's an emergency."

The Roughie dialed another number and during this second phone call (in which he carefully avoided saying anything about gaijin, grinning and giving me three or four conspiratorial winks), the Smoothie took the opportunity to lecture me on how I mustn't wear a knife on my belt unless I intended to use it at least once every thirty minutes.

"Well," I said, "I've been in police boxes all over Japan and you're the first person who's ever told me that."

"That's because you're a gaijin," he huffed. "They'll have known you wouldn't understand the language."

The Smoothie wanted to make me take the knife off there and then and pack it away at the bottom of my rucksack, but the Roughie said tomorrow would be soon enough for that, gave me directions to the ryokan where he had succeeded in booking a room for "a young man," winked again and wished me luck.

The ryokan carried it off pretty well at first, though as the evening wore on I got the feeling they thought they'd somehow been swindled. And, for my part, I was getting so fed up with apologizing for myself, and having to be apologized for, that I ended up having a brief, bitter row with them. I told them I wanted to phone Tokyo and they said I would have to use the pay phone, which only took ten-yen coins one at a time. That was ridiculous, I scoffed, since I should need to insert about two hundred coins at four-second intervals. So I insisted, to their unconcealed annoyance, on phoning the operator on the ryokan's private phone and getting her to tell me the time and charges. They fumed all the way through the call, and when I had finished it and gone back upstairs, I heard them ring the operator again to make sure I'd quoted them the right amount. I expect it was my language skills they mistrusted.

In the coffee shop I stopped in for breakfast one whole wall was decorated with a picture of the Matterhorn which the owner illuminated for us with the flick of a switch. There was also a pile of comic books to amuse the breakfasting customers; the one I glanced at (*Eros*) featured a naked woman tied up in an automobile body shop being assaulted with a breathtaking variety of spanners, jacks, and big ends. An hour down the road I came across a reminder of the comic books of my own less mechanized childhood: a very old carved Buddha, seated by the roadside with his hands clasped in prayer, had been decapitated and now had a small, perfectly egg-shaped stone cemented to his shoulders where his Buddha head should have been. One of the rarer phantoms in Japanese demonology has a smooth, egg-shaped head like this, and in a famous ghost story he reveals it to a customer at an all-night noodle stall. But the old stone figure reminded me more of the intergalactic enemies of Dan Dare, who was forever struggling through the innocent pages of the *Eagle* against a great host of alien eggheads armed with all manner of big ends.

Autumn was in the hills now. Not a tree but had some brown in its leaves, and many leaves had already fallen, fluttering along the sides of the broken road, or through the wilting bamboo groves, or lying sodden in the potholes. Again the road wound higher and higher, and the railway and stream that ran looping far below looked like a snail track racing a piece of twine. Near the top of one hill, I came to a cleft that several generations had used as a rubbish dump. There was a little wooden shrine above the stinking heap of cans and cartons, and again I couldn't help pitying the deities for the slums that they are lodged in. "There are thirty thousand gods in Japan," a friend had once boasted to me. "Yes," I had retorted, in a bloody mood, "and about three of them paid any respect."

Between villages I passed an old country grandmother with so much greenery strapped to her back that she looked like a bit of Birnam Wood. It was five o'clock on the ninetieth afternoon of my journey when I reached the wooded crest of the hills and crossed out of Oka-yama Prefecture into the bluish haze of rural Hiroshima. The Tojo Bowling Center was the first Hiroshima landmark I came to, with a great phallic ten pin on its roof like a Dan Dare missile. Down in the valley, over the little town of Tojo itself, a pall of smoke drifted as the people in the outlying fields burned their leaves, and clouds rose smokily over the river, purple-gray and pale creamy pink.

I found a ryokan near the town's main bridge, and the moment the crinkly faced old woman appeared in the entrance hall we started giggling at each other like five-year-olds.

"Ooo! You *surely* can't want to stay *here!*" the old woman giggled, rubbing her hands on her apron.

"Oh, but I surely *do!*" I giggled, unloading my pack onto the entrance hall floor.

"But you won't want any *food,* will you?"

"Oh, yes I will. I'm *starving* to *death!*"

"Ooo! Ooo!" she giggled, pattering about the step. "Why don't you go *out* and find something you *like?*"

"I'm sure I'll like what *you* give me," I giggled, while she brushed the dust off my shirt and out of my hair and I sat unlacing my boots.

It is how I imagine all the great love affairs begin—which is probably why so many of them end in disappointment. The nearest I can come to explaining it is to blame it on some mysterious electrical discharge, and electrical discharges are by nature unstillable; they result in shocks, not marriages. Electricity has to flow from contact to contact; static electricity is an irritant. But for the evening I spent in love with that old woman our eyes never stopped popping and our breaths kept coming out of our throats in chortly spurts. She did all my laundry for me—we thought it was uproarious—and when I insisted on drinking a beer before going down to the bathroom, I thought I'd given her a stitch. I've always got on well with old women—they seem to like my conversation—but conversation here in Tojo was out of the question; we'd have ruptured each other's lungs.

After dinner I went out to a small bar that served skewers of grilled chicken and sat and half listened to two slurpy customers recite the names of the months to each other in ill-remembered English. The old woman had gone to bed early, her battery in need of a recharge, and here I was sitting with two silly men who thought I was a joke but lacked the wit to share it with me.

That night I chuckled myself to sleep, thinking of the sparks coming out of the old woman's nostrils and hair, and as we slept, each plugged into our dreams, the first snow fell on Mount Fuji.

In the hills to the west the construction of the ever-lengthening Chugoku Expressway was in full swing, and dump trucks rattled past me up the narrow road to Taishaku at the rate of about one a minute. The sooty dust they raised made my windpipe feel like a blocked-up flue, and I sat out of the dust for a while in a bus shelter until a workman in a tin helmet told me that they were just about to dynamite the hillside above my head. I heard the deep boom of the explosion some three minutes after trudging away, and the birds, instead of shrieking in panic, were as silent as if their vocal cords had been ripped out of their throats. In the brief intervals when the air was clear I could smell the bittersweet pines. The fields were brown and autumn-stripped, and the rice straw hung in neat rows from its frames, covered with transparent sooty plastic.

At about ten-thirty I reached the little village of Taishaku, which stands at the northern end of its own famous limestone gorge. Both the village and the gorge are named after one of the Buddhist gods of thunder whose task it is to watch over the world and protect it from catastrophe. In one of the small souvenir shops in the village a woman told me that forty to fifty schoolchildren had died not many years before on an excursion through the gorge when their pleasure boat had capsized and sunk. Now, she said, school authorities warn children to keep well away from the gorge, and perhaps the thunder god has his eyes peeled more keenly now than he had then.

The temple in which he is worshiped is a small, steeply roofed building, founded in the early eighth century and dwarfed by a massive limestone cliff that must predate his tenancy by at least a hundred million years. On the trees near the temple hung little knots of folded white fortune papers, the printed letters faded and the papers stiff and crumbly from the rain. Across a small vermilion drumbridge, in a cave scooped out of the gray side of the gorge, stood the same sad piles of prayer stones as at Osorezan, some two or three hundred wooden grave markers, and a tray of white candles all unlit—the signs and symbols of the thunder god's half-hearted watch over the Hiroshima countryside.

I had lunch in the village and then marched on along a high wooded road dappled with the autumn sunlight that came slanting and dancing through the still-green leaves. I stopped to have a beer at one of those puzzling little shops (not the first I had been in) that combined a chemist's with a liquor business. The woman who ran it was fat and talkative, and I sat for about an hour at the table she kept for drinkers with afternoons to waste, eating the peanuts she had opened for the two of us and listening to her talk about her ninety-one-year-old mother and about her two sons who lived in Tokyo and whom she saw once every twelve months if she was lucky. Hiroshima was such a long way for them to come. And me? What was I doing here? And where was I headed? The city? Did I mean Hiroshima city . . . ?

". . . when the bomb fell I was staying with relatives in a little village across the hills in Okayama. I heard the news on the radio and couldn't fathom what had happened, so I went into the city to see for myself.

I saw people jumping into the river in their working clothes to try and cool their peeling bodies. There were schoolgirls in their uniforms with their arms and half their faces burned away. Later on, when it was all over, they took them to America to have skin grafted onto their faces from their thighs, and when they came back and you saw them from a distance you thought how pretty they looked. It was different when you got close up. Walking through the rubble of the streets I recognized my old schoolteacher from the funny bald patch on the back of his head. We always used to make jokes about it. I ran up and called out to him, and when he turned round the lower half of his face looked exactly as though there was a fungus growing on it. I went to Tokyo shortly afterwards and saw people carrying armfuls of potatoes through the streets as though they were precious jewels. . . ."

She looked at me across the table.

"Do you believe it?"

"Yes, I believe it."

"Young people today don't know what to believe. Their fathers sit in bars and sing the old soldiers' songs again. Nostalgia, they call it. I call it something else."

I quoted her a poem that I remembered seeing in a Japanese magazine:

> *The war songs drone on,*
> *deafening the survivors.*

She nodded and repeated it two or three times to herself, and gave me three hard-boiled eggs to take with me, and I sat and ate them on a rock further along the road while the afternoon sped by faster than my feet could keep up with it.

The dead frogs in the gutters looked unnervingly human, with their back legs splayed out straight behind them and their front legs folded neatly across their chests. Even more unnerving—from the back and at a distance—were two blond-haired people sitting dead still in a parked car. Their stillness was as shocking as the color of their hair—until I drew abreast of them and saw that they were a couple of life-sized mannequins for use in seat-belt demonstrations. They stared straight ahead through the windscreen as though they had been paralyzed, and the complete absence of any living thing on the road made it seem that the inhabitants of all Hiroshima—frogs, blonds, schoolchildren and their teachers—had unwittingly crawled into some blind angle of the less-than-all-seeing thunder god's eye.

A comic book at the restaurant I stopped in for coffee was entirely devoted to the raping of uniformed schoolgirls—by their gym teachers, by doctors they consulted, even by their uncles and aunts. The waitress was fascinated by my grasp of the menu. "Ooo!" she warbled, "can you read *that?*" But the bill she brought me was a stiffer test because, unlike the menu, it was printed in what the restaurant imagined to be English. There was a space to tick off "ko-rudorink" (cold drinks), another for "hott dorink," and the total was scribbled under the word "aum," which I took to be a misprint for "sum," and not some esoteric name for the Godhead. "Hurro! Hurro!" said a man into the telephone as I walked past him out of the restaurant. Perhaps the mannequins had finally called for help.

The last hour of my trudge that day was along a highway where headlights blazed like tracer bullets, and I reached a ryokan long after dark, too dazzled to notice the cigarette burns in the sheets and too tired to complain about the wails of the cat that sat on my window ledge keening through the night.

On a battlefield scarred with the tracks of tanks and pitted with the craters of mortar shells crows were battening on Japanese corpses, ripping eyes out of sockets and tearing the flesh down to the skull. A stone's throw away, in a makeshift stockade, two young Japanese soldiers were tied with barbed wire to wooden stakes and a grinning American Marine sergeant, who had just emerged from a barracks where he had been lashing the behinds of two screaming Japanese women with a studded leather belt, was mustering a firing squad. The young Japanese soldiers cried out as they died. One cried, "I am a Japanese!" The other, "Long live the emperor!" The bullets tore fist-sized holes in their chests, and within minutes of their deaths the crows were alighting; the eyes went first, then the tongues.

I put the comic book back on the pile and spent the rest of breakfast staring at my maps. The large drive-in was almost empty, and when he saw that I was no longer occupied by cultural pursuits, the owner came and sat with me and we had a chat. He was a youngish-looking middle-aged man with gold teeth and a long chef's apron, and we discussed the Japanese economy.

He told me that America, Britain, and West Germany could no longer be taken seriously since they were all more than halfway down the tube. Japan, by contrast, was the only country in the world where identical consumer goods, sealed and date-stamped for extra freshness, were as available in the smallest rural hamlets as they were in the metropolis. There were drawbacks to this convenience, he suggested. Fifteen years ago the Japanese had had something to work hard for. Now it was all there for them on a plate, and the young people no longer understood the value of dedicated labor. Fifteen years ago, too, the future had seemed a straight line; now there was a jittery awareness of the future's limitations. And then the litany began: tiny country, no natural resources, misunderstood by everyone. . . .

He was an amiable chap, disarmingly honest about the things that impressed him personally:

"Sometimes foreigners—Americans mostly—come in here on their way from Iwakuni to go skiing on Mount Daisen. If they order 'morning service' (coffee with a free egg and a slice of toast) they always wait quietly till it's ready, no matter how busy I am or how long it takes. Japanese customers who order the same thing will be howling for it within five minutes. They're very patient, foreigners. It must come from having to do without conveniences. . . ."

The television was on full blast in the drive-in, and our conversation fizzled out when a newsreader reported that nine Japanese terrorists had just hijacked a JAL flight to Dacca and were demanding six million dollars in cash. The owner disappeared with an embarrassed cough into his kitchen, and I swung on down the narrow road that followed the local railway track in its plunge through commuterland toward the city of Hiroshima.

Commuterland or not, these valleys and low rolling hills were among the greenest and most eye-pleasing I passed through on my journey. Hiroshima seemed a neat, well-manicured prefecture, and despite the drive-in owner's all-too-tiresome urging of the work ethic, the people struck me as a gentle, unhurried crowd who felt it important to spare time for chats like ours. Among the conveniences available to them in their shops was a wall clock set into a large photographic panel showing Oh Sadaharu cracking the home run that flushed American baseball down its own tube: from camera to clock factory to rural Hiroshima in twenty-six days—there's industry for you!

As I approached Mukaihara, toward the end of a long, overcast day, three little girls ran after me to ask me where I'd come from. Hokkaido, I told them. They shrieked and ran away. And in the shabby streets of the little township I was serenaded on my search for a ryokan by four boys of about the same age—alerted, perhaps, by the little girls—who trailed after me, shouting "I-me-my, you-your-yours" for something like five minutes till I snapped at them to shut up and, incredibly, they did. There were no ryokans in Mukaihara, and no policemen by the look of things, either. The station was little more than a shed, but the old man I found dozing there told me that there was a ryokan near the next station down the line, at a place called Ibaraichi. How far was that, I asked.

"Fifty kilometers."

It was half a minute of agony before I realized that the old man had a less than perfect grasp of the metric system.

"How many *ri?*"

"One and a bit."

"Then it's *five* kilometers, not fifty."

"Yes," he agreed, "it could be, too. Things are never the same for very long nowadays."

Dusk fell, and again it was night by the time I reached a place I could stay. The ryokan was in darkness, but the little bar next door had lights on, and so I opened the back door, hoping that the bar and the ryokan were parts of the same establishment. They were, and I was welcomed to both by two gushing hostesses and a jubilant mama-san who also ran the ryokan and who sat with me as I ate my dinner, addressing me all the time as *O-niisan* (the polite, affectionate term that means brother).

"Ibaraichi is a very old town, O-niisan. It's only five or six years since they made it a suburb of Hiroshima city. It has a long history of its own to be proud of. This ryokan itself is seventy years old, and in the temple across the road one of the great Mori lords is buried. Each year in spring an old man in his eighties with long white hair and a flowing beard comes from the city of Hagi, a hundred and twenty kilometers away, to spend the night here in this ryokan, and in the

208

morning he climbs the hill behind the temple to pray at the grave of the lord, his ancestor."

The woman knew her history. Hagi, she said, was the city to which the Mori lords had retired after losing Hiroshima due to one of them's siding with the wrong faction against the shogun in 1600. He had attempted to make amends by cutting off his own son's head, but the shogun preferred stability to murdered children and Hiroshima passed into more reliable hands. Recent history, too, was a preoccupation of the mama-san's, and it crept up on our dinner conversation without awkwardness or fanfare.

"Do you know what an *omiai* is, O-niisan?"

"Yes, it's the meeting between a potential couple and their families as the first step toward an arranged marriage."

"That's right. You know a lot, O-niisan. Before the war, if the man was satisfied at an *omiai* the marriage would go ahead with no thought at all for the woman's preferences or affections. That was how it was with me, though I saw little enough of my husband to know whether I could love him or not. We'd been married a year and a half and I already had one child. My husband was a soldier in Hiroshima city. . . ."

I waited without saying anything, turning my sakè cup round and round in my fingers.

". . . I remember it was especially fine weather that day. We lived about two *ri* from the center, and my husband was stationed near the naval yards. It was a quarter past eight in the morning and suddenly all the paper doors and screens blew down and everyone shut their eyes because it seemed the day had grown brighter. I'd just watched two planes fly over and when I looked up again they were still there. One of them had turned and was climbing away but the other one was circling a great cloud that seemed to be rising like a tornado out of the earth. We couldn't make out what the planes were doing. It was two days after that they told me my husband was dead. . . ."

"I remember going out and walking the streets. Some of the people were burned on every part of their bodies except where they had tied the sashes round their summer kimonos. All the rest of their clothes had disappeared. Others you couldn't see any marks on; their skin looked perfectly normal, but there was something itching underneath it. When you took them to the doctor's, they said it was a vitamin C deficiency and gave them an injection. Ten days later their hair began to fall out and they bled from all their orifices, and then they died. I remember a fourteen-year-old boy pulling great chunks of his hair out and asking his mother why. The next day he complained of a stomachache and his mother took him to the doctor, who sent him to hospital with suspected appendicitis. The next day he bled from his ears and nose; the day after that they cremated him.

"Later on they told us that no plants or trees would grow in Hiroshima for ten to fifteen years. Around the point where the bomb dropped they were selling land for a yen and a half a *tsubo* (about the size of two tatami mats). But the next year the grass grew just the same and the trees bore leaves again. . . ."

An old woman with perfectly white hair tottered round the doorpost of the room we were sitting in, clutching the paper screen for support, and peered at me, still seated at the dinner table with the same sakè cup between my finger and thumb.

"Where's auntie?" she asked me.

"Here," the mama-san said, standing up with a puff of breath.

"What about my dinner?" the old woman moaned. "I've been waiting and waiting and waiting. . . ."

I slept on a hard rice-husk pillow, and the second-to-last night of September had a chill in it.

Next morning the mama-san made me a packed lunch and, still clucking with pleasure and calling me O-niisan, told me which road would bring me soonest into the city that had fueled all her life's conversations.

✄

It was a beautiful bright sunny day with the mountains crisp and clear, and white autumn cumulus piled up on their peaks like cushions. Despite the growing nearness of the city, the little villages along this railway line preserved a great deal of country charm. In the narrow main street of one, an old woman pushing an empty pram waved and flashed me a lovely smile, and in the course of the day perhaps a dozen drivers stopped to offer me lifts.

From the crest of a hill in midafternoon I had my first view of the hazy city, with high hills to the east of it and, pale beyond, the islands of the Inland Sea. Cranes towered above the islands, and high over the

210

cranes, at the edge of a wisp of cirrus cloud, a tiny rainbow hovered. I tramped down through the northeastern suburbs and was swiftly lost in a maze of streets and railway sidings, managing to take my bearings once or twice from the briefly glimpsed NHK radio tower. At last in the distance I saw the gleaming blue-and-white bullet train snaking slowly along its elevated track, and I knew I was approaching Hiroshima station and two packless, trampless days of ease.

In the streets I met people who seemed eager to speak English to me. An old man sitting on a corner said "Hello." A vegetable seller in a straw hat said "How are you?" A young man in a sports shirt said "Where do you go?"

"To find a ryokan."

"I go play pinball."

And an American with gray hair pointed at my pack and asked me what mountain I was planning to climb.

"Can I help you? I know Hiroshima pretty well."

"Perhaps you could recommend a ryokan."

"A what?"

"A ryokan. A Japanese-style inn."

"Hell, no. I stay at real hotels."

As I was crossing the last of the shunting yards on a long empty iron footbridge, four boys who had been throwing stones at the coal trucks threw them at the footbridge I was walking across instead. One of the stones ricocheted off a girder and caught my pack about six inches below the nape of my neck. I yelled at the boys and they scuttled away across the rubble and the rusted points of the railway track, and vanished behind a warehouse over which the sun was setting like a bloodied eye.

211

8

A Thousand Cranes,
A Thousand Suns

AT THE POINT where the atomic bomb was dropped on Hiroshima there is a Peace Park, and in the Peace Park there is a museum. I visited the museum with no illusions that I would be able to write about what I saw and little real hope that I would comprehend it. The three hours that I spent there, forcing myself to look at every item, reading each caption in English and again in Japanese, brought me no closer to an understanding but they knocked a gaping hole in my spirit.

It is not the vastness of the destruction that moves you so much as the relics of individual suffering. These speak with the most eloquence: a melted desktop Buddha, a burned watch, the scorched blazer of a thirteen-year-old schoolboy, one of more than six thousand who had been led out to participate in an air-raid defense program and so were on the unprotected streets when the bomb fell. There are photographs of a little girl, her will snapped, refusing the cup of water that might have made her death easier; of a young soldier bleeding obscenely from the pores, who died two hours after his picture was taken; of keloid formation on the face and body of a teenage boy, bald as an egg; of a young housewife who had put on, in these last breathless days of the war, a bright cheerfully patterned summer kimono and the dye of the cloth had burned lines and squares into her back and arms and neck so that she looked, in her death agony, like a plaid doll.

There is a display in which two or three department store mannequins have been dressed in rags and smeared with rubber latex to represent the peeling off of their skin. They slouch through a yellow

212

cardboard inferno, so gross, so like a comic strip that I could not bear to look at it. For the three hours I was in the museum my eyes kept drifting to the windows and, through them, into an impossibly remote world where fountains played in the sunlight of the park.

I was staggered to see so many schoolchildren being shepherded round the exhibits by their teachers. They were very young and very quiet, shuffling along wide-eyed in their little yellow hats, some holding each other's hands, some pointing and asking their teachers questions that were answered in an almost inaudible drone. I did not see a single child smile, and the seriousness of their faces made them appear very much older and wiser than they were. Many stared as they passed me, and I could feel the bewilderment and tension in their little bodies. One boy turned round from an exhibit to find me standing close behind him and threw up an arm as though to protect his face from a slap. None of the children laughed at me or shouted greetings, but several whispered to each other, quietly and seriously, "Look, it's a foreigner. Look, it's a foreigner." Slowly I shuffled past the exhibits toward the exit with my sunglasses on my foreigner's face, breathing easier because I was almost out of the museum, and quite unprepared for what happened next.

I was looking at one of the last displays—a shelf of melted rooftiles and bottles that had fused together in the twelve-thousand-degree heat of the bomb—a heat sufficient to melt human bones. I felt a nudge at my elbow and looked round to find a man in his early thirties—too young, I think, to have remembered much about the bombing—standing beside me wearing workman's clothes and smelling (or perhaps I imagined this) of sakè.

He said: "Your country did this."

My eyes must have altered behind my sunglasses. I slid away from him and stopped in front of a large photograph of a junior high school girl with half her face missing. I felt the same nudge and now the man was grinning.

"Do you like this picture?" he asked. "Do you find it interesting at all? Does it amuse you? Do you find it amusing?"

And suddenly the part of the museum where we were standing was very still because, suddenly, it contained no other people, only a young man with a camera—a student, I think—who came up and slipped quietly between us and said to the workman: "Stop it, please. Please, stop it. Please, leave him alone. He's not an American. Please, stop it."

213

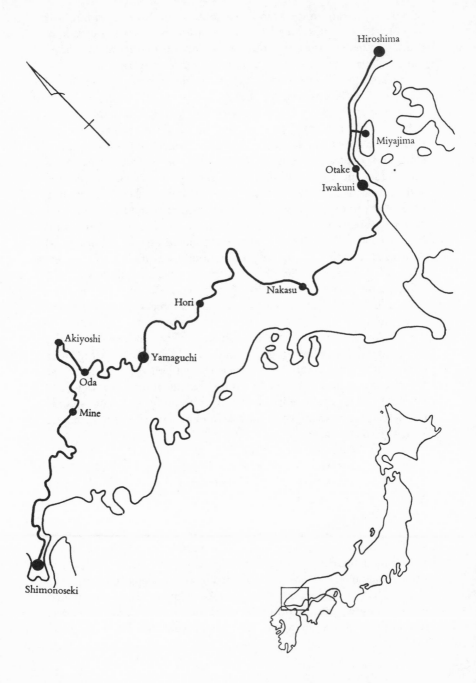

Hiroshima

Miyajima

Otake

Iwakuni

Nakasu

Hori

Akiyoshi

Yamaguchi

Oda

Mine

Shimonoseki

But the workman would not be stopped now, and his voice had begun to rise.

"He was rude to me," he said. "He turned his back when I spoke to him. He mustn't do that to me. I'm Japanese!"

I drifted on toward the exit, past another group of staring children whose teachers had stopped answering their questions and were looking vacantly at the windows or at the walls. I could hear the workman and the student still arguing and I managed to pause at the souvenir stand long enough to buy some books I wanted—one that contained poems by survivors of the bombing, one with the photograph of the schoolgirl who had no face. When these were wrapped and paid for, I turned round to find the workman waiting for me in the doorway.

At first I pretended I hadn't seen him and tried to walk past him, through the pool of space that other visitors had left around him, out into the impossible world where the fountains played. But it was a narrow doorway, and as I stepped through it, he prodded me and I took a deep breath and swung round and looked him in the face.

"I'm very sorry," he said.

"It's all right," I said. "I'm sorry I was rude."

"I'm sorry I was rude," he said.

"No," I said, babbling like an idiot, "I'm sorry. I'm sorry. This is the Peace Park."

"I'm sorry," he said.

"No, I'm sorry too," I said.

I left him in the doorway and went and sat on a bench with my books still wrapped in their paper bag and watched the autumn sun light the leaves of Hiroshima trees.

It was from a cloudless sky like this that the bomb dropped—"brighter," say the people who saw it, "than a thousand suns." Later on, in the north and east of the city, the sky turned dark and a "black rain" fell. As painful as the deaths and the lingering disease was surely the bewilderment of the stunned survivors: no such suns, no such rain had ever before intruded into mankind's history.

From my seat under the trees in the Peace Park I watched an old man sweep colored garbage into a heap that he arranged very carefully beside one of the park's stone monuments. When I passed it on my way to the gate I saw that it was not a heap of garbage but thousands upon thousands of tiny folded paper cranes.

There is a story told about a little girl who fell desperately ill some two or three months after the bombing. For a long time the exact nature of "A-bomb sickness" was only dimly understood, and treatment was haphazard and ineffectual. This fact, combined with the soaring black-market prices of foreign medicines in postwar Japan, condemned most of those who contracted radiation-induced diseases to an agonizing death. But the girl's mother was stubborn and resourceful and hung onto her wits far longer than most mothers would have. Patiently she persuaded her little daughter that if she could fold one thousand paper cranes and string them together like a rosary she would recover. Millions of these tiny cranes—the work of well-wishers and pilgrims—hang today in colored festoons from the stone monuments in the park, and it was these that the old man was arranging in heaps. The little girl began to make her cranes, but daily her fingers lost their strength, and eventually the sheer effort of folding them was a torture both to her and to her mother. Still her mother—by now, and of necessity, a believer in the myth she had concocted—stubbornly urged her daughter to fold another crane and then another, and painfully the little girl folded her cranes and one by one the number grew. She died after making nine hundred and sixty-four.

I have found it extremely difficult and depressing to write even this much about Hiroshima, but others have taken greater pains. Among the pieces of writing that move me is a short childlike poem by Toge Sankichi—a man of twenty-eight when the bomb fell, who died of radiation disease eight years later. The poem is reproduced in stone on a Peace Park monument.

> *Give back my father, give back my mother.*
> *Give back the old.*
> *Give back the children.*
>
> *Give me back myself, give back*
> *all people who are part of me.*
>
> *For as long as this world is a human world,*
> *Give me peace.*
> *Give me peace that will last.*

The sun was still bright when I walked out of the Peace Park, past the fountains and the monuments and the paper cranes. It was hard on this cloudless autumn day—95 days since the start of my journey, 11,890 days since the dropping of the Hiroshima bomb—to realize how quickly time had passed and, in passing, how completely it had stolen away memory. Some 200,000 people are thought to have died as a result of the world's first atomic holocaust, and their names are contained in a stone chest that is one of the park's simplest and most eloquent memorials. But looking at the words carved on the chest, I couldn't help wondering whether the passing of time had not transformed their ringing promise into a strangled, wholly incredible prayer:

Sleep in peace.
The mistake will not be repeated.

I left the Peace Park and walked along the broad, tree-lined avenues of Hiroshima and through the jangling shopping arcades with their mirrors and coffee houses and their pounding sense of well-being. I watched the young people of Hiroshima crowd round the counters of a Kentucky Fried Chicken shop and a young female member of the staff wash down the statue of Colonel Saunders outside, soaping his back as a daughter might soap her father's as he sat on the tiled floor of a bathroom.

I had my boots reheeled by a man squatting on the sunny pavement outside the arcade. He had his sleeves rolled down and buttoned at his wrists, but when he saw my face he rolled them up to reveal the livid purple burns that snaked up both his arms. I watched three Americans ask directions of a middle-aged Japanese woman at a bus stop, thanking her with waves and exaggerated smiles, bowing absurdly low. In a bookshop I found a display of books in English, books by foreigners— *The Kimono Mind, How the Japanese Think.* I left them alone. I bought a book of essays by Richard Hoggart for his Englishness. I wanted no kimono minds; I was tired of how the Japanese think. I bought new jeans in a shop where a poster read, "For Those Who Assent to the Spirit of America. . . ."

I walked back with the jeans and the book to my ryokan and lay down on my mattress in the middle of the afternoon. I spent three hours reading Richard Hoggart, and in the evening I went out to get stone drunk in places where Hiroshima workmen drink.

Next day, too, I wandered aimlessly about the arcades, passing groups of workmen taking their lunch breaks on the sun-spattered pavement. There was a small film theater on the museum's upper floor, and I had planned to go to a showing there. Three times I got as far as the gate of the Peace Park, and three times I turned and walked back into the arcades. By early afternoon I was lying on my mattress in the ryokan again. I read more Hoggart and his cool Yorkshire sense washed through me like an opiate. At dinner I sat with a middle-aged American couple, just back from a sponsored goodwill trip to China, who explained to me patiently and emphatically why the Japanese should abandon their writing system, just as (they assured me) the Chinese were abandoning theirs. The couple understood not a word of Japanese, but this did not prevent them from enjoying their brushes with exotic languages.

"You speak good British," the man assured me. "Wash yer faysin the baysin." And they chuckled happily.

After dinner, to my surprise, an old friend from Tokyo turned up at the ryokan. Seiichiro had found out from my wife that I was likely to be in Hiroshima on the same dates as he was. He had then tracked me down through the ryokan information office at the station, where I had gone to inquire about lodgings, and he stood now in the foyer mopping his brow and looking as lost and out of place as he had on every occasion since the first time I met him.

We went out to stroll together through the narrow, neon, bar-lined streets, past topless cabarets and cinema hoardings advertising *Ilsa, Harem Keeper of the Oil Sheiks,* a film that featured blond women being tortured in ingenious ways. Hostesses in velvet dresses clip-clopped up and down the alleys, calling out to passers-by or grabbing them by the arm and hauling them toward the doorways of their clubs and bars. But at a bar whose prices were displayed on a winking sign outside, Seiichiro and I were politely turned away.

"Oh, don't come in here, O-niisan. You won't enjoy yourselves in a place like this. Those prices are not the real prices, you know." And as a suited businessman stumbled past: "Hello, Mr. President! Come on in! What a wise choice! You'll love it!"

"There's tax, you see," explained Seiichiro, mopping his forehead, "and service charge and a cover charge. . . ."

We had a quiet drink in a workmen's haunt, devoid of workmen. Seiichiro had a book to give me—a hard-covered novel that I glanced at and handed back.

"Have you read it, then? It's *Black Rain*. All about the bombing of Hiroshima. I've finished with it now. You're welcome to take it."

"No," I said, "it's too heavy for my pack."

"There's a paperback edition. Maybe one of the shops here has it."

"No, it's all right," I said. "I'll read it when I get back to Tokyo."

We sauntered back to the ryokan, where Seiichiro, too, had taken a room, and in the night a hard rain began to hammer down onto the streets. While I sat having breakfast in the dining room next morning, the manager of the ryokan stood over a guest at the next table and spoke in clipped sentences to the red back of his neck while the guest stared down at his rice bowl:

"Just go back and look at what you've done to that room! Go on, go back and look at it! How can I let that room to other guests? What excuse have you got for doing a thing like that?"

Seiichiro came in, dripping from the downpour, carrying a three-hundred-yen plastic raincoat and a transparent plastic hat that he'd gone out to buy. He had made up his mind to walk one whole day with me, and though I warned him that twenty-two fume-choked kilometers along the teeming wet growl of a national highway was the lousiest possible introduction to the joys of long-distance walking, he tugged on his brand new raincoat and hat, and we began tramping out of the center of Hiroshima, across the gray babble of the swelling rivers and into the bleak industrial suburbs.

Seiichiro was perfectly equipped for the adventure. In addition to his new plastic clothes, he had an Asahi Pentax, a Canon 8mm movie camera with a microphone on a telescopic rod, and a Sony cassette recorder slung across his shoulder. Throughout the day he used these in turn, sometimes skipping on ahead to take pictures of me as I strode grimly through puddles with my anorak zipped round my face, or sitting across a coffee shop table from me with his telescopic microphone three inches from my nose. He began each of these coffee shop sessions by recording in his own voice the date, time, and place. Then, with the recorder running, he aimed his movie camera at me, pressed the trigger and whispered, "Go on, say something!"

"I can't think of anything. Ask me a question."

"How do you feel?"

"Rotten."

"Is this a long day?"

"No, it's one of the shortest."

"What gear are we walking in?"

"Reverse."

"How do you feel?"

"Rotten."

It was actually one of the worst days of the journey. The rain never let up for a moment, and we sloshed along the highway sulky and bored, cursing the trucks that sent tidal waves up our thighs. The road hugged the southwest sweep of the coast, and in gaps between gray factories we glimpsed small shrouded islands in the stinking wash of the Inland Sea. By late afternoon we had reached the amusement park near the ferry port for Miyajima island. The park's huge ferris wheel was churning slowly round with no one on it, looming out of the dusk at us like the ghost of some infernal rain machine. We queued up at the ticket counter for the ferry, and Seiichiro bought two cardboard cartons of cold sakè that we swallowed in three gulps each.

In the twilight the great Itsukushima Shrine stood empty except for the tame deer that huddled in the doorways of shuttered souvenir shops or squatted in concrete porches to sleep. The tide was out, and we trod through the island's oozy mud flats and over the slippery flagstones of the shrine till we reached the government lodging house where Seiichiro had managed to book us a room. There we got painstakingly slewed and played umpteen games of electronic ping-pong, which I lost by unbelievable margins. At dinner we sat with a group of bakers who had come to Miyajima on a two-day company outing and who questioned Seiichiro closely about his eccentric choice of pet.

"What's its name?"

"Alain Delon."

"Where does it come from?"

"London, England."

"Do you think it'd mind if we talked to it a bit?"

And so the conversation piece joined the conversation.

Did I know what *giri* and *ninjo* were? No, only Japanese knew that. Did I realize that Japanese was the most difficult language in the world? And that Japanese blood was a different temperature from everyone else's? And that Japanese brains were arranged in a different way?

And that Japanese bread was the best ever baked? And Japanese beer the best ever brewed...?

I went and played electronic ping-pong with myself and then sat on a Western-style lavatory trying to read the small print on a label stuck to the door. The label explained, by means of words and pin figures, how men must lift the lid of the seat before pissing and women must lower it before sitting down; and there was a large mirror on the wall, too, so that you could watch yourself performing these exotic operations. Outside the window of our room, cleaning women were chasing deer from the rubbish bins with mops. The rain had stopped, the moon was out, and Seiichiro had primed his camera for one last session.

"Monday, October third. Ten-thirty p.m. Government lodging house, Miyajima island. How do you feel?"

"Better."

"How many days has it been now?"

"Ninety-seven."

"How much longer will it take?"

"Maybe a month."

"How do you think you'll feel at the end of it?"

"Tired, relieved, boastful, empty."

For much of the night the bakers stumbled up and down the corridor outside our room, and when the cleaning women had gone to bed the deer rolled the rubbish bins down the slope and the saplings on the lawn collapsed like ninepins.

It was a warm blue morning, and after prodding his blisters for a while and telling me how much he had enjoyed our miserable walk, Seiichiro took the ferry back to the mainland, and I spent the next couple of hours exploring the chief sights of Miyajima island.

Like Amanohashidate, Miyajima is considered one of Japan's Three Most Beautiful Scenic Places, and since ancient times the island has been recognized as an abode of powerful gods. The ceremonies of Shinto— Japan's indigenous religion—are almost entirely concerned with purification, cleanliness being not merely next to godliness, but far and away the preferred choice. Until the Meiji Restoration of 1868, for example, no births or deaths were permitted to occur on Miyajima, since both are regarded as forms of pollution. Even today, there is neither a crematorium nor a graveyard here, the dead being sent to the mainland for burial and the mourners undergoing ritual cleansing before taking the ferry back to their island homes.

Japanese people are inclined to boast of the religious tolerance that has characterized their history; and it is true that no such religious warfare as Europe saw for centuries between Catholic and Protestant ever occurred between Japanese converts to Buddhism, the foreign faith imported in the sixth century, and those who adhered to the older pantheistic-animistic religion, parts of which survive today as Shinto. (It is, however, worth noting that this tolerance did not extend to Christians, against whom, for more than two hundred years, a policy of harsh persecution was carried out and for whom were reserved the most imaginative forms of torture and execution.) Buddhism and Shinto were early seen to complement each other. Temples and shrines often nestle close together on the same city sites or mountaintops, and membership of a Buddhist sect has never deterred Japanese people from getting married in Shinto shrines or taking part in such rituals as the first shrine visit of the New Year—rituals that are far closer to gestures of national identity than of religious faith.

Yet no two warring European churches could present a more striking architectural contrast than the Buddhist temple of Eiheiji and Itsukushima Shrine on Miyajima island. Where Eiheiji was all earth colors, the shrine is brilliant red and white. While the buildings of Eiheiji seemed laid out in a comfortable anarchic jumble, the buildings of the shrine are symmetrical and crisp and the corridors that connect them are composed of uncompromisingly straight lines. The bright shrine colors, standing in sharp contrast to the greens and dark October browns of the hills, and the mathematical precision of the rectangles combine to create the impression of an imposition on nature, as though the shrine had been placed here to subdue the hills and suck all of their sanctity into itself. Where one could imagine living a comfortable —if restricted—life in a temple like Eiheiji, it was more than I could do to imagine living for twenty-five minutes in Itsukushima Shrine. It is a monarch's palace, not a home for humble monks, and I wouldn't mind betting there are blither gods swinging about in the maple trees of Miyajima island than cower in the geometry of its cathedral.

The sea plays a major part in enhancing all three of Japan's Three Most Beautiful Scenic Places, and at Miyajima the shrine has been built on platforms over the water so that when the tide is in the whole edifice seems to rise away from the shore and float above the reflecting surface of the channel. The most famous of the shrine's attractions is a bright vermilion torii gate—the largest torii gate in Japan and easily the most photographed Shinto structure anywhere—and this stands well away from the shore on the bed of the sea itself. But it was still quite early in the morning when I wandered round the precincts of the shrine and the tide was at its furthest ebb, so the interplay of shrine and sea was a little less magical than I had anticipated. The stilts of the platforms stood revealed above beds of mud and shallow seaweed-clogged pools, and the salt-smeared concrete and faded paint at the bottom of the legs of the torii gate anchored it in the ooze like a mired giant.

But the revealed mud flats provided the morning's visitors—especially the thousands of schoolchildren who were being herded about by megaphone-wielding guides—with the perfect opportunity for indulging in that most important of all Japanese shrine-going rituals, the Taking of the Souvenir Photograph. Teachers, guides, and cameramen arranged row after row of them on benches spread carefully out on the exposed seabed, and all the arrangements meticulously ensured that each child had his back to the shrine so it didn't matter an iota to them whether it was floating or sinking into the mud. Smaller groups took their own photographs. One neat-suited businessman had himself snapped in front of an ancient dance stage practicing a golf swing with his rolled-up umbrella; another was committed to posterity as he fed the pages of a comic book to a hungry deer.

And as I walked through the corridors of the shrine, I couldn't help noticing how different was the determinedly sanctimonious atmosphere that pervades most Christian churches from the breezy nonchalance with which visitors treat the religious monuments of Japan. In a Christian church one is urged to speak in whispers; at Itsukushima Shrine groups of visiting businessmen bawled at each other as though they were on a golf course.

"Oi, look at this!"

"Where's Honda? Is he drunk again?"

"Have you got my camera?"

"Which way to the bus?"

The priests who sat behind strategically placed counters selling fortune papers and travel charms never once asked the visitors to speak more quietly. In fact, they ignored the visitors altogether except when money was changing hands.

"Is the other side of the shrine just the same as this side?" one businessman asked as he bought a charm.

"More or less," yawned a priest, slipping his coins into a cash box.

"Well, there's no point in looking at it, is there, then?" said the man, and he turned and strode purposefully back the way he had come.

The road from the shrine to the ferry terminal was lined with souvenir shops where the commonest items were deer—wooden deer, clay deer, plastic deer, inflatable rubber deer—and there was a waxwork museum where I could just make out, beyond the dim recesses of the foyer, two lifesize figures: one a court dancer in a magnificent lacquered lion mask and the other Oh Sadaharu swinging the baseball bat that most visitors would have given ten chips of the true cross to possess.

The tide had turned by the time I took the ferry, and where the children had squirmed on their wooden benches, the cosmetic water rose inch by inch to hide the mud, the flaking paint, and the worn, earthbound foundations of the platforms. When I reached dry land and set off along the highway, Miyajima's godly geometry was floating clean and prim again above the mirror of the sea.

In some ways the Chugoku District is a microcosm of the whole island of Honshu. One coast—the one along which I was walking—is over-populated and depressingly "developed." Industrial debris has scarred the shores of the once-romantic Inland Sea, and the innumerable smokestacks that were the only monuments to Japanese civilization I saw on the ninety-eighth day of my journey were made no prettier by being painted with red and white stripes. The other coast—the one washed by the Sea of Japan—is as comparatively unspoiled this far west as it is in the more northerly parts of Honshu, and the mountainous area in the center, into which I would shortly begin trekking, is rugged and sparsely populated, with almost all the major towns and cities of the region crowding the shores.

The fearsome efficiency of the private sector of Japanese industry is to some extent offset by the startling financial losses regularly reported by parts of its public sector. The Japanese National Railways

224

in particular has come under increasing fire for the inefficiency with which it is run (though this "inefficiency" hardly ever affects the clockwork punctuality of trains). Overmanning struck me as a problem: for as I tramped along beside the main line out of Hiroshima I passed gang after gang of workmen replacing sleepers, each gang provided with two or three lookouts whose sole job was to warn them through megaphones (they were mostly standing within four yards of each other) whenever a train approached. There was a very efficient stink in the main street of the city of Otake which seemed to emanate from the Bank of Shikoku. It didn't bother the local people, though—the young car salesman with dyed auburn hair, the old grocer carefully washing and polishing a bit of ornamental driftwood, and the dozen or so long-distance drivers eating curry at a roadside cafe, all of whom had left their engines running, so that the bank stink and the truck stink combined to usher me smartly out of Otake wondering which sector of the medical industry—public or private—sold the residents spare sets of lungs.

Within minutes I crossed out of Hiroshima into Yamaguchi, and so entered the last prefecture in Honshu. I had dawdled in Hiroshima, and October was almost a week old now, which—together with the stinks and smokestacks—lent my feet a fleetness that surprised me. I passed a shed in which a woman was molding the headless torsos of pink shop dummies, and by five o'clock I had struggled through the growling suburbs of Iwakuni city and found a room in a dingy little ryokan where the woman confessed within seconds of meeting me that her sister had married an American marine, and then made up for this appalling revelation by explaining that she herself had been in Hiroshima when the bomb was dropped, had been told that she could therefore have no children, had adopted two on the doctor's advice and promptly given birth to four more. Later that evening, to demonstrate the cosmopolitan nature of her family, she brought me a knife and fork with which to eat a bowl of noodles.

When I went out for a walk after dinner the woman's husband strolled to the corner with me and warned me against three-quarters of the bars in the city. He didn't warn me against the fast-food outlet that advertised "Mexican Bugers" or against the publication called *Nasty Gals* which was available from a nearby vending machine. A cabaret on the same street had a selection of photographs outside in which the grinning hostesses all displayed mouthfuls of jet-black teeth, the work of some dissatisfied client with a felt-tipped pen who had obviously not had the benefit of the husband's warnings. I played safe and strolled into an ordinary working man's *akachochin*, and thereby set in motion one of the oddest adventures of my journey.

It began with my being asked to leave because the *akachochin* was off-limits to the American marines who are stationed at the nearby naval base. I explained that I was not a marine, and not even an American, whereupon the stony silence in which a one-yen coin could have been heard drop gave way to the normal hollers and belches, and I was bought a beer by the two men sitting next to me at the counter, one of whom (an R.S.M. in the Japanese Maritime Self-Defense Force) drew from his pocket a fistful of American money and flung it dramatically onto the concrete floor.

"That's the only money we're allowed to spend on base," he growled. "Look at it! And this is Japan!"

The dimes and cents continued to lie where he had flung them till he stooped and picked them up again a bit shamefacedly, and put them back in his pocket.

"Why is this place off-limits?" I asked. The other man (whom I shall call H, because he was also in the forces and anything like his real name had better stay unrecorded) told me sheepishly that it wasn't really off-limits, but that a number of Japanese servicemen came here to get away from the base atmosphere and the master obliged them by discouraging any Americans who happened to wander in.

"I'm really sorry," H said seriously, and the R.S.M. bought me a second bottle, at which point I had a beer-inspired brain wave and asked whether it might be possible for me to visit the base.

The R.S.M. was silent. H thought about it for a moment or two and then told me that it would be perfectly possible and that he would conduct me on a personal tour of inspection.

"When do you want to come?"

"Tomorrow morning, if it's all right."

"Yes, that will be fine. Come to the main gate. There you'll find two checkpoints, one after the other. The first will be manned by an American marine. Pay him no attention whatever; just walk straight past him and go to the Japanese guard who'll be in a sentry box further inside the gate. Ask for me and he'll phone my extension."

In the lubricated mutter of the cheerfully lanterned bar, with a third bottle of beer to banish all misgivings, nothing in the world had ever seemed more straightforward. Walk past the American marine at his checkpoint: but of course, who would think of doing anything else? Get the Japanese guard to phone H's extension: nothing simpler surely—have another beer. . . .

And next morning, to my own surprise, this mood persisted long enough for me to march the four kilometers to the main gate of Iwakuni Base under a cloudy, busily windy sky, stroll past a spotty baton-wielding American M.P. in my jeans and patched denim shirt with a dusty rucksack on my back, greet the startled Japanese guard in Aomori dialect (which I tend to lapse into when suppressed tensions are cooking up the manic phase) and ask to be connected to H.

And here came the first thump of sobriety.

"H?"

"Yes."

"What's his rank?"

"Haven't a clue."

"What's his first name?"

"Couldn't tell you."

The Japanese guard groaned and tapped the telephone with his fingernails. And the American M.P., now partly recovered from the shock of a British hiker declaring independence in this incredibly un-military manner, marched up to the door of the Japanese sentry box and demanded to see my I.D.

"I haven't got any I.D., I'm afraid," I said. "I've come to pay a call on Mr. H." (The "Mr." brought a louder groan from the Japanese guard.)

The M.P. made me stand against the wall outside the sentry box while the Japanese guard dialed the number I had given him and asked, with a small, marvelously timed cough, for "Mumble . . . mumble . . . H, who knew a foreigner."

H arrived within minutes, driving a huge black limousine and wearing a dress uniform with (an unrecordable amount of) gold braid on the sleeves. My eyes almost popped out of my head, but the two guards must have had near heart failures. They sprang to attention and saluted us both while H pumped my hand, slapped my back, signed me in, and stuffed my pack into the boot of his limousine. Then we drove off on a tour of the base, leaving the guards to curse all comers.

Iwakuni houses twelve hundred Japanese servicemen who operate seventeen PS1 seaplanes (classified information; guard this book with

227

your life). They spend their time, I learned, playing two games of baseball a day, and the R.S.M. who joined us said he couldn't make out why the Americans on the base didn't do the same.

During the Vietnam War some protesters, including Jane Fonda and her husband, demanded that the Japanese government search Iwakuni for nuclear weapons. The government politely declined to do this, repeating its faith in the "three-point principle," cheerily agreed upon with the United States, that no nuclear weapons will ever be manufactured, maintained, or brought into Japanese territory. This last prohibition includes the frequent visits to Japanese ports by U.S. vessels with nuclear capability, so presumably the armament is offloaded onto small rubber dinghies that are left floating on the high seas for the duration of the call. I taxed H with this joyful fiction and he brightly refused to discuss it. Instead, he told me that a big American transport had docked during the night, and we went to see it unloaded, clambering onto the deck of a moored tender where H and the R.S.M., chortling loudly, took it in turns to pose with me for souvenir photographs. (I begged them to send me prints but they never did.)

We drove slowly round the perimeter of the base, passing vastly overweight Americans jogging, and H told me that he hated using a car but that you couldn't survive on an American-designed base without one. He hated going to the officers' club, where the Americans outranked and ignored him; he hated the fuss the M.P.'s made, such as not issuing passes to enough taxi drivers; in fact he hated the whole setup and longed to be transferred.

When we said goodbye back at the gate the two guards sprang to attention again and saluted me smartly as I passed. H waved me out of sight with a broad, satisfied grin on his face, and I stopped to look in the windows of the tailor's shops which, together with the pawnshops and bars with names like Linus and Popeye, were the only native enclaves in the district. You never see tailor's shops like these except near the gates of American bases. They all display gaudy Chinese dressing gowns which the proprietors impishly call kimonos, and specialize in embroidering the backs of colorful silk jackets with texts to please their unique clientele. Examples from the tailor's shops at Iwakuni:

And the Good Lord said "Let there be Marines,"
and the Gates of Death sprang open.

228

*When I die I'll go into Limbo because Heaven doesn't
want me and Hell is afraid I'll take over.*

Both these jackets bore a picture of a huge U.S. marine in combat
gear grasping the hair of a small Oriental man with large protruding
teeth. The marine was sneering, surrounded by a ring of flames; the
Oriental was dangling from his fist, crying tears of blood.

But the most extraordinary jacket, given the nature of the customers,
was surely the one with this on it:

> *Beneath the spreading mushroom tree,*
> *the world revolves in apathy,*
> *as overhead a row of specks*
> *roars on, ground out by discotheques;*
> *and if the secret button is pressed*
> *because one man has been outguessed,*
> *who will answer?*

The M.P.'s had displayed a text of their own, brisk and to the
point: "The roads outside this gate are among the most dangerous in
the world," warned their sign—"Drive Defensively!"

All day I walked in the Yamaguchi mountains, among startled people
and snakes made lazy by the autumn heat. My map called it Highway
376, but in the reality of the hills, thirty kilometers on from the M.P.'s
warning, the road was no more than an empty dust track, forking without signs in the middle of woods, surfaced briefly at the one or two
villages where I smelled chestnuts roasting or heard the screams of a
pig being slaughtered. When I asked directions I caused nothing but
confusion. A truck driver pointed me down one fork, a cyclist pointed
me down another; and the old lady who owned the shop we were all
standing in blinked at them both and kept quiet till they had gone.

"I didn't like to contradict them," she said, "but if you'd done
what they suggested you'd be sleeping with the foxes."

I was still eight kilometers from the nearest town when I tramped
into the tiny village of Nakasu. Work had ended for the day. Wives

were hurrying home to cook the evening meal, husbands were standing about in the street or sitting drinking sakè outside the grocer's shop, comparing the fish they had spent the afternoon hooking out of the reservoir. And dusk was settling rapidly, but it was more than I could do to pass the shop without stopping in for something to fortify me against the two-hour trudge that still lay ahead.

As I took my pack off outside the grocer's a small middle-aged man in a grubby white vest stood up from his stool and exclaimed, again and again, his eyes sparkling with excitement:

"England! England! England! England!"

I nodded and went into the shop and the grubby-vested man followed me, jigging about from foot to foot.

"Where are you going?" he bubbled as I poured myself a beer.

"I'm trying to reach the next town."

"Tonight?"

"Tonight."

"What ever for?"

"I need to find a ryokan."

I had only half emptied my beer glass, but the man grabbed the bottle and refilled it for me, pouring beer till the froth spilled out of the glass onto the concrete floor.

"You don't need a ryokan," he bubbled. "You can stay with me."

Behind the counter the grocer sneezed.

"That's very kind of you," I said, "but I'd hate to put you to any trouble."

"No trouble at all," the man beamed, turning to the grocer who was wiping his nose. "It would be a pleasure, wouldn't it?"

The grocer examined the contents of his handkerchief.

"It would be . . . er . . . interesting," he conceded.

"Come on," beamed the man, "no trouble at all." And he even paid for my beer.

I shouldered my pack, and we climbed the slope behind the shop, past two slavering dogs who mistook me for their dinner, and through the tangled undergrowth of the man's back garden to the front of his old wooden house. There, as he slid open the door, still jigging from foot to foot, we were met by a mess such as anyone who has ever seen those elegant photographs of Japanese interiors, but has never actually set foot in one, would find very hard to credit. On the living-room floor lay pile upon pile of boxes, tins, books, papers, plates, kettles, dishes, picture frames, bottles, fruit, ashtrays, washing up, and a dozen large squares of orange foam rubber. On the wall above the color television the Mona Lisa smiled down at the mess and at the glorious centerpiece of it all—a huge black treadle sewing machine around which, in a circle, sat six oblivious cats.

Mr. Takahashi—the jigging man—swept mounds of papers off the low wooden table and moved enough of the boxes so that we could sit down on two of the foam-rubber squares.

"England," he mused, thumbing through one of the large books which turned out to be an atlas of the world. "Here we are—they've got it the wrong way round again. This island"—he pointed at Ireland —"is Scotland, but they always call it Ireland; whereas this pink country"—he pointed at Scotland—"is Ireland, but they never get it right."

"Have you been to Britain?" I asked, thinking it a silly question.

"Oh, yes," said Mr. Takahashi. "Yes, I've been there. The River Thames. Australia, too. They sent me from one to the other. Actually . . ."

There was a long moment during which a cat licked its paw and I realized what was coming.

" . . . I was a prisoner of war. They caught me in Burma."

"Really?" I said, and counted the next ten seconds by the ticking of the wooden clock. Mr. Takahashi closed his atlas.

"Oh, yes," he said. "I like the English."

Out came his beer and in came his wife. She was a plump woman with lively eyes and not a trace of a wrinkle on her face. She was loaded down with shopping bags and explained that on her way home from the school where she cooked lunches she had passed the grocer's shop, and the grocer had rushed out to warn her about the "interesting" evening she was in for. So she had bought a great pile of meat and fruit and vegetables and sakè and ordered a whole crate of beer. For the next half hour she took charge of me, finding me one of her absent son's kimonos, making sure I had put it on properly, and introducing me to her cats by name. Three of their names were Danshaku ("Baron"), Jerry (of "Tom and Jerry"), and Julien Sorel (out of Stendhal). I can't remember the other three, but I expect they were something like Wyatt Earp, Olive Oyle, and Chrétien de Troyes. The television had been switched on, and as the Mona Lisa continued to titter down at Telly Savalas advertising Master Blend coffee, Mr.

231

Takahashi steered me over to the alcove where a carved wooden chest contained a rare hand-printed edition of the eleventh-century classic *Genji Monogatari*.

"I can read this," said Mr. Takahashi proudly while his wife sighed and raised her eyebrows, "but these days there's not one in a thousand who can. I bet there's not one in *ten* thousand."

While his wife cooked dinner—a huge beef stew—Mr. Takahashi and I took a bath together. We had already drunk a fair amount of beer and exchanged addresses and telephone numbers, and we sat in the bathroom soaping each other's backs and singing odds and ends of folk songs. The couple lived alone in the old house, among drawers and cupboards full of their son's possessions, and I caught in their busy desire to please me a snatch of the loneliness in their lives—the loneliness of an entire rural generation whose sons and daughters have swapped the hills for the cities.

In the bath I happened to mention that today—the hundredth day of my walk—was also my wedding anniversary. Mr. Takahashi climbed out of the tub, dried himself hurriedly and left the bathroom. I spent ten minutes in the tub by myself, humming songs and warming to Yamaguchi Prefecture, and when I had put on my kimono again and come back into the living room, I found to my astonishment that the couple had phoned my wife, whom I had not seen for more than three months, and who was waiting eight hundred kilometers away in Tokyo to wish me a happy anniversary.

At dinner Mr. Takahashi drank a vigorous amount of sakè and began to ask me odd questions such as whether I had my passport with me.

"You never know," he said, squinting at the window. "You can never be too careful with people here. A lot of schoolchildren saw us together. If they go home and tell their parents and their parents happen to phone the police . . ."

"Don't be so daft!" scoffed his wife.

". . . then the police might come up here with truncheons . . ."

"Take no notice of him, the silly fool!"

". . . and bang on the door and there's no back way out . . ."

"Don't talk such lunatic drivel!"

". . . and then we'd have to show them your passport," Mr. Takahashi ended, somewhat lamely.

After dinner we played *shogi* (Japanese chess), but as soon as he had

232

lost the first game, Mr. Takahashi complained of an unbearable agony in his eyes which was causing him to see the *shogi* pieces on the wrong squares of the board, and loudly demanded to be put to bed.

"Can't you wait ten minutes?" asked his wife, deep in a TV soap opera.

"Agghh!" moaned Mr. Takahashi, rubbing his forehead and banging his feet on the tatami mats.

"This happens regularly," his wife explained as she put him swiftly and efficiently into his futon, and then came back to sit at the table with me and tell me of her plans to buy a mink coat when her endowment policy matured in ten years' time and to go alone on a trip to Paris and Egypt and Turkey, in preparation for which she was studying French.

"Not English?" I asked.

"No," she said firmly, "I don't like the Brontës; I like Flaubert."

I woke in the morning in their son's room, in their son's futon, in their son's kimono, and Mr. Takahashi had already left for work. After breakfast, when I had laced my boots and we were about to leave the house together—the wife to go and cook school lunches, me to hike forty-three kilometers—I offered to pay for the meals and the room, and Mrs. Takahashi flew into a mock rage and threatened to box my ears for such a suggestion. We said goodbye on the main street of tiny Nakasu, bowing to each other while neighbors gaped. Mrs. Takahashi plucked a small pink handkerchief from her sleeve, dabbed her eyes with it, and stuffed it into her bag, and I left her village the sadder for a kindness that I could not repay because I was not meant to.

For a while Highway 376 continued to wind through remote pear orchards until it disappeared altogether and I had to find an alternative route. I trudged along by a river that trickled between its banks as though from a leaking tap, and for an hour or so the overcast sky disgorged cold, spiteful rain. I came across a live frog by the side of the road with one leg missing and guts spilling slowly into the mud; so I slit its throat with my knife. It was like stabbing a punctured rubber ball, and I was horrified at the time it took to die.

The signs of civilization were few. Outside a little junior high school a battered bronze copy of Rodin's *The Thinker* wore a Yomiuri Giants' baseball cap, and further on a disembodied voice welcomed me through treetop loudspeakers to a recreation park called Woodyland—swings, climbing frames, obstacle courses—all half buried under dead brown leaves and not a soul in sight.

It was a long day, and by six in the evening darkness and mist had combined to shroud the landscape. Beyond the far bank of the river, smoke rose from wooden houses and an old man tottered out to feed twigs into the stove that heated his bath. I switched on my torch to find the batteries had died, and so picked my way by the pale light of uncurtained windows into the little town of Hori, where a woman in the shop at which I bought new batteries directed me to the town's two ryokans. The first was full. At the second the maid who came to the entrance hall was so thunderstruck by my appearance that I had to ask her four times for a room before she could summon the strength to nod her head.

In the room next door workmen roared with laughter at the idea of me eating raw carp with a fork, and the owner's wife, who sat with me over dinner, told me that workmen were her only guests. There had once been a railway station at Hori, but the line had been closed fourteen years before and tourists were a pipe dream. The building of the Chugoku Expressway was bringing regular groups of workmen to stay (it was workmen who had filled the other ryokan, too), but when the expressway was finished and the workmen gone, both ryokans would close. Halfway through the meal her mother telephoned to announce that the new rice was ready at her farm, and the woman said that each year when her mother told her that, the old rice lost its flavor.

After dinner a tall gray-haired man talked to me for an hour about the history of the valley. It was here, he said, that the luckless Heike clan had settled at the end of the twelfth century after fleeing the site of their last defeat. I am astonished how many remote places in Japan claim this distinction. I have heard it said of central Shikoku, of the Shinshu mountains in mid-Honshu, of the isolated villages of southern Kyushu, and of the tiny Goto islands off the coast of Nagasaki. The bulk of the Heike are supposed to have perished at sea in the Battle of Dannoura, but if all the local claims are true, enough were left over to populate half the country.

In the morning, when I left the ryokan, shreds of blue sky had begun to appear, and I strode out of Hori past its one little coffee shop (called

234

Liver because it was beside the river) and over a steep, bare, bulldozed pass toward the prefectural capital of Yamaguchi. It was a windy day, and though I was in shirtsleeves, expressway workmen stamped about the pass with their hands deep in their overall pockets. I arrived in Yamaguchi city at about four o'clock, took a room at the fifth ryokan I tried, and spent an hour doing my laundry, which entailed several trips up and down the front staircase, on each of which, as I passed the hallway, a thin old man in a gray suit hopped out of the room where he was sitting and shouted "Whiskey! Whiskey!" at me. Eventually the woman of the place took pity and showed me how to reach the washing machine by a different route.

That evening I found a small grilled-chicken bar where the only other customer was the proprietor of a shop that sold Omega watches, as a result of which he had decided to send his son to university in Switzerland.

"We Japanese must become *kokusaijin*," he told me, using a word much in vogue that means, literally, "international person." He wore a black striped suit, a red striped tie, cuff links, and a Homburg at a rakish angle, and he repeated the word *kokusaijin* at least three times a minute, so that after a couple of beers I felt inclined to ask him what the hell he meant.

"Do you mean the Japanese must become like Arabs?"

"*What?*"

"Or like Somalis or Ethiopians?"

"Of course not."

"Cambodians, Indonesians?"

"No."

"Koreans, Peruvians, Pygmies, Eskimos?"

" . . . "

"What you mean," I growled, "is that they must become like white genteel Americans and live in detached bungalows with lawns and jacuzzis and sip Lipton's tea in the afternoons."

Instead of getting angry with me, the watch shop proprietor nodded very seriously, as though I had just shown him how to do a particularly tricky piece of origami.

"Thank you very much," he said.

"Why not send your son to Tibet?"

"Thank you very much indeed."

235

We parted friends. The night was cool and the twin green towers of St. Xavier's Cathedral rose above the city like the upraised arms of a surrendering foe.

It was a Sunday and the streets of Yamaguchi were full of uniformed Japanese soldiers, many of whom said things to my back like "Wass yah naymu?" The shops seemed as ruthlessly middle-class as those of distant Toyama had been. There was a hair salon with a "menu" of styles—Desir, Belle Fé, Mignon, Ambre—and a mannequin in the next-door window had jet-black hair and bright blue eyes: surely a *kokusaijin*.

Yamaguchi is a small city—a little over a third the size of Toyama, which is itself not large—and I was briskly out of it and back in the hills, climbing steadily along an almost empty road toward the karst plateau and limestone caves of the Akiyoshidai Quasi-National Park. Signs along the snaking road warned that it was dangerous in heavy rain, but the day was bright and dry, and after an hour or so a fine panorama of the little city of Yamaguchi opened up below me—neat, clean, unashamedly provincial, stretched thin between the encroaching hills and lit by the silvery autumn sunlight.

Higher, a crisp cool wind blew. Cars stood idle by the roadside and Sunday drivers lay snoring in their seats, while their children made heaps of the black gravel or gazed at a dead cat, its mouth churning with maggots. In a grocer's shop where I stopped for a beer an old unshaven workman in black split-toed boots and a tattered straw hat stared at me with undisguised suspicion, and when I asked for a second bottle he thumped the legs of his stool and swore.

There was a traffic jam outside the little town of Oda. Cars and buses were crawling away in an unending stream from the Akiyoshi plateau; and it struck me that I would be lucky to find a room. The following day, Monday, was a national holiday, and the long autumn weekend would certainly have brought hundreds of families into the park. I asked a man at a petrol station about ryokans, and he jumped in his van and offered to take me to one. When I explained that I wanted to walk, he drove slowly ahead of me down the single main street of the town, and by the time I caught up with him he had already discovered that the place he had in mind was full. He drove on to a second ryokan, and though that was full too the owners offered after some head-

236

scratching to turn their son out of his bedroom and make him sleep on the couch downstairs. By the time I had taken my pack off, they were already tossing all the poor son's possessions—plastic model motorbikes mainly—out in a jumble onto the landing. I had my dinner in the kitchen, where the maids kept sneaking in apologetically for surreptitious cigarettes, and then spent the evening in the family's sitting room where I took part in what amounted to a wake.

It turned out that the family had taken their daughter into Yamaguchi city that day for an *omiai*—the first meeting between a potential couple and their family representatives to test the waters for a possible marriage. The *omiai* normally occurs after an exchange of photographs, and it is arranged by a go-between, often an old friend of one of the families, who has unearthed what he considers an eligible prospect. The young people and their families meet, usually at a hotel restaurant or coffee lounge, and talk about nothing in particular, smiling with studied politeness while they furiously size each other up. Marriage will not be mentioned, although jobs and hobbies may be discussed, and afterwards the young people will decide separately whether they want to see each other again, and if they both do, dating can commence.

The daughter was busy serving us all sakè with a twinkling smile on her face, and everyone else, including her mother and father and the go-between—Mr. Kobayashi, an elderly reporter for the local newspaper—sat staring glumly at the floor.

"How did it go?" I asked the daughter when I found out how they had spent the afternoon, and if looks could kill, the father's and mother's would have flushed me straight down to the Ninth Circle.

"Not a success," the daughter said brightly, and I then compounded my felony by pouring her a cup of sakè with the remark that it would do her good after such a hard day.

Eventually they all cheered up, even Mr. Kobayashi—until I beat him in a game of *shogi* which was watched by a cluster of the ryokan's guests who kept congratulating each other on witnessing an international sporting event. Public defeat was the last straw for the poor go-between, and he ended his day of sorrows peddling home on a wobbly bicycle while the twinkling daughter got happily sloshed for what I suspect was the first time in her life.

Next morning I asked a policeman on traffic duty the way to the Shuhodo cave. He spent two minutes giving me detailed instructions, pointing all the while down the road on the right; but no sooner had

I thanked him and started to walk away than he called me back, told me he had thought better of it, and gave me a completely new set of directions, pointing all the while down the road on the left.

It was Sports Day, an annual holiday which, according to the Japan National Tourist Organization, aims "to promote the mental and physical health of the people." For about a kilometer and a half the road was absolutely jammed with buses and cars all searching for parking spaces that obviously didn't exist. Shuhodo is one of the largest stalactite caves in the world, and on this national holiday the walkways that permit you to tramp round it were at least as crowded as the platforms of Tokyo Station during the morning rush hour. A determined mass of holidaymakers, all grimly concerned for their mental and physical health, each tried with practiced hands, feet, and shoulders to get round a bit faster than the person in front. At the cave's special attractions—most of which were limestone pillars that evoked the shapes of natural objects: Pumpkin Rock, Big Mushroom, Straw-wrapped Persimmons—blue-jacketed guides seized the inevitable loudspeakers to enlighten us all about the pillars' dimensions, while between times the Percy Faith Orchestra played "I Left My Heart in San Francisco." I was surprised to come across an elevator in the middle of a Paleozoic cave (just as several years previously I had been surprised by the one in Osaka Castle), but having neither legs nor Sports Days, the trilobites must regard its installation as a kindness. When I surfaced at the other end of the cave a notice told me that the walk back to the bus center would take me thirty-four minutes. I set off with the few brave souls who had shunned the elevator and who looked as though it was more than their lives were worth to take thirty-five.

Walking away from the plateau down a road that was mercifully much less jammed, I found a fully dressed man lying unconscious outside the gates of a small town hall. Undecided what to do, I stood on the other side of the road and watched several cars pass in and out of the gates without their drivers paying him the least attention, so I told myself that they knew best and tramped on into the city of Minè where I found a ryokan and spent the night.

Minè, I learned, is the second smallest city in Japan (the residents call it Mini), and it was designated a city some twenty-odd years before when its mining industry was in full swing. Then it had a population of about forty thousand, but the seam was quickly mined out, the population fell to barely half that, and the fact that Minè is still a "city" is regarded as a curiosity by most of the people who live there. Certainly the place is tiny: when I went out for a walk after dinner I found I had crossed it in about six minutes.

Sports Day ended with me sitting in a bar—the only customer for two hours—listening to the same Paul Anka sing the same "Diana" that he had sung a hundred and one days before in a bar in distant Hokkaido, while the mama-san in a bright orange kimono sat beside me at the counter drinking my beer and telling me that I had "quiet eyes."

On the twelfth of October—the 106th day of my journey through Japan—I walked into the city of Shimonoseki at the extreme southwestern tip of Honshu. From far back on the coast road I could see the streams of cars and container trucks grumbling across the Kammon Bridge that joins Honshu to Kyushu, the southernmost of Japan's main islands. The Kammon Bridge, the longest suspension bridge in the Orient and the tenth longest in the world, was opened to the public in 1973, and I had been looking forward to walking across it. But, although in the early months pedestrians had been allowed to use it, the rules were changed when the city authorities noticed that too many of the pedestrians were jumping off.

The smell of the sea was contaminated by the smells of oil and rust and tire rubber and the dry, day-and-night tickle in the throat of carbon monoxide. On the busy main road—the tail end of National Highway 2—a lot of tiny dead globefish lay matted with dust and half mashed to pulp, their entrails spilling out of them like little nests of earthworms.

Shimonoseki is the nation's globefish capital. In the six months between the autumn and spring equinoxes some three thousand tons are netted by the city's boats (about half the entire national catch) and are sold in a traditional auctioning process where buyers hide their fingers in canvas bags to conceal their bids from competitors. Globefish are notorious because the ovary, liver, and other organs contain significant amounts of tetrodotoxin, a poison that is said, in its purest form, to be a thousand times more deadly than cyanide. Chefs in restaurants specializing in globefish have to obtain licenses from the government to ensure that they are able to gut, slice, and dress the fish for safe consumption. Nevertheless, an average of thirty Japanese people die each year from globefish poisoning. One of the most publicized cases occurred in January 1975 when the Kabuki actor Bando Mitsugoro—who had been designated a Living National Treasure—died after eating globefish prepared by a licensed chef at a restaurant in Kyoto. The five or six companions with whom the actor had dined that night were rather less keen than him on the delicacy, so he gobbled all their portions, too—despite which the chef was charged with professional negligence and received an eight-year suspended prison sentence.

Basho has a haiku poem on globefish:

> *Would you believe it—nothing's happened!*
> *Yesterday's vanished, and so has the globefish soup.*

But another poem describes how one night two men sat down to eat globefish together and the next day the one carried the other's coffin. There are many ways of getting round city authorities, and though the Kammon Bridge may be closed to jumpers, Shimonoseki has thirty-five globefish restaurants.

Beneath the Kammon Bridge flows some of the most famous water in Japanese history. It was here, in these narrow straits, eight hundred years ago, that the great Battle of Dannoura was fought between the two most powerful clans in the land—the Genji, whose victory changed the shape of Japanese history, and the Heike, whose defeat, with the drowning of the eight-year-old emperor Antoku, gave subsequent centuries of Japanese art, theater, and literature an inexhaustible fund of material with which to celebrate the melancholy and transience of human life. After Dannoura, for the first time ever, real power left the old imperial capitals of western Japan and moved east, to within thirty miles of Tokyo. Generals became more important than emperors, and the arts of war eclipsed the arts of peace.

Fourteen ancient moss-stained graves—all that remain in tangible form of the drowned Heike—perch on a little stone-walled mound in the precincts of a tiny temple called Amidaji, now unfortunately part of the large, garish Akama Shrine on the main road into the city. To stand before these graves, reading their inscriptions, is to stand at the vortex where history and legend collide. The names are real enough—Tomomori, Tsunemori, Arimori, Kiyotsune—but their deeds have so often been played and sung that the heroes themselves, like Robin Hood, have half disappeared into fable.

240

The Amidaji temple is also the scene of one of the best-known ghost stories in Japan, the story of Hoichi the Earless. Ironically, this tale—originally part of an eighteenth-century collection—would probably have been lost to the modern reader if it had not been retold in a book called *Kwaidan* (Ghost Stories) by the expatriate author Lafcadio Hearn, who came to Japan in 1890 and stayed until his death in 1904. Hearn's version is deeply moving, and his elegant English both enhances the legend and magnifies its horror. But the English of the handwritten, mimeographed pamphlet presented to me by the old priest at the temple is well worth preserving too, since, in its way, it is quite as remarkable as Hearn's:

The History of Earless Hoichi

The blind priest, Hoichi lived in the Amida Temple. As he was too famous as a biwa priest, the ghosts of the Heike clan should like to listen to his biwa (lute) and came out secretly one night. The warriors sitting in a row waited on Hoichi in a dignified. Someone commanded, "Welcome. Please play and talk the state of the battle of Dannoura." When Hoichi did so, the warriors who assumed a grave air were shedding tears and the ladies were in a blubber. "We've been very satisfied with your performance this night. Please come and play tomorrow and the day after tomorrow for a week night." Hoichi was asked so, and bid farewell to them. Thus, as he kept going out every night, the priests in the temple noticed his suspicious action. The priests were keeping watch for Hoichi with bated breath from behind of a sliding door. They followed him at once but he disappeared. When they returned to the Temple inevitably, the sounds of biwa was heard loudly in the wood. They ran up to him in a great hurry pushing aside grass. Hoichi with a grim look seated alone in front of the graves in darkness and played the biwa with all his might. The friar's lanterns flickered around him and the ghastly scene was too ugly to look at. They felt a shudder in spite of their social position of the priests. They woke up and brought back him. When they told everything to a Buddhist priest in the Amida Temple, he was very surprised. "The ghosts of the Heike clan having a grudge are about to take away to the beyond," he told Hoichi and wrote down the Hannyashin sutra on Hoichi's whole body.

On that night, when Hoichi seated alone as usual, he sensed the ghosts coming up at last night. The lukewarm wind blew and the steps stopped in front of him. While Hoichi wondered. He was called, "Hoichi!" Though the ghosts called Hoichi in a loud voice again, they could listen to nothing. "We can't listen to his voice and watch even his figure to night." When they saw casually they could see only his ears in the darkness. They hold his ears with their cold and iron hands, and pluck off them. Then they left somewhere. The Buddhist priest thought that Hoichi had been safe very today. But he was surprised. "Oh," he was petrified vacantly. He watched at Hoichi's loosing his own ear and murmured, "Oh, I was under the impression that I had written the Buddhist scriptures on his whole body, but forgot writing on only his ear." Since then, this is called "Earless Hoichi."

Another pamphlet in English about the history of the shrine (which has clearly invested in its own copying equipment) explains that "Once it was a first-class Government shrine" and that at its annual festival in April "a prostitute parade on 24th is famous all over the country." I bitterly regretted not being able to see this, though later that evening, down near the docks, between the Korean Education Center and a street full of yarrow-stalk-rattling fortune tellers, I ran into something that, while not a parade, was at least a congregation.

The third pamphlet given to me in Shimonoseki was part of the stock of a young American called Dennis, whom I met while browsing in a bookshop next day. Dennis belonged to a group called the Children of God and had been sleeping rough in Japan for two years without money or a job. He was on his way to Korea (there is a boat that leaves from Shimonoseki), and the pamphlet he gave me, by "Moses David," predicted among other things the destruction of the motor car ("All of a sudden they are turned into carriages, wagon wheels and buggies!"). Dennis himself went a step further and predicted the destruction of America. This was a shame, he admitted, because his parents continued to live there, but every time he went back to America he was forced to be humble and polite because the people were all so much bigger than he was, and it was time God took a hand. Dennis also told me that spirits travel in bottles, and that at an exhibition of Chinese antiquities in London some spirits had jumped out of ancient bottles and entered carefully selected Englishmen. I escaped from Dennis fairly briskly and spent much of the afternoon in a coffee shop chatting to an old workman with large spaces between his teeth, which I glimpsed often because when he paused for breath he opened his mouth wide enough to trap half the bottled spirits in Shimonoseki.

We sat at a corner table. A young businessman had been trying out his English on me when the workman came up and asked if he could sit with us and, when he did, the businessman grew bored and went away with a polite goodbye but without paying for his coffee. I hardly noticed he had gone. The workman was telling me the story of his life—or the story of his death, which was more intriguing.

"They told my family I'd been killed in the war—told them I died on Saipan. Sent them a telegram—very polite. Gave them the date and everything. Said I was killed on the fifteenth of August at three o'clock in the afternoon."

Carefully, the old workman tore a page out of the notebook he used for his jobbing accounts and wrote the date out for me with a red felt pen—August 15, 1944—so that I wouldn't forget it.

"I've got a grave in Horyuji temple in Nara. A really splendid affair it is. I went to see it when I got back home. My little daughter didn't recognize me and screamed whenever I came near her. Then, when she finally realized it was me, she kept saying over and over again, 'August fifteenth, three o'clock; August fifteenth, three o'clock.' Over and over. Like the time on the telephone."

We had an argument about who would pay for the coffees. The old workman wanted to pay for them all, including the businessman's, but I wouldn't let him. So outside in the street he took a tiny silver-colored bell from his pocket and tied it to my belt with a red cord.

"For luck," he said, like a man who knew what luck was.

My hike through Honshu was over. I had crossed a dozen prefectures —2,048 kilometers—in seventy-eight and a half days, and had had my share of good luck and bad luck. Kyushu lay ahead of me now, and the route I had planned would take me through the mountainous center of the island, over the volcanoes Aso and Kirishima, round the skirts of Sakurajima, till the last of all the roads to Sata brought me out on the island's southernmost tip. Five hundred and fifty-odd kilometers to go. I expected it would take me another three weeks. October was flying, the nights were closing, and I reckoned I would need as much of the old workman's luck as he could spare me.

9

Landscapes of the Moon

THE KAMMON PEDESTRIAN TUNNEL, which links the suburbs of Shimonoseki with the port of Moji in Kyushu, is less popular with strollers than the bridge was. At noon on the 108th day of my walk I had all four-fifths of a kilometer of it to myself, and the elevator attendant on the Shimonoseki side was so delighted at having a foreign patron that he waived the twenty-yen fee I owed him. I emerged on the last of my three Japanese islands to find trams rumbling along the roads, office workers playing volleyball in a car park, and small dusty palm trees doing their best to enliven one of the grimmest, clangiest, and therefore most prosperous industrial complexes in the country.

Moji was once a city in its own right, and it is still the largest international port in Kyushu. But in 1963, in a move seemingly aimed at stifling municipal pride in favor of "rationalization" (that shoddiest of bureaucratic terms), Moji was lumped together with four of its neighbors to produce the sprawling, bureaucratically named "North Kyushu City." The other four small cities had mostly owed their livelihoods to heavy industry—in particular, coal mining and iron and steel—so the resulting industrial hybrid is not the cheeriest of environments to walk in. For four hours I trudged through the built-up strip between the tanker-clogged straits and the smoky, gray-green conical hills. In the doorway of a little ironmonger's an elderly man in long white underwear fenced a grimy gilt wall clock with a pink feather duster, and a workman in gray overalls and a yellow steel helmet had a long public piss in the middle of the high street. By late afternoon I was still nowhere near leaving the five-cities-in-one behind

244

me, but I had managed to reach one of its less clangy sectors, so I took a room in a quiet little ryokan called Spring Beauty on the banks of a scummy river.

The fish market and the shopping arcades, lit up in all their nightly neon, were a lot livelier and more flourishing-looking than the gas tanks and steel mills that had loured at me all afternoon. For dinner I wandered into a restaurant where the staff greeted each new customer by smacking a massive iron gong—music to your ears if you knew it was coming, the fright of your life if you didn't. There I sat next to a professional cyclist who spent his days ("like a masterless samurai," he told me) traveling from one race track to another—fifty tracks scattered the length of the country. He asked me if I liked raw sea urchin (a specialty of the Shimonoseki straits) and when he discovered that I loved it, but that the restaurant had none, he made them send out for a special order. We sat at the counter with the wooden dish of sea urchin between us, and the cyclist told me, over and over, what a pleasure it was to watch me eat.

On the banks of the scummy river a huge brown rat sniffed nonchalantly at a pile of rotting cardboard boxes, and gray-suited salarymen staggered up and down with their arms round one another's necks. North Kyushu City on a mid-October Friday night is a bouncy, bedraggled place to be. I lost my ryokan and found it again by remembering that an office cleaning agency called Happiness stood on a corner of the same street. In the night—too late to wake the owner for a coil—silent mosquitoes launched kamikaze raids from the river and scored eleven bites on my face and neck and fourteen on my fingers, arms, and wrists.

It is hard to say whether the haze that hung over North Kyushu City next morning was natural or bureaucratic. The scum on the river was supporting more cans, bags, and detergent containers than I remembered from the night before, and it was with a great deal of relief that I set off south again—the direction that sooner or later must bring me to the uncluttered hills I recalled from past journeys. Still, for more than three hours I trudged through the dreary built-up sprawl, stopping once for coffee in a shop where the owner spent ten minutes eulogizing

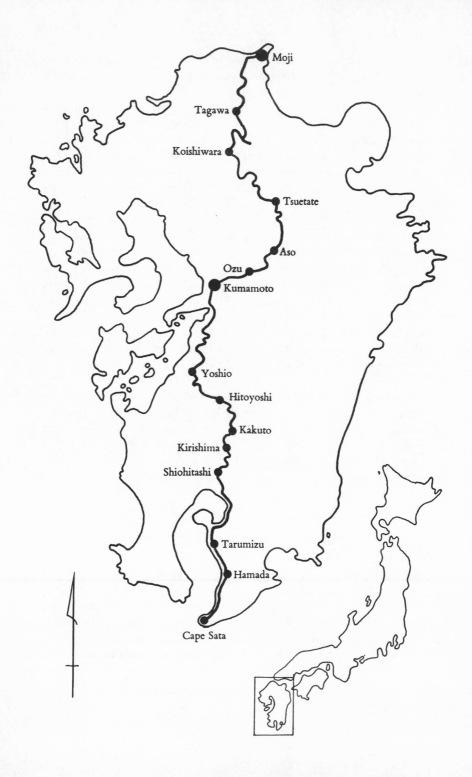

Moji

Tagawa

Koishiwara

Tsuetate

Aso

Ozu

Kumamoto

Yoshio

Hitoyoshi

Kakuto

Kirishima

Shiohitashi

Tarumizu

Hamada

Cape Sata

the dapperness of a regular customer: Oh, his new *sebiro* (Savile Row) was so *sumaato* (smart) and she was astonished how *hansamu* (handsome) he looked in a *suutsu* (suit)! It was good to be leaving the city behind me, and the city vocabulary as well.

The road continued fumy and congested, even when it began to pass between rows of wooden buildings instead of grimy concrete ones, and finally into less hazy air through which high hills and mountains loomed dead ahead. In a little supermarket where I stopped to get some apples, a woman with dyed red hair who worked at one of the cash registers had a good old giggle about me with the customer she was serving.

"Don't laugh too loud," the customer warned her. "He might understand Japanese, you know." And this notion struck the red-haired woman as so outrageous that she giggled frantically till I was out of the shop.

By the time dusk had fallen I was still not into the real countryside, though I had walked more than thirty kilometers since morning. At a taxi company office outside a small suburban station I asked if there were any ryokans in the neighborhood. The old man in charge made me an exquisite reply:

"Well, it wouldn't be true exactly to say that there aren't any, but it's a little difficult to say precisely that there are."

I fled on in top gear to the little satellite city of Tagawa, where I found a room, dumped my pack, and went out for a dinner of grilled scallops and peppers.

For dinner companions I had two businessmen who sat next to me at the restaurant counter and who struck up a depressingly familiar sort of conversation. The younger of the two would ask me a question, such as how old I was or whether I could eat fermented beans. Then, before the first three words were out of my mouth, he would turn to his more senior colleague, ignoring my answer completely, and marvel at length and very loudly at how fluently I spoke Japanese. This is sometimes a bit of a backhanded compliment because the Japanese word for conversational fluency—*pera-pera*—has a lot of the sense of "to gabble" about it, so that the businessmen were not so much admiring a serious attainment as congratulating me on my sleight of mouth. In point of fact, they were not really congratulating me at all; they were congratulating each other on having landed an evening of cheap entertainment, and their irritatingly loud offers to buy me more beer

247

("*Don't* worry about the *bill!*") were meant, I felt—albeit ungratefully —to impress the other customers in the shop as much as to quench any thirst of mine.

When they had finally gone—after insisting on an ostentatious exchange of addresses, followed by a long round of hand pumping and back slapping—the older man sitting on the other side of me, who had remained completely silent throughout, tapped me on the shoulder and said, "You're a very good-natured man, aren't you?"

"On the contrary," I said, "it was they who were good-natured. After all, they bought me two bottles of beer."

"If I had been you," the man said seriously, "I would have poured the beer all over their heads."

It turned out that he was a businessman too, though while the others had been dressed in their eternal suits and ties, he wore a dark red open-necked shirt and an old pair of corduroys, and he confessed that he didn't much like company life and frequently took days off to go fishing. I had been scratching a large red mosquito bite on the back of my hand—one of the twenty-five souvenirs of my overnight stay at Spring Beauty—and the man told me he'd taken it for an "anger spot" that had come up in reaction to my two companions.

"I thought you were exhibiting great self-control," he said, "just like Winston Churchill used to. Churchill always had a radiance in his face, even when he was dealing with nincompoops like them."

Winston Churchill remains a hero to an astonishing number of Japanese men in their fifties and sixties, an age which presupposes firsthand memories of the war. I probed a bit, observing that Churchill's had been one of the three signatures on the Potsdam Declaration, which had called for Japan's unconditional surrender and threatened the "prompt and utter destruction" that Nagasaki and Hiroshima had suffered.

"Potsdam was one of his off days," the man replied, "but even then he had a radiant face." And he told me, too, that if I wanted to be a real author, I must write "a novel as good as Churchill's—Churchill's or Bernard Shaw's."

When we said goodnight and I got up to leave, I was stopped in my tracks by two sharp pains that shot up my legs as far as my knees. Perhaps more "anger spots" were lurking in my feet, or perhaps the chill that was threading these mid-October nights had joined the ranks

248

of the other perils—mountains, mosquitoes, businessmen—which called down at last on the long-distance walker a weariness he was bound to succumb to.

In some ways the island of Kyushu is as "foreign" as Hokkaido. It was in Kyushu that the first Western ships anchored, in Kyushu that the first Westerners were permitted to live, in Kyushu that the first Western languages were learned—under the tutelage of Spanish and Portuguese Jesuit missionaries, the pioneer among whom was Saint Francis Xavier—and in Kyushu that Xavier and his successors built the first Christian churches. Even during the 215 years of *sakoku* (national isolation), when the doors of Japan were double-bolted to the world, when Japanese people were forcibly prevented from traveling abroad and the foreigners who landed in Japan were beheaded, there was a foreign settlement in the west of Kyushu (the tiny Dutch and Chinese trading post at Dejima in Nagasaki), and, through Kyushu, foreign goods were imported into the country—tobacco, oil paints, medicine, and guns.

Kyushu has long been a center for pottery—and despite the Korean origins of many local ceramic techniques, pottery is an art that one thinks of as typically Japanese. Yet, Japanese pottery owes some of its character and current popularity to Kyushu's foreign contacts, too, for it was in the tiny Kyushu village of Onta that the English potter Bernard Leach lived and worked, and Leach was instrumental in bringing about a significant revival of the folk pottery upon which some of the rural areas of Kyushu now thrive.

About nine kilometers from Onta lies the larger village of Koishiwara, the principal pottery center in Fukuoka, the prefecture through which I had been tramping for the last two days. Almost all of the shops in Koishiwara are pottery shops, many of them doubling as restaurants to cater to the tourist trade. In the stream you can see the old communal water wheel that, in pre-electric days, pounded the clay. And in the narrow sloping main street of the village you can watch the potters throwing, glazing, firing, lazing, boozing, and making money. Koishiwara attracts a fair number of visitors, foreigners included, and it never occurred to me that I would have any trouble finding such a well-known place. But it was on the way to Koishiwara that, for the first and last time on this long journey, I got hopelessly lost.

The day had begun well. The weather was good, the city at long, long last was behind me, the knobbly mountains to my right were sharp and blue in the autumn sunshine, and near the small town of Soeda I was photographed by a genial man in a car who clearly felt that I was a form of wildlife requiring conservation. I strolled cheerfully along till, at about two o'clock in the afternoon, I reached the little village of Masuda. My map indicated that to get to Koishiwara I would have to leave the road I was on and take a narrower track over the hills, so I stopped an old man in khaki dungarees on a bicycle and asked him which track I should follow.

"Go straight on as far as Hikosan," he wheezed. "Then take the right fork where the road crosses the railway. There's only one road going that way and it's clearly marked. You can't miss it."

Pleased that the way was so straightforward, I decided to make a lazy afternoon of it, so I took my time about ambling to Hikosan and stopped off on the way for a bottle of what I had begun describing to grocers as "foot gasoline."

"Where are you going?" asked the woman in the grocer's shop as she rinsed me out a mug.

"Koishiwara," I said.

"You've come the wrong way, then."

I gulped back a mouthful of froth and set the mug down on the table.

"You'll have to go back to Soeda. That's about six kilometers. Then take a bus."

"I don't want to take a bus. I want to walk."

"It's a very long way," she warned. "I don't think you'll make it."

I opened my map and glared down at it. From here to Koishiwara as the crow flies was about eight kilometers.

"But is it really necessary to go back to Soeda? I thought I could get there from Hikosan."

"Humph!" said the woman, and disappeared into a back room to reemerge a moment later with her mother.

"*Koishiwara?*" said the mother, breathing hard, as though I had named the Isle of the Cyclops. "You want to go to *Koishiwara?*"

"That's right," I said. "I was told I could get there from Hikosan."

The mother made an odd noise in her throat, half laugh, half death rattle.

"You've no need to go as far as Hikosan," she coughed. "Go straight on for another kilometer and you'll find a sakè shop on a corner. The road that starts there goes straight to Koishiwara, but if you're not too sure you can ask at the shop."

I had now collected three separate and quite different pieces of advice on how to get to Koishiwara. I finished my beer fairly hurriedly, lurched into my pack, and struck off down the road again, but my worries disappeared when, a kilometer further on, just where the chuckling, half-dead mother had said it would be, I saw the sakè shop and poked my head round the door.

"Hello," I said, "can you tell me which of these tracks"—there were several—"goes to Koishiwara?"

"None of them," said the owner of the sakè shop. "You'll have to take a train and change at Daigyoji."

"No, he won't," snapped a customer with a sharp red face. "He can walk there along this road to the left." And he pointed up a narrow dirt track to the right.

I unhitched my pack and pulled out my tattered map.

"Would you mind showing me which road that is?" I asked.

The customer and the owner both bent over the map and there was silence for about a minute.

"Here it is," said the owner finally. I looked at the map. He was pointing at Highway 212 from Hita to Oguni at a point approximately twenty-five kilometers to the south.

"Don't be silly," said the customer, "that's not it. Here it is. Here's the one." He was pointing at the main trunk road to Fukuoka city, which went off to the north. Koishiwara was west.

"Well, thank you," I said, and there being nothing else for it, I took a compass bearing and began to climb the most promising-looking of the steep, empty mountain tracks.

The afternoon had grown cooler, but as the track rose the vista of a perfect green valley opened up below me, softened by the gray smoke from fires burning chaff that drifted across the valley like mist in a scroll. Higher up, the wind was stronger, and the track followed the dry bed of a stream in which, to my puzzlement, all the larger boulders had numbers painted on them. I slipped on boulder 51 and used enough English for my puzzlement to vanish sharply.

251

At its highest point the track divided with no indication of which fork I should follow.

"Excuse me," I said to a little girl who was sitting outside the only dwelling for miles—a sort of combination barn, cowshed, and parlor— "excuse me, but which of these tracks goes to Koishiwara?"

The little girl stood up, glared at me for five seconds, then burst into tears and fled among the cows. Her mother came out to see what the commotion was, and when I had smiled my most harmless smile and repeated my question about Koishiwara, she pointed, trembling, down the track to the left and ducked quickly behind her cowshed door.

One hour later I was back at the same spot. The track had ended in an impossible tangle of undergrowth, I had slid up to my shins in a pool of mud, discovered that I had lost my map somewhere back near boulder 98, and would have got great satisfaction from kicking the mother and her little girl all the way back to Hokkaido.

It was six o'clock when I got down out of the hills onto a surfaced road, which I found by following the thin green trickles of a dammed river. A van driver who stopped to offer me a lift told me that Koishiwara was still ten kilometers away and that the road there took a turn back into the hills. I thanked him and began to walk as quickly as I was able. By seven the moon was out, horned and half hidden in clouds. It was eight o'clock and pitch dark when I came at last, through the smoke of the potters' fires and the fires burning chaff, into the empty streets of the village. I had covered, as the crow flies, twenty kilometers and, as the Japanese hikes, more than forty-five.

"Give me a beer," I sighed to the sakè shop owner as I leaned my pack against his wall and slumped down at the counter. "I've been lost in these hills all afternoon."

The man gave me a beer and a curious look.

"Why didn't you ask someone the way?" he said. "It's a straight road. Everyone knows it."

In the morning Koishiwara presented a more urbane face. The restaurant-cum-souvenir shops on the main road contained pot-bellied businessmen in Arnold Palmer golf shirts saying, "Um—ah—yes, yes—um—I see," as they appraised the bowls and fruit dishes, and "Um—ah—um—a gaijin—um," as they turned from the pottery to

252

appraise me. The previous day's hike had left my calves feeling as though chunks had been bitten out of them, and though the steamy road had few cars on it and the sky above was sprinkled with clouds like puffy white kites, it was one of those days I wished was over before it had really started. I left the businessmen, each with a parcel of pots and plates and a little white cloud of tobacco smoke floating over his head as speech bubbles float in comic strips, and tramped off south past the last kilns of the village into the rolling green hills I had been aching after for days.

A little later, I crossed the prefectural boundary from Fukuoka into the thin western hook of Oita. Within yards of each other a cat with its guts splayed out like a dancer's fan and a freshly dead dog with blood oozing out of its nose helped register the change from country road to Highway 211. But the highway was mercifully empty and meandered along, sticky and bright, beside a still, green river.

The sakè shops I stopped in for refreshment were unmistakably Kyushu shops. Each had a wooden counter to prop up, a notice offering credit terms to regular customers, and on the shelves the 1.8-liter bottles of shochu (a potent liquor made from either rice or potatoes) easily outnumbered the bottles of sakè that had been the principal tipple throughout the rest of rural Japan. (Further south, beyond Kumamoto, the bottles of sakè would disappear altogether, and in Kagoshima— the last prefecture of my journey—the only choice as often as not would be the rough, impossible-smelling potato shochu, from knocking back which the locals have earned the unadmiring nickname of "potato samurai.")

In the eating shops and restaurants the rice was flaky and new harvested. The morning TV news had shown the first bales of Tohoku rice being dispatched to Tokyo on painted trucks while the farmers danced to send it off and their wives gave the truck drivers bouquets. My road continued to follow the river, zigzagging through the sun-spattered countryside, and I swiftly discovered that, whatever it smelled like, the shochu I had been drinking at the counters of those little shops was having a notable effect on my ankles and calves and had gone a good way toward banishing the moodiness that had been clouding my higher parts since I got up.

Outside a small wooded shrine a couple of ornamental halberds were propped against two chipped stone lions, and a decorated wooden palanquin stood ready to carry the invisible god on his annual tour of the harvested fields. From the way the palanquin was parked, it seemed likely that the god was having his hair permed in the beauty parlor called Little Cut Bomth next door (this, the shrine, and the lions being the only man-made structures in sight), though if he had any sense he was out in the orchards admiring the clusters of heavy gold persimmons that hung like elfin globes from the trees and scorned the need for any other thanksgiving ornament.

Further on, a sixteen-year-old schoolboy waited patiently for me on his Honda motor scooter and then rode slowly along the empty road beside me asking me all the usual things: "Did I like Japan? Wasn't Japan marvelous? Wasn't it easy to live in Japan . . . ?" We said goodbye at the gate of his high school, which had "Yankee Doodle" blaring out of the upstairs windows, and at three o'clock, sweating undiluted *shochu* and beaming at everything under the sun, I crossed the river at the giant Matsubara dam where a largish party of uniformed schoolgirls came skipping out of an ice-cream shop to shout "Doesn't he look hot!" "Doesn't he look weary!" and "Good luck, Mr. Gaijin!" in chirpy thanksgiving voices.

Beyond the dam the river had been transformed into a deep blue-green lake, and halfway along the eastern bank of it, at four o'clock on a still-sparkling afternoon, I stopped to dilute the *shochu* with a beer at a tiny shop run by a youngish woman who showed—in the eight minutes I was in her company—many of the classic signs of deep-seated hysteria. First she asked me if I were a Christian, and when I said no, she asked me why not. She, it turned out, was a Roman Catholic (Kyushu still has a far higher proportion of Christians than any other part of Japan), and this meant she was a member of the local church, which had a congregation of five. Would I like to attend the service there that evening? Would I like to spend the night at her house? And would I like to meet her younger sister, who had been thinking seriously about marrying a foreigner because they were so much kinder than Japanese men? Then, before I could answer any of these questions, or even before I could catch my breath, she changed her tack completely and told me, in a Christian sort of way, to bugger off. Well, she didn't say exactly that, but she kept looking at the clock and frowning and warning me that her husband wouldn't like it if he caught me here in a beer shop drinking beer. So I left the place in a state of mild confusion ("Japan is paradise" was her parting comment) and slogged on up the road toward the hot spring resort of Tsuetate—

crossing on the way the unmarked prefectural boundary between Oita, into which I had made the briefest of excursions, and Kumamoto, the prefecture which would have to suffer me for the next eight and a half days.

Tsuetate took me by surprise. First a bowling alley came into view in the middle of a completely deserted glade. Then the first of a string of eight-story hotels, their grubby pink facades crowding both river banks and squashing like concertinas the older wooden ryokans on which I had set my sights. On the bridge I met an old man in an artist's beret who swore that his ryokan was the finest in the prefecture, so I let him lead me to it. There, in the foyer, three kimonoed maids apologized cheerily for having no rooms that overlooked the river (if I'd come five minutes earlier, they assured me, I could have had my pick). So I settled into a room with a view of steamy bamboo poles on which the blue-and-white yukatas of a dozen large hotels were drying, and then went down to the bathroom for a long, shameless soak.

One day I'll write a book about hot springs. They and beer and splashes in the ocean were the great bodily pleasures of this four-month lunacy. If it weren't for hot springs, I could never have lolled in the pink evening water of Lake Shikotsu, would not have seen the Oyu Stone Circle or met TIT cyclists or myna birds or the truck driver from Yamagata whose groin I remembered better than his face, not watched the old women at Tamagawa soap each other's slate-gray breasts nor, here at Tsuetate, sat in the same bath as the white-haired gentleman who had learned by heart all the poems of Basho and could tell me with profound nods of the head on which narrow road each one had been composed. Basho never visited Kyushu, but there is a song—older than his poems, probably, since the history of Tsuetate is said to stretch back seventeen hundred years—that celebrates this spa and its curative powers:

All who are healed in the Tsuetate waters
need lean no more on staffs as they leave.

Basho might have said it with a bit more style, but the white-haired gentleman swore that the baths here had done wonders for his wobbly legs, and I told him I'd be grateful if they would do a few wonders for mine.

255

The white-haired gentleman came to my room to have dinner, but left discreetly when the chubby-faced maid—who had changed from her kimono into a short tweed skirt—announced that she would like to sing me a lullaby. Not that I was the remotest bit sleepy, but that did not bother her for a second, and as she cleared away the dinner things and made a space for my futon, she sang me in a soft Kumamoto voice the first part of the "Ballad of Tsuetate":

The hot spring smoke, the hot spring smell,
the flowering cherries in the dell—
spa of our dreams, our hot spring home
would grace a painting, would liven a song.

But livelier songs than this had begun issuing from the large party room at the end of the corridor where, the maid said, smoothing down her skirt, the members of the Oguni Amateur Sumo Wrestling Association were celebrating their defeat in the tournament just past. They were the reason she had changed, she told me ("You've got to be able to nip out of their way; the shorter your skirt, the faster you can run"), and this confession, more than the songs, prompted me to ask if I could join them.

Seventy-one days earlier, on a rainy night in Akita, I had helped the Matsuba Phoenix Baseball Team celebrate a victory. I had thought it one of the most raucous celebrations I had ever been privileged to attend, and the lees of that evening had hammered at my skull for several trying days. But I was about to learn two important lessons: that sumo wrestlers out-celebrate baseball players by about the same margin as they outweigh them; and that if you think victory parties are raucous, you've never celebrated a defeat.

I entered the party room to wild applause, and looking back, I think this owed something to the fact that I was wearing nothing under my yukata, which must have been obvious as soon as I sat down. Anyway, during the course of the evening, I swapped sakè cups at least twice with each of the more than thirty wrestlers who were sitting or lying round the perimeter of the room watching the entertainment that took up the space in the center. There was a man who could make remarkably lifelike puppets out of ordinary hand towels and then cause them to copulate in striking ways. There was another man who, with the lights dimmed, performed a striptease at the climax of which, still

256

dancing, he hid his penis miraculously between his thighs so that it looked for all the world as though he'd changed sex in mid-strip. And there was the auctioning off and parceling out of the bodies of the younger members of the association—an event that sent the three chubby-faced maids (all of whom, I noticed, wore short tweed skirts) shrieking and prancing to the far corners of the room. Finally I realized —though it no longer mattered—that none of the association members was wearing anything under his yukata either, and this discovery prompted me—for reasons perhaps one day some well-wisher will explain—to challenge their Grand Champion to a sumo contest.

I know I lost. I remember rolling across the surprisingly hard tatami mats in a circle of hugely grinning faces, and that's the last thing I was conscious of until, in the dark of my own room, with my yukata wrapped snugly round me and a thin futon across my aching rib cage, I opened my eyes and saw the chubby-faced maid sitting on a cushion staring down at my face and singing in a voice I could barely hear:

> *Don't weep, little fawn; cling to your memories.*
> *I can stay for but a single night.*
> *Tomorrow, with the sky for my companion,*
> *I travel to far towns, to far towns. . . .*

By eleven o'clock the next morning I was sitting groaning on a mound of grass, rubbing my ankles, massaging my ribs, and watching a dozen young men in spotless white judo outfits jog barefoot along the narrow road that winds up till it meets the crater of Mount Aso. If I looked back down the road I saw mountains, dense as ocean waves. If I looked up I could just make out the thin wraith of white smoke that floated steadily out of the distant volcano into the empty blue sky.

Along the sides of the road about a hundred schoolchildren sat in their uniforms or in bright blue track suits, sketching the fields and the brown rice drying on frames. Each tried to hide his sketch from me as I passed—except for one who was so deeply engrossed in plotting the shape of the paddies with a small plastic protractor that he didn't see me.

A girl of about fourteen screamed and jumped up and told me, giggling breathlessly, that only Japanese people lived in these mountains, so *what* could I *possibly* be *doing* here?

"Aren't you American?"

"No, I'm English."

And this, to my surprise, brought a wilder scream.

"Do you know the Bay City Rollers?"

"Not personally."

"They're English too! Oh, they are! They are!"

The girl began jigging about from one foot to the other with her fingers crammed into her mouth and her cheeks flushed and wet, and she kept gasping out, when she had caught enough wind:

"Oh, they are! Oh, yes! Oh, yes they are!"

Two of her friends came up to calm her eventually, and one asked me the price of an air ticket to England. I suppose they had decided on drastic remedies. They were friendly between the gasps and wails and I concluded that it was better to come from the country that produced the Bay City Rollers than from the one that failed to produce Lamborghinis.

By two-thirty in the afternoon the moon had already risen and was hanging, white as the smoke from Aso, in a sky still blue and cloudless. The rice had given way to grass—the greenest I had seen on the whole journey—and as the road curved more and more steeply upward, the grass turned greener still. Here on the great caldera there were no schoolchildren—only cows who flicked their tails and looked up at the white moon, wondering where evening was. Sparse ricks of straw still dotted the landscape, but there were few trees, just a dark tangle of shrubs; while behind me, like a painting, the gray-brown shape of Mount Kuju rose and the sun touched it, turning it orange, then gold.

By three-thirty I was standing on the rim of the greatest crater on earth, having walked there from Hokkaido, staring down into the flat round hollow, big enough to contain three widely spaced towns, at the smoke from the towns and the shadows it made drifting lazily in the afternoon light, at the walls of the crater, like landscapes of the moon, and at Mount Aso itself, huge in the center, and the purple volcanoes beyond it to the east. I walked down into the hollow, wanting to cry.

October was more than half over, and the little hot spring spa of Aso was quiet and mostly deserted. Many of the ryokan windows were shuttered and piles of old newspapers lay damp and yellow in the entrance halls. The only sound that came from the ryokans was the

258

muted babble of huge color television sets that had been on since break-fast with no one watching them. The sun had gone down behind the rim of the crater, and a long shadow was creeping up the main street of the little spa. With it came the evening wind.

"What's the English for *geemu?*" asked Manabu, the eleven-year-old son of the couple who owned the ryokan. We were sitting in the roomy old hot-spring bath together, and Manabu had asked me to teach him some English. He had a small notebook and a pencil with him, and he was managing to write in the notebook without getting it wet. That was very clever, I thought. He was a very clever boy.

"What's the English for *geemu?*"

"Game," I told him. He wrote it down.

"What's the English for *juusu?*"

"Juice."

"What's the English for *robotto?*"

"Robot."

"What's the English for *kamera?*"

"Camera."

"What's the English for *pitchaa?*"

"Pitcher."

He wrote them all down.

"They're the same!" he told me happily.

The evening had turned chilly, and I wandered through the streets of the little spa in a thick autumn kimono and a pair of geta with split heels. The geta made a sharp noise that echoed through the empty streets, and amplified their silence. Manabu's mother had a small bar about a kilometer from the ryokan that consisted of one tiny counter and a cramped back room that could seat four at a crunch. There had been no customers all evening and at ten o'clock, bored half out of her mind, she had walked back to the ryokan to ask me if I would get up out of bed and go and sit in her bar with her.

We sat for an hour on the burned tatami in the back room, drinking sakè and eating raw fish. It was colder in the bar than it was on the streets, and still no customers came. Manabu's mother sat smoking one cigarette after another, lighting the next cigarette from the butt of the last, and I supposed this was her way of keeping warm. She was an odd, scowling, shabby figure with the red dye fading from her gray frizzy hair, in her baggy trousers and patched jumper, coughing over her cigarettes, staring at her bottles of whiskey that no one was drinking, waiting for the New Year to come and go and for spring to come back to the crater.

At eleven the mama-san from the next-door bar came in. She wore a blue-and-gold embroidered kimono and her long hair was piled up in exquisite rings. I wondered how long it had taken her to dress and to pile up her hair like that, and what had occupied her mind for the last five hours, sitting with no one in her bar, listening to the radio. She saw me, bowed quickly, and turned to leave.

"It's all right," said Manabu's mother. "He's not a customer."

The mama-san had come to ask if she could use the ryokan bath, so we closed both bars, padlocked the mama-san's bicycle, and walked back through the empty streets. The mama-san had changed into a pair of blue jeans, but her hair was still coiled into the elaborate rings, and I had a vision of how we must look the three of us—two Japanese women, one in jeans, one with red hair and a cigarette stuck in her teeth, and walking between them, a tired Englishman in a kimono too short and geta too small.

I folded my arms, feeling the cold. It was the coldest evening of my journey. The stars were very bright in the sky and a light wind blew the smell of the volcano through the shuttered streets. In two days I would be in Kumamoto city. In less than two weeks I would be at the tapering rocks of Cape Sata. I looked for the moon, but I couldn't see it—only the empty space in the sky where the stars were hidden by the shape of Mount Aso.

In the post office at Aso Spa, where I went the next morning to withdraw some money, the computer deducted 80,000 yen from my 300,000 and left me with a balance of more than 9,000,000. I pointed this out to the post office clerk, who frowned, grinned, wagged his finger at the computer, and corrected the error with a stroke of his pen, thus confirming my belief that the leaky biro is mightier than the silicon chip. Though bright, it was the chilliest morning of my walk and the first on which I wore a sweater. In a little optician's I had a new screw put into the arm of my sunglasses, but forty minutes later a nose tab fell off, so I suppose they are self-destructing.

I searched for a coffee shop and found several in the quiet little villages of the crater, but all were closed; and the woman who was scrubbing down the windows of one of them scoffed openly at the idea that any self-respecting hot-spring coffee shop would be operating at ten-thirty in the morning. I slogged on, the sky still bright, smoke drifting lazily out of the silent volcano (signboards at intervals along the road welcomed tourists to "the Fire Country"), and followed a wooded path round the rim of the crater until I reached the point where Highway 57 broke through the towering caldera wall and rushed off down its western slope toward the city of Kumamoto, some forty kilometers further on. All afternoon tourist-filled buses passed me on the highway with their uniformed guides chirping mechanically into microphones, and between the buses, taxis ferried gray-faced company presidents into the crater, grimly bent on enjoying themselves in the spas that the autumn had wasted. A beautiful white dog came limping along with blood trickling out of its hind legs, yelping whenever a taxi passed and cringing at each bus.

There seemed little point in making an all-out effort to reach Kumamoto city that day—particularly since my ribs, hips, and thighs were still celebrating my defeat at sumo wrestling—and so I took it fairly easy and, at about four o'clock that afternoon, I strolled past a wooden shack called *Ari* (Ant) which stood on the edge of a paddy field and advertised itself as a nightclub, and then into the little one-road town of Ozu, which seemed half asleep. A hot dog stand called *Guudo Doggu* occupied one end of the almost empty road, and midway along it I found a little ryokan where the young woman who came to the entrance hall said to me in exquisitely polite Japanese, "Would you be kind enough to wait an honorable moment while I ascertain the availability of a room?" and then skipped back into the kitchen and shrieked, "It's a gaijin!"

"It can't be!" gasped another voice, which turned out to be her sister's. She sat me in front of their television set to watch the kiddies' cartoons for half an hour while the first young woman fled upstairs to prepare the room with an honorable hoover.

The special language that attaches to ryokans is worth a moment's study. Sitting in front of the television, watching robots demolish galaxies in about the time it took me to peel my tangerine, I learned, for instance, that the hotels in the Fire Country get a lot of *abekku* in autumn. *Abekku* is the French word *avec*, but transmogrified into Japanese it means a (usually unmarried) couple. So the sister was informing

261

me—why, I'm still not sure—that a lot of illicit humping goes on in the neighboring inns as the leaves fall. Then, too, a guest who says to a ryokan person—as I did shortly after dinner—"I'm just going out for a short stroll" is always understood to mean "Expect me back incapable of speech at about midnight," and is automatically told what time the door is locked and shown the back way in.

I did go out for a short stroll, but Ozu being the kind of town I suspected it was, I was back at the ryokan before the sisters had ever dreamed of locking the door. I had one encounter in the town: two second-year high school boys shouted at me from the other side of the road:

"Hey, are spik English? Are spik Jap'neze? Hey, you, Amerika people!"

These boys had been studying English for four and a half years, so I expect in another six years' time they'll be able to say hello.

Back at the ryokan the elder sister told me about her trip to Europe two years before (five countries in ten days), and all her stories were about the horrific difficulties she had had with language. In Rome she had wanted to say Gucci but had kept saying Bucci, Kucci, Ducci. . . .

I slept with a tingling cramp in my feet and next day followed the unraveled cassette tapes that wound along beside Highway 57 into the hazy prefectural capital. Trams clanged past the Hotel Mink and on the horned castle the roosting pigeons looked like ornamental tiles.

That evening I learned that raw horsemeat was a specialty of the area, so instead of eating dinner at my ryokan, I went to a little restaurant near Kumamoto station with my mind made up to try some. It was disappointingly stringy and, having come straight out of the refrigerator, was hard with bits of ice. I sat for a long time sipping beer, waiting for the horsemeat to thaw, while the only other customer in the restaurant had a private conversation with the owner.

"Foreigners are a weird lot, aren't they? I had my fill of them when I was in the States. So impolite and opinionated. Always on the lookout for a confrontation. I kept telling myself how lucky I was to have been born a Japanese."

I asked for another beer, and the owner brought it over and put it down on my table without a word.

"I tried to buy a raincoat in New York, but I couldn't find one to fit. It wasn't just that they were all too big. Foreigners are a funny shape. Japanese bodies are so much better proportioned."

My second beer bottle was still full and I'd hardly touched the horse-meat, but I got up and went over to the cash register to pay my bill. The conversation had been going on for twenty minutes and I no longer found it amusing.

"I don't speak English," the owner said to me and winked at his customer.

"Wah yah frum?" the customer grinned.

I paid the bill and left the shop. The night in Kumamoto city was cool, and I was still hungry and wanted a drink, so I strolled twenty yards up the road by the station and sauntered into another, similar shop. But no sooner had I slid the door closed behind me than I knew how impossible the night would be. One of the three customers sitting at the counter turned to his friends and announced in a voice loud enough to fill the place:

"Look! A *hen na gaijin* (funny foreigner) has arrived!"

I sat down and took the warm towel the master offered me and rubbed my hands and face with it.

"I'm not a funny foreigner," I said. "I'm an ordinary foreigner."

There was a short silence, and the master coughed.

"Er . . . what . . . er . . . would you like to drink?"

"He heard me!" laughed the customer.

"Yes," I said, "you have quite a loud voice."

The traditional pantomime followed, in which the customer went through the motions of an elaborate and completely insincere apology, ending with an offer to buy me some beer.

"No thanks," I said. "I've ordered some of my own."

After that, for ten minutes, the man's two friends kept glancing at their watches and saying, "Well, shall we make a move, then?" and "How about another down the street?" Finally, when I had passed up one more offer of beer and not touched the peanuts that had been thrust along the counter at me, the men got up and paid their bill, leaving three whiskeys-and-water undrunk.

"Goodnight," the man said as he passed my stool. And, behind the counter, the master sighed and allowed himself a little smile.

"Where you from?"

"The moon."

"Oh?"

"The North Pole. Mars."

The master bowed twice and topped up my glass.

"I'm very sorry."

"It's not your fault."

"Really, I'm sorry."

"I fancied a quiet drink."

"It must be . . ."

"You know . . ."

"It must be difficult being so . . . well . . . so . . ."

"What?"

"Being so difficult."

I left and went back to my ryokan to sleep with a mouth smelling of ginger.

If you compare a medieval European castle with a Japanese castle you are at first struck by the similarities. Each consists of a series of fortifications arranged in roughly concentric circles. Each has a keep—or donjon—at the center of these circles, and each contains numerous turrets and angles from which the defenders, in relative safety, can inflict damage on the attackers. Kumamoto Castle, completed in 1607, is one of the three largest castles in Japan (the outermost of its concentric circles is nearly thirteen kilometers in circumference) and was the last to suffer a medieval-style siege (during the Satsuma Rebellion of 1877). Strolling round the castle on the warm 116th day of my walk, I was struck not so much by its similarities to European models as by one significant difference.

The strongest point of a European castle is almost always the central keep. (The walls of the White Tower of London are twelve feet thick.) But the donjon of a Japanese castle such as Kumamoto is almost invariably its *weakest* point. Often, this part of the castle is constructed, not of stone, but of wood and plaster (the present donjon at Kumamoto was rebuilt in ferroconcrete in 1960), and its elaborate tiled roofs and templelike facades give it the appearance of a fragile bird poised for flight, or of a decorative plume on a suit of stone armor. The European castle is based on the strategy of a last-ditch stand in which the keep at the center must be held for as long as possible. This strategy has governed military practice in the West from Masada to the Alamo and from Hastings to the Battle of Britain. But the Japanese donjon by itself is indefensible. The strongest point is invariably the outermost of the concentric walls, and the builders of such castles must have known that once the last of these walls was breached the donjon would very quickly fall—most likely to an attack by fire.

It is interesting to apply this observation to the campaigns of the last war. In Europe, Churchill was telling the world that Britons would "defend our island, whatever the cost may be; we shall fight on the beaches, we shall fight on the landing grounds, we shall fight in the fields and in the streets. . . ." The Japanese, meanwhile, were busy erecting a set of far-flung concentric defenses (on the island chains of the Pacific Ocean) in the belief that no last-ditch battle for the homeland would ever become a necessity. The Allied forces then attacked the rings of Japanese-held islands in precisely the same way as a medieval army would have laid siege to a Japanese castle, and once they had breached Okinawa, the last of the concentric walls, the homeland—the indefensible, fragile bird—lay spread-eagled and helpless before them.

The area around Kumamoto Castle has nowadays been turned into a park, and the authorities have erected signboards in English which introduce visitors to the botanical side of the city's history: "Kumamoto has several kinds of its own traditional plants handed down from the old times. These flowers stand for the traditional character of the people in Kumamoto who esteemed 'purity.' . . ." In a gravelly car park not far away some old-age pensioners were playing a rather intense game of croquet (popular among old-age pensioners in Japan, who organize leagues and tournaments and call it "gateball"). Each player had a large number taped across his back and chest as though he were an Olympic contender, and as I passed them, an old lady was berating an old gentleman for holding his mallet like a radish.

The evening was tamer than the last. I had a dinner of raw yellowtail and was back at my ryokan by eight o'clock. The hotels next-door were full of excursioning high school pupils—boys on my side of the road, girls on the other—and they spent an hour or so after their meal shocking the local esteemers of purity by propositioning each other out of third-story windows. From my own higher window I could see across the rooftops to the donjon of Kumamoto Castle, dwarfed by the neighboring TV transmitter and floodlit in the darkness. More than ever, in the floodlight, above those flat concrete roofs, the donjon looked like a white-breasted bird that had perched there today and tomorrow would be gone.

For a fortnight now there had been no rain, and though the autumn nights were getting colder, the days were still bright and the cirrus clouds drifted high, without menace. My pace had picked up in Kyushu, and with Kumamoto city behind me, I could watch the hills rising pale ahead, sloping up eventually toward Mount Kirishima, the last major obstacle between me and the sea at the end of Japan. A truck driver treated me to a lunch of boiled vegetables and told the woman in the restaurant that her tea was too bitter, but we drank three pots of it as he listened in puzzled silence to my tales of the roads he had known all his working life.

In the fields on the furthest outskirts of the city the yellow rice stalks, still uncut, had been hacked at and flattened by the wind from the sea, and no combine harvester would ever cope with them. Construction workers in yellow steel helmets lay on scaffolding planks in the afternoon sun with their transistors tuned to the year's last baseball series, and outside a dusty railway station a lunatic dog flung itself in the path of every truck that passed.

In the entrance hall of a little ryokan three elderly people greeted me with bows and smiles. They paid not the least attention to my foreignness, but brought me an evening paper and a bowl of tea and told me that the pass at Kirishima was the hardest in all Japan to cross on foot. The trains to Kagoshima banged and thundered by within ten yards of my window and the sound was oddly consoling. I watched Alain Delon play Zorro on a black-and-white television that nearly died with every passing train, and slept early, nursing the cramped feet I had begun to think would be mine for life.

The next morning—as on most mornings now—I searched for a coffee shop to sit in while I got used to the idea of lurching off on another thirty-kilometer day. Partly it was sheer procrastination and partly a real need for something to banish the taste of breakfast pickles. This 118th morning of my trek there were other reasons for prolonging my departure. There was the girl behind the coffee shop counter, for a start, who wore an apron that said "Prick Up" in big black letters and who fluttered her eyelashes at me while I outlined to her the state of trade unionism in Britain. There was, too, the nature of the shop itself, one of those shops—perhaps unique to Japan, but at least typical of the infinite pains for detail that Japanese proprietors can take—where a request for coffee is as meaningless as asking merely for beer in a British pub. There were at least ten different kinds of coffee, a map on the wall to indicate where each was grown, a chart displaying the taste, strength, and aroma of each, and a choice of sugar granules in two colors and four grades. On the counter stood a dispenser for breath fresheners called Mouth Clean—a good example of the no-nonsense use of borrowed English that I found more attractive than the euphemistic French of the crater hotels. It reminded me of the loan office called Money Shop, and of the yacht named Pipe Cut because it is owned by an advocate of male sterilization.

After an hour I had pricked up satisfactorily, so I left the girl with her tinted hair singing "Scarborough Fair" to a collection of empty stools, and turned south onto the remote road which ran dead flat through marshy land that looked as though it had been reclaimed from the sea. The hills rose ahead in grades of mistiness, and the wind blew the chaff smoke from October fires into my eyes and mouth and hair.

But even on a remote road like this there were large electric shops and shops selling armchairs: testaments to the growing American-style dependence on motor cars, which is alarming when you consider the narrowness of most of the roads and the conviction of so many Japanese people that their country is impossibly tiny. For kilometer after kilometer I would see no drive-ins and then find a string of four or five together, as though, like primitive settlers, they had formed armed camps for protection. They were no different from the drive-ins I had seen in Hokkaido, three thousand kilometers further north, nor were the little towns different from those of Tohoku, nor the factories and their smoke less gray than those of Naoetsu. The people spoke with different accents, but the same proportion were gracious and kind and the same proportion treated me like a freak, explaining, if they got the chance, that Japan had had so little contact with for-eigners (in modern times for *only* five generations) and that it was their native inquisitiveness, and not rudeness, that had got the better of them. Walk the length of Japan: what for? To hear a nation with a two-thousand-year history complain of growing pains?

The road bent east eventually to follow the meanders of the deep green Kuma River, dammed at intervals along its length into quiet, shady lagoons. Here, in the still bright afternoon, fishermen drowsed in motionless boats, and on the tiny dirt road I walked along, children

267

cycled silently home. Across the river a military convoy growled toward Hitoyoshi along a highway regularly flooded by the summer rains that are this lovely valley's curse. And in the hills beyond the highway, hidden by the mist that clung to the high passes, lay the lonely, impoverished village of Itsuki, soon to be flooded forever by the opening of another dam. It was from this village, in times not long past, that the daughters of the poorest families were sent as nursemaids into the neighboring towns before they themselves had outgrown their playthings, and sang in remorse the lullaby that I had hummed to myself eighty nights before in the sulfur springs of Hachimantai on the eve of the festival of O-Bon:

> *And if I die dig my grave by the road.*
> *Let each passer-by sprinkle flowers.*
>
> *What flowers shall they be?*
> *The wild camellias, watered by*
> *   the rain from heaven.*

At the little hot spring resort of Yoshio, a kilometer or so down a quiet tributary of the river, the woman in the single concrete ryokan showed me to a room that was entirely bare of ornament—no calendar, no plastic flowers—and in which the paper screens were half in tatters and the strong stink of sulfur—the same as from the Hachimantai volcanoes—clung to the tatami and the cupboards and the walls. Now was their busiest time, the woman told me, as she brought me a river fish pregnant to bursting. But in my three trips down to the yellow-stained bathroom I met only one other ryokan guest, an elderly man from the room next to mine who peppered the night with a rumbling snore while I lay awake flexing my toes and grimacing—growing pains of my own.

A thick white mist came down in the night, and I got up shortly after dawn and hobbled to the window where I stood staring out at a valley that had vanished. I went down to the bathroom but a woman was using the hot spring tub to do her pillow cases and sheets, so I had to wait until after breakfast before human ablutions could begin again.

By ten o'clock the mist had risen and the hills sparkled like polished mosaics in the autumn sunshine. All five women of the ryokan came to the entrance hall to bow to me as I left, and they all waved and called out "*Sayonara*" as I crossed the little concrete bridge and turned east again toward the river and the road.

The river had begun to flow more swiftly now as it swept round the long jagged curve from Hitoyoshi, and half-submerged boulders and river-wide faults created a churning stretch of shallows down which old wooden boats plied. Each was poled by a boatman at the stern and steered through the swirls by another in the bow, and they were full of white-shirted salarymen on company outings with jackets and ties and towels knotted round their heads to remind them that they were in the country. Just as the boatloads of city tourists had clapped and sung on the Mogami River seventy-six days earlier in the choppy cool of the northern summer, so here in the warm autumn these salarymen clapped and sang, and the loudspeakers in their boats carried the songs of the guides and the grunts of the boatmen across the river to the highway where they were drowned by pneumatic drills.

Some of the salarymen had paper hats on their heads instead of towels and some had covered their legs with green blankets because the Kuma rapids are eighteen kilometers long and the knees of salarymen on such outings are easily intimidated. Along the highway, on the opposite bank, trucks hauled the old boats and the older boatmen two at a time back to Hitoyoshi where they were dumped in the river to start their long journey over again—reminding me of the prodigals in Dante who are condemned eternally to push heavy weights in a half circle and then reverse course and push them back again the way they had come.

I sat and watched boat after boat pass, and then ate a workman's lunch in a little restaurant overlooking the river where some of the guides had come to rest. They were women with frizzy red hair and red gaiters and dark blue checkered yukatas, who leaned out of the restaurant windows and made elaborate arrangements in sign language with the red-faced salarymen in the boats below—arrangements which suggested that shooting the Kuma rapids was but a prelude to a salaryman's country adventures.

As the afternoon wore on, the hills fell away and the road and river wound together into the Hitoyoshi basin. I sat for a while in a tiny,

269

totally empty railway station—no staff, no ticket barriers, no sign of a train; only a little notice to remind travelers that this was "Everybody's Station"—and then crossed the river onto the highway from where I glimpsed, towering beyond the little city, the mountains of Miyazaki. Hitoyoshi was flat and quiet with fewer industrial scars than most cities its size, and perhaps this was because a large hot spring resort occupied the area nearest the station. But the ryokans all looked too expensive, so I searched the back streets and found a smaller place where a nervous woman with metal teeth did all my laundry for me while her two pet monkeys thumped their cage, and one reached out— as an old man had eighty-nine days earlier on a road near Osorezan— to peel a flake of sunburned skin from my nose.

In the evening I went to a place that did skewers of grilled chicken. I chose it because the outside walls were plastered with posters advertising draft beer. The red lanterns hanging over the doorway all had "Draft Beer" printed on them and the inside walls, too, were covered with pictures of Teutonic women in dirndl smocks serving mugs of draft beer.

I ordered a draft beer.

"We haven't got any," said the owner.

After that our conversation took a desultory turn. The owner's wife made two attempts: "Do you drink a lot?" she asked me, and "Are you with a large group?" A young man with long sideburns in a fawn-colored drape jacket came in and slouched up the stairs without a word. Then he slouched down again, went behind the counter, and broke a plate. The owner and his wife stood looking at the floor, and the young man left as wordlessly as he had come.

In the morning the Kuma mist had invaded the city, and though it had vanished by the time I left the ryokan, the sky was dark with clouds and for the first time in two weeks it looked like rain. On the way out of Hitoyoshi I passed an elegant old lady with white hair and a shopping basket walking slowly along the main street and bending down every five yards with considerable effort to pick up trampled cigarette packets. Out of the city the road grew steep, laboring up between drab brown harvested fields toward the prefectural boundary with Miyazaki. The rolling slopes of the plateau soon replaced the somber fields. I passed a roadside stall, decorated with Union Jacks, that had once sold pears but was shuttered now and dead as the landscape. In the gutter lay a dried-up tortoise—somebody's pet—and I was startled to find my shirt speckled with the corpses of half a hundred baby flies.

Just after one o'clock I came to the Hitoyoshi Loop Bridge, a towering red metal structure that soared into the air in a huge double helix as it lifted Highway 221 on an ingenious short cut toward a two-kilometer-long tunnel that burrowed through the top of a mountain. The bridge had only been open six months but the old highway below was already overgrown and completely unused. Incredibly, the builders had provided a set of steps for pedestrians which joined the two loops of road almost vertically and reduced my hike by a couple of kilometers. The wind in the exposed valley was strong, the clouds lower as I climbed toward them, and the metal girders of the bridge whistled softly with only me for miles to hear them. My last view of Kumamoto was an aerial one of crimson maples hiding the lowest approaches to the bridge, and then I plunged into the tunnel and emerged nineteen minutes later in Miyazaki Prefecture on a high terrace overlooking the Ebino valley.

Across the valley, silver mist formed a shimmering chain that joined the hills to the clouds, and barely visible—like ghosts—beyond, rose the three tallest cones of Kirishima. Below lay the flat little town of Kakuto, a silent railway snaking in and out of it and the town hall the only building over two stories. I trudged down the silent slope of the valley wall, and when I reached the streets of the little town I found them as deserted as the pass had been.

The room at the ryokan was completely bare, and I had to ask for a cushion and a small collapsible table to write my notes at. The last guest had signed the register on September tenth, and in the seven weeks since then the family had gone painstakingly and critically about the business of assimilating into the household the young woman from Hitoyoshi who, that spring, had married their eldest son.

I saw how the assimilation was progressing when I joined the family in their living room for dinner. The young wife was ordered about like a servant girl—first by her husband, then by an uncle from Tokyo who happened to be staying the night, and last and most ferociously by her mother-in-law, who sat magisterially on a sofa in the corridor, framed like an icon between the paper screens which stood open so that she could scrutinize every move made during the meal.

"Bring the gaijin his pickles at once!"
"Open another beer!"

"Isn't the bean soup ready *yet?*"

The young wife rushed about smiling uncertainly, making no complaints whatever to her adopted family members who had not shifted off their cushions for at least three-quarters of an hour.

After dinner an old grandmother was summoned from a neighboring house to entertain me. I had mentioned that I was fond of shamisen music and someone had remembered that the grandmother owned a shamisen. So we sat and watched her lower herself carefully onto a cushion in the center of the room, unwrap her instrument with meticulous care from its embroidered cover, select a plectrum, tune each of the three twisted-silk strings with her ear pressed hard against the neck; and then look round contentedly at her awestruck audience and confess that she had never learned to play.

"But it's a shamisen all right," she said to me. "Here, would you like to touch it?"

To make up for the disappointment, the uncle from Tokyo sang a pop song very badly, and then turned the television on with the volume up so that no one would get a chance to improve on his performance. The grandmother, meanwhile, told me that she was stone-deaf and kept repeating this information at intervals for the rest of the evening.

"I'm deaf as a post," she kept saying; and then she would turn and growl at the young wife to make some more tea or fetch us some more crackers.

At about eight o'clock the young wife disappeared for fifteen minutes and came back looking sheepish and pregnant in a brand new blue-and-white track suit.

"Do you mind if I go to volleyball club?" she asked.

"Oh, it's volleyball, is it?" said the mother-in-law archly. "And I suppose we must all sit here dying of thirst until you get back! We've got a guest tonight, remember!"

"I won't go, then," the young wife said, grinning.

"Oh, you go, you go," said the mother-in-law. "The dishes will wait until after volleyball. And stand up properly so the guest can see what you look like in your outfit!"

The young wife, blushing and grinning, stood and posed in her track suit in front of the paper screens, while her mother-in-law pointed out what was wrong with her body, her husband smirked, and the grandmother reminded us that she was deaf as a post.

272

The young wife told me later that she had known no one in the town when she arrived and had joined the volleyball club so she'd have a chance to make some friends. She joined it in May but had only managed to get away three evenings during the five months since then, so the volleyball club had scolded her for not being serious and she was lucky they let her practice at all. There was no way they would have her on the team, she said; and she sighed and smiled: "That's country life."

"Country life," said the mother-in-law when the young wife had gone to volleyball, "means that you've no need to get up early in the morning. You take it nice and easy as long as you're here. We don't rush about like they do in the city. Have a late breakfast. Have a lie in."

"He's my son," said the deaf grandmother. "He can stay as long as he likes," and she handed me a persimmon that had taken her twenty minutes to cut and peel.

I was upstairs in my futon when the young wife got back from volleyball, and the rest of the family were in theirs. I lay awake for some time listening to the clatter from the kitchen, and then from the living room as she laid out the dishes for breakfast. She was not up late, not past midnight. The pace is easy in the country.

The young wife had given me a map of the roads to the Ebino plateau —a web of red biro lines on a page torn out of a pocket notebook— and I spent the first hour of the next day trying to make sense of it. I gave up near the Ebino Fish Center, a little shed in the middle of nowhere, where an old man was carefully stacking logs for the winter. He drew me another map with a flint on the ground, and we crouched over it and discussed the state of the trails like a couple of Indian scouts. On these lowest slopes of Mount Kirishima the only buildings were pigpens and coops full of clucking scraggy chickens. The smell of the land was an English smell, and the sounds were the sounds of my childhood Sundays.

"You see, it's only Japan that has four seasons," the mother-in-law had explained over breakfast, and as I emerged at midday on the road I had been looking for since I left her ryokan, the season burst on me with a display that took my breath away. Finest were the deep crimson maple trees, but as I climbed higher up the northern slope of the volcano, the golds and yellows and scarlets thickened till I imagined myself shrunk to the size of an ant that had wandered into a kiddies' kaleidoscope. Round a bend, as though the whole of Kirishima had turned into a fairy tale, stood two harnessed horses that might have been waiting there a hundred autumns ago to haul their logs down to the valley farms. The road was silent but for the rustle of the leaves. Three cars passed me in the space of an hour, and in the one or two that stood parked by the roadside, honeymoon couples stared sleepily out at the century-old horses and at the fiery trees and me.

By midafternoon the leafy canopy had thinned and I saw, beyond the highest maples, the stark gray-green cones of Mount Kirishima belching streams of white vapor into a slowly clouding sky. Soon the road lurched downwards, and I heard the familiar sound of a woman's voice chirruping at tourists through a loudspeaker. The cloying smell of sulfur rid the air of all trace of pigs and English loam, and I emerged from the kaleidoscope onto the Ebino plateau, four thousand feet above the sea, and saw the sun go down behind the jagged cones of the volcano that towered over a landscape devoid of fairy tale and light, a landscape as seething and lunar as Osorezan's.

It was cold, too, on the heights of the mountain, and the eight busloads of schoolchildren who had just begun to wind their way up for a last look at the crater, accompanied by megaphone-wielding guides, half skipped and half shivered as they shouted out above the megaphones, "Hey, this is a pen!" and "How do you doooo?"

I had two beers in the *Bijitaa Sentaa* (Visitors Center) and then booked myself into the almost empty government lodging house, which I could tell had been built for honeymoon couples because the souvenir postcards were heart-shaped. There was one honeymoon couple there that evening, and they sat at a safe distance from each other across the table and ate their dinner in total silence. Breakfast was a bit livelier: a small busload of businessmen had arrived and by a quarter to eight in the morning they had emptied seventeen bottles of beer between them.

When I left the government lodging house it was spitting with rain, and so I didn't spend very long touring the plateau's attractions. All the ponds and paths were neatly signposted, clouds of stinking vapor were billowing about, and hordes of teenagers in freshly laundered mountaineering gear were scrambling in and out of buses and paying so much more attention to me than they were to the ponds and craters

274

that if I had stayed there much longer I expect I would have been sign-posted too.

At twenty past ten I set off down the toll road, past a bus whose driver smiled at me and told me he'd take me down for nothing, past five elderly women on their hands and knees scrubbing the curbs with pumice stones, and past the small sign that told me I was leaving this corner of Miyazaki and entering Kagoshima, the last prefecture of my journey.

All day the sky mounted a frantic pantomime in which patches of blue and thunderclouds chased each other about at the speed of a Chaplin film. Occasionally, through the trees that lined the road, I could glimpse the sea far below—the first I had seen of it since Moji. The road dipped toward the rash of hot springs that speckles the southwest slope of Kirishima—first a small abandoned ryokan, its windows smashed, its old tiled roof caved in, then the enormous nine-story Hayashida Spa Hotel, flanked by a bus terminal, a bowling alley, and a vast department store which I trudged round, partly to make sure it wasn't a hallucination (not many department stores are plonked down halfway up an active volcano) and partly in search of somewhere to have lunch. It was an eerie experience. I was the only customer in the store, and between the lingerie and the escalator I was bowed to by nine uniformed shopgirls who stood like automatons behind their counters in a hall that was silent as the grave. At the foot of the escalator an officious little manager in a blazer came bustling up saying *"Basu! Basu!"* and pointing toward the terminal.

"I don't want a bus," I snapped, "I want my lunch." And he gaped at me so thunderstruck that three of the shopgirls forgot they were automatons and tittered into the backs of their hands.

The department store—as I should have known the moment I clapped eyes on it—contained nothing I wanted to eat. There was a sort of palm court restaurant, completely empty, with a stage at one end equipped with half a dozen conga drums; and I quickly left and found a little shack further down the road where I ate a plate of fried rice and ran briskly through my life history for the benefit of a toothpick-chewing customer who, though he wanted all manner of personal information about me, addressed every one of his questions to the cook. It was like having to use a simultaneous interpreter, an experience made particularly bizarre by the fact that we were all speaking the same language. The only remark the customer made directly to me was when

275

I had finished eating and was halfway out of the door: only Japan, he told me, has four seasons.

That afternoon I tramped through more Kirishima hot springs as the road wound down toward the coast. All of them boasted eight- or nine-story hotels and red-brick steak houses, and one of them had a *Herusu Sentaa* (Health Center). A high school girl who had been sitting on a grass bank came bouncing across the road to have an English chat.

"My school stands on a hill," she told me.

"What hill?" I asked.

"It has no name," she said mysteriously. Then she confided that she wanted to be a simultaneous interpreter (there must be a call for them in shacks that sell fried rice) and she handed me a packet of bubble gum and told me she was glad to have met me. Two high school boys who saw this happen yelled obscenities at her from the safety of their bicycle saddles, and I walked on past a snack bar called Al Capone and left the last of the plush hot springs behind me just as it began to rain.

Lower down, the resorts were less plastic and more inviting. Some had little corrugated-iron shelters that served as changing rooms by the side of the road, and I passed a group of elderly women sitting about five yards from National Highway 223 with their naked breasts and bellies hanging out over their petticoats, waving at me with vigor. Overhead, invisible above the rainclouds, jetliners growled toward Kagoshima airport, and after snaking for thirty minutes through a wet gray gorge, the highway dumped me at the entrance to the Shiohitashi Hot Spring ryokan, which was so crumbling and shabby that I hadn't the heart to pass it by. I spent the evening there, the only guest, with a painfully hot sulfur bath all to myself; and for conversation, a tired-looking woman with dyed red hair, an azalea-leaf kimono, and a fag hanging out of the corner of her mouth, who lent me her Givenchy soap.

At three o'clock on the afternoon of the 124th day of my walk I reached Kagoshima Bay and turned south to follow the coast along the last of all the roads to Sata. Immediately ahead loomed the magnificent gray-brown cone of Mount Sakurajima, topped by its own little beret of cloud. The road was flat, and all the way the smell of the ocean—of fishing nets drying, of petrol on the water, of open drains, of rubbish tipped onto the beaches, of castor oil and rotting fish heads—floated up to remind me that Japan where the Pacific meets the East China Sea is the same Japan that is lapped by the Sea of Okhotsk.

Twenty piglets lay one on top of another in a sty, flapping their pink ears and trying to sleep. In the house next-door an elderly woman in kimono lay on the floor in front of a huge color television, snoring through the late afternoon news. A girl at a shop I stopped in spent five minutes admiring the hair on my forearms, and a man with a red nose told me that he'd saved two million yen as a wedding present for his son. Evening drew on: fishing boats purred past the winking red lamps of tiny harbors. Across the bay the amber lights of the city of Kagoshima flickered on behind the dark lava slopes of the volcano, and as on the very first road of my journey—that hot June road—so here on the last, an old man said to me "*Gokurosan* (thank you for taking the trouble)."

Next morning I picked my way lazily round the foot of Sakurajima, which until 1914 had been an island in the bay, but which spewed out enough lava and ashes that year to form the neck that now joins it to the mainland. The Kyushu sea is much more placid than the earth. The great chunks and mounds that rise around the volcano look as if they have been flung there by some giant playing at mudpies, and over everything I passed—the palms, the cactus plants, the fruit trees by the roadside—lay a thick coat of moon-gray dust.

I stopped for lunch in a little restaurant that was completely deserted. The woman who ran it saw me from the window of her house across the road and came bustling over to tell me that her daughter had just given birth to her grandson, and so she hadn't much time to mess about but would fry me some noodles. I sat there alone eating the noodles and drinking beer that I fetched myself from the restaurant's refrigerator. When I had finished the woman was nowhere to be found, so I left a thousand-yen note under one of the empty beer bottles and slept for half an hour on a white, silent beach.

For kilometers that afternoon I walked not along the road, but along the top of the crumbling sea wall that offers a whisker of protection to the shacks and houses of this bare coast. An old woman gave me a piece of salted fish, and an angler scrambled up from his stool on the beach to shake my hand. Though the sky was clear for most of the time, sheet lightning kept flashing along the Pacific horizon, and by five o'clock thunderclouds had swarmed across the bay with gaps

277

among them that the rays of the sinking sun shot through in a perfect imitation of the old Japanese flag.

The sea had grown restless too, and as darkness fell the waves rose, and the rain came all at once in a torrent. There was nowhere to shelter and I raced on to the little village of Hamada, where the woman at the minshuku brought me warm towels and tea and slippers in the pauses for breath that she managed to snatch between serving pork cutlets in her restaurant and packets of soap powder in her grocer's shop. I was left to myself and made friends with the cat. But at dinner, when the woman had closed the grocer's and turned the lights off in the restaurant, we sat together in her living room, and she told me that Hamada was a nothing, a nowhere, a place where weekend fishermen dropped off rubbish as their cars sped through it on their way back from the cape.

"How far is the cape?" I asked.

"Fifteen *ri*," she told me. "An hour by taxi. A day and a half if you're mad enough to walk."

Her husband came home at ten-thirty, having driven the secondhand car he'd just bought from North Kyushu City. It had taken me eighteen days to walk that distance, and he had driven it in a little over twelve hours. They spoke in whispers for a while and I gathered he'd had some sort of run-in with the police. But they soon perked up and showed me a picture postcard that they had once received from distant Cape Soya and had kept for the amusement of their guests.

"That's the northernmost point of Hokkaido," they told me. "You'd be astonished how like Cape Sata it is."

November third—a national holiday—a day that, according to the Japan National Tourist Organization's official guide, is "set aside to foster the love of peace and freedom as well as the advancement of culture." South of the village of Sata the road curved and climbed into the hills. Occasionally, the blue sea appeared below with tiny white fishing boats bobbing on it, and across the bay on the Satsuma peninsula, Mount Kaimon brooded like a pyramid.

I stopped in at a grocer's shop that appeared to be managed by two small children: all the faces on the posters and placards had beards and gaps in the teeth drawn on them, and the youngest child clutched a small red cushion which screeched with laughter whenever it was pressed, and which reacted to my presence in the shop with as much hilarity as a cushion could. It was at this shop that I first met the reporter from the *Minami Nihon Shimbun*—The South Japan News—who was driving past and recognized me from the description given him by my wife. She was waiting for him—and for me—at the cape, where the reporter planned an interview; but he seized this opportunity to snap a photo of me with the perfect cone of Mount Kaimon in the background and another with an old grandmother who owned a wooden frame for humping vegetables and things about on her back and who was made to explain to me, for the sake of the picture, what it was.

"Your rucksack is much nicer," she told me. "I wish I had a rucksack like that. They're better than these old . . . what d'you . . . what d'you call 'em . . . ?"

"*Shoiko,*" I suggested, which is what they are called in the north of Honshu.

"Could be," she said, giving me a funny southern look.

The reporter drove on ahead, but kept lying in wait for me at unlikely spots that he thought would make backgrounds for picturesque photographs, which was a nuisance because I was dying for a piss and never knew where he was going to pop up next.

The last stretch was a toll road lined with palm trees. To right and left the sea rolled in to break heavily on the rocks below, and the road itself rose and fell sharply as it wound toward the end of land. The next day, sitting on a bus for the first time in four months, I would travel back along this bumpy road and be as sick as a dog.

I tramped past a picnic area ringed by small round straw-thatched huts that resembled a travel agent's vision of Tahiti, then paid a hundred yen to walk through the tunnel that led to the lighthouse at Cape Sata. Hawaiian guitars serenaded me out of loudspeakers, uniformed schoolgirls tut-tutted about the state of my jeans, and the admission ticket to the tunnel informed me that I had arrived at latitude 31° N—the latitude of Alexandria, Shanghai, and the Punjab.

Waiting for me at the top of the winding steps that led up to the lighthouse were the reporter and Yukie, my wife. The reporter took a picture of me standing in front of the signpost that marks the southern extremity of mainland Japan, then bought me one last beer in the empty restaurant and asked me these questions:

"How long has it taken?"

"A hundred and twenty-eight days."

"How far have you walked?"

"It's difficult to be exact. The maps weren't always reliable and the roads in the mountains often doubled back on themselves. If I include the 'rest' days I spent wandering round large cities (because even then I walked), the nearest figure I can come up with is 3,300 kilometers, but that is probably too low."

"Did you never take a bus or a train?"

"No."

"Didn't drivers stop to offer you lifts?"

"Often, especially when the weather was bad, but I always resisted the offers."

"How do you feel?"

"Nine kilograms and three toenails lighter."

"What was the hardest part of the journey?"

"Parts of Hokkaido, when my body was still adjusting, and the mountains of central Hyogo and Yamaguchi, where some of the roads that are marked on the map as highways are actually dirt tracks that seem to run in circles."

"Did you have any trouble with the food?"

"Of course not."

"Or with local dialects?"

"Not much."

"Did you ever feel like giving up?"

"Once, early on, when I thought I might not be up to it, and once in Hiroshima when I began to wonder what the point was."

"Can you say now what the point was?"

"No."

"Did you enjoy it?"

"Yes. I would do it again if I had the time and energy and money."

"Why did you decide to do it in the first place?"

"Because I'd lived in Japan for a quarter of my life and still didn't know whether I was wasting my time. I hoped that by taking four months off to do nothing but scrutinize the country I might come to grips with the business of living here, and get a clearer picture, for better or worse."

"Have you managed to do that?"

"No."

"Do you like the Japanese?"

"Which Japanese?"

"The Japanese."

"Which Japanese?"

"Do you feel at home in Japan?"

"No, I think it would be a peculiarly thick-skinned foreigner who was able to do that."

"Do you think you've learned much during the last four months?"

"Yes, I think I've learned a bit about Japan and a lot about myself."

The reporter closed his notebook and we shook hands and said good-bye, and I sat at the restaurant table with Yukie, scribbling postcards to friends in Tokyo, and feeling that I had answered those questions as well as I was able . . .

. . . but I couldn't help remembering a conversation I'd had in Hokkaido in July, a fortnight into my journey. I was sitting outside a little grocer's shop in the sun, talking to an old man. The old man had asked me where I lived, and I told him I lived in Tokyo.

"Tokyo is not Japan," he said. "You can't understand Japan by living in Tokyo."

"No," I agreed. "That's why I'm taking this time off to have a good look at the rest of it."

"You can't understand Japan just by looking at it," the old man said.

"No, not just by looking at it," I said. "Not by looking at it as a tourist might out of the window of a bus, but by walking through the whole length of it."

"You can't understand Japan just by walking through it," the old man said.

"Not just by walking through it," I argued, "but by talking to all the different people I meet."

"You can't understand Japan just by talking to people," the old man said.

"How do you suggest I try to understand Japan, then?" I asked him.

He seemed surprised by the question, and a little hurt, and a little angry.

"You can't understand Japan," he said.

281

About Alan Booth

Born in 1946 in London's East End, Alan Booth, by the age of 10, had already read most of Shakespeare's works. He studied drama at Birmingham University and went on to join the London Shakespeare Center, where he worked as both actor and director.

Booth went to Japan in 1970 because of his interest in the idea of theater as ritual—an idea very much in vogue in the 1960s—and studied the Noh theater. As time went by, however, Booth grew increasingly disenchanted with Noh, but more and more fascinated by the country in which he had now made his home; he also began to realize his true vocation as a writer. For two decades, he contributed regularly to various English-language publications in Japan with commentaries on Japanese films or socio-political issues. During this time, he also became fluent in the Japanese language and extremely adept at singing classic Japanese folk songs, *enka*, which endeared him to his Japanese hosts.

What Booth has become known for, and perhaps what he enjoyed most, was traveling to remote corners of the country, visiting rural inns, meeting the local folk, drinking bottles of beer with his hosts, and then using his witty writing style to chronicle the events. Originally published in 1986, *The Roads to Sata* has become a classic of its kind.

Booth died in 1993 of colon cancer and is survived by his wife, Su-chzeng, and their daughter, Mirai. Booth's other major work, *Looking for the Lost*, is also available from Kodansha Globe.